An experiment that works

in teenage religious education

An experiment that works

in teenage religious education

Bernard Lipnick

BLOCH PUBLISHING COMPANY, N.Y.

Published with the help of the Dushkin Publication Fund of the Institute for Contemporary Jewry, Hebrew University, Jerusalem.

Composed and produced by FOCUS/TYPOGRAPHERS, St. Louis, Missouri
Text is set in Journal Roman, display type in Bubble

Designed by Daniel Pearlmutter

Printed in the United States of America.
Published simultaneously in Canada.

Library of Congress Catalog Card Number: 75-39795

ISBN: 0-914536-02-8

First Printing March 1976

Bloch Publishing Co.
915 Broadway
New York, New York 10010
Telephone: (212) 673-7910

To Harriet

And our children

Daniel, David, Jayme, Jesse, Mark, and Tammy

Contents

In Appreciation

While it is not possible to identify all who fostered the concerns which this book treats, the following are deserving of special mention:

Rabbi Jerome Lipnick, who demonstrates, both personally and in his work, the integral relationship between Judaism and the quality of life.

Dr. Louis L. Kaplan, formerly Dean of the Baltimore Hebrew College, whose lifelong dedication to Jewish and general education sets a standard yet to be matched by his students.

Mr. Louis Newman, formerly Director of Camp Ramah in Wisconsin, who has demonstrated that John Dewey's faith in young people is capable of realization in real life.

David Lipnick, for whose benefit, to a greater extent than he might ever know, the whole enterprise described herein was conceived.

Mr. Obbie Price, a rare combination of business man and educator, whose faith in the program assured its being given an opportunity to prove itself.

Dr. Ronald Wolfson and his wife, Susie, whose past and future contributions to Jewish education can only be measured in the attainments of the fortunate young people whose lives are touched by theirs.

Drs. Louis M. Smith, Richard deCharms, and Arthur G. Wirth, of Washington University, whose searching questions and expert guidance assured that the experiment underwent the full rigors of scholarly research.

Mrs. Harry (Miriam) Freedman, who not only typed the material contained in this volume and researched a considerable portion of it, but saw to it that its author survived what were at times very difficult circumstances.

Mr. and Mrs. Charles Klotzer, whose children benefited from the program and who in their desire to distribute its benefits more widely placed their publishing firm — FOCUS/Midwest — in its service.

Dr. Alexander Dushkin and Dr. Moshe Davis, whose convictions that new and better alternatives in Jewish education may yet be found, helped to make the publication of this book possible.

Congregation B'nai Amoona and its good people who for almost a quarter of a century have encouraged the author to devote himself to the service of God, Israel and Torah.

To them all — my heartfelt gratitude.

Bernard Lipnick

Preface

The introduction to the latest comprehensive report on Jewish education in the United States, completed in 1959, likened Jewish education, nationally, to Mark Twain's characterization of the Platte River — a "monstrous big river — a mile wide and an inch deep." Similar, implied the report, is American Jewish education, "useful to wet the feet, to cool the atmosphere and to improve the scenery," but certainly no "source of water supply for the life of a thirsting, industrious community."[1] The report went on to detail and document its indictment and ended with numerous recommendations for improving the situation.

That there was little or no improvement in the condition of Jewish education during the ensuing decade is indicated by a number of subsequent appraisals.[2] With the passage of time the situation if anything seemed to deteriorate. There was well-nigh universal agreement, irrespective of the segment of the educational establishment under consideration, that Jewish schools were imparting neither cognitive skills nor positive attitudes towards Jewishness. In fact, there were those who suspected that Jewish schools were counterproductive. Instead of communicating to their students a body of information needed in order to identify Jewishly and instead of fostering in their charges the desire to so identify, the schools were at least partly responsible for their rejection of Jewishness. Some observers, on the basis of long experience in the field, went so far as to posit an inverse relationship between the number of years of Jewish schooling and students' Jewish identification; that is, the longer students attended the less willingness to identify Jewishly, even though additional time spent in the classroom may have resulted in some cognitive gains.

Against this background and as a reflection of its own growing concern, the Jewish community of a large midwestern urban area, which for the purposes of the present investigation shall be called Graceville,[3] commissioned a local survey of its Jewish education which was completed in 1966.[4] The survey not only corroborated the national findings, but supported the judgment, based upon several criteria of educational excellence, that Graceville was one of the most backward Jewish communities in the nation. While nationally, for example, Jewish children were distributed almost equally between one-day-a-week schools and those of a more intensive nature, 86% of Graceville's students attended one-day-a-week schools with only 16% in either all-day or weekday afternoon schools. Nationally, 7% — 10% of all students were enrolled in secondary Jewish schools of one kind or another. In Graceville, by contrast, the figure was a "shockingly low" 2%, to use the author's descriptive terminology. Graceville's teachers were well below the national average in terms both of Jewish background and professional training. Curriculums in Graceville tended to be text-centered and unimaginative — all of which led the surveyors to assert that such "investment in Jewish education" as they found in Graceville, had produced "only minimal and perhaps even negative returns . . . ."[5]

Within this setting, one congregation, B'nai Israel, the larger of two Conservative congregations in the area, attempted to develop and maintain a religious school for the children of its thousand affiliated families. The school was divided into three major departments: the Sunday School with an enrollment of approximately 500 students, a Hebrew School whose 200 students attended three afternoons a week in addition to Sunday School, and an after-school High School Department with 35 students. Enrollment in all departments was restricted to members' children and entailed no expense to the parents beyond congregational dues. The School was headed by Rabbi Sol Katz, Associate Rabbi of the congregation. Staff comprised some 40 teachers, specialists, and assistants. Approximately one hundred of B'nai Israel's teenage youth were involved in synagogue sponsored youth groups.

An informal appraisal of B'nai Israel's educational system reveals it to have been guilty of most of the insufficiencies enumerated in both the national and local studies. Yet, over the years, its leadership, particularly the Senior Rabbi, Bernard Levy, felt considerable torment at the "job" that it was not doing with its young people. This may have been a significant achievement in itself, in accord with Polanyi's statement that "to be tormented by a problem is to believe that it has a solution."[6] In B'nai Israel's case, the torment gave rise to a belief and the belief gave rise to, if not a solution, then an experimental alternative. It is the story of that alternative which forms the subject of the present study. It is proffered in the hope that its example will inspire similar efforts by others, that Judaism increasingly may work its unique and ennobling influence upon Jewish young people and through them upon society at large.

Chapter One

Introduction

The Working Hypotheses or Guiding Hunches
of a New Program

The one major area in which Rabbi Levy long felt the need for improvement was the Hebrew School. The reason was that the Hebrew School, the most intensive Jewish education offered by B'nai Israel, was generally acknowledged to be the least successful of all the departments, especially in its upper grades, a quality which it seemed to share with other Jewish schools throughout the community and country. A typical problem concerned schedule. How could children, after a long day at public school, be expected to come to after-school classes and derive benefit? There were frequent conflicts with after-school activities which grew in number and intensity from year to year. Hebrew School attendance averages were seldom better than 80 − 85%. Even when present, students' fatigue and the desire to be out playing "like everyone else" robbed the experience of whatever interest was brought to it by the students or engendered by even the most enthusiastic teachers.

In thinking about desirable alternatives, the example of Jewishly oriented camps kept recurring to Rabbi Levy. His experience convinced him that Jewish camping exerted such a uniformly positive influence that whatever change would be contemplated would do well to be guided by its example. In the course of time and after several abortive attempts, he identified four guiding hunches or working hypotheses which he regarded as necessary ingredients for an alternative Hebrew School program.

The first was that, like camp, a new Hebrew School program should dissociate itself from that with which the children and even their parents were familiar. Based upon their own previous experience and the experience of older siblings, the students were so repulsed by Hebrew School that anything which smacked too much of the past would, he thought, be rejected out of hand. Whatever the alternative, in other words, it would have to represent a significant departure from the conventional Hebrew School pattern which had been in effect at B'nai Israel and at other Jewish educational institutions for as long as anyone could remember.

A second hypothesis had to do with the need to have participants, particularly the children, view themselves as Origins.[1] Although the term "origin" was not known to Rabbi Levy, at the time, the concept conveyed by the term was known and honored.[2] A conventional Hebrew School tends to view students as well as teachers as part of a chain of command emanating from, if not a person, then a tradition which dictates certain procedures. If the participants are in any way responsible for their own experience, it has to do with the mode of study only, and even then in a minimal way. The fact is, however, that Judaism sees man as ultimately responsible for his own decisions. Judaism eschews determinisms and regards the human being as essentially free in matters of moral choice. The need therefore for everyone's involvement at every level of planning and execution, the need for everyone to be treated, in other words, like an origin of his own behavior, was deemed crucial.

The influence of camping was present, as well, in what came to be the third working hypothesis; namely, the need for a total living situation.[3] It seemed reasonable that if religious education was to influence children the amount of influence would be related to the amount of exposure. Nor was it just a quantitative matter. Qualitatively, much of what Judaism teaches, whether in the form of dietary regulations or rules of social interaction, is no more than disembodied principle in other than a total living situation. In addition, it was felt that a community-like, total living situation would be important due to the fact that Jews live in a milieu which is at times inimical to Judaism and its purposes. On the most basic level, there are serious differences and even conflicts between Judaism and the secular-Christian culture which holds sway in America.[4] On a more practical level, Jewish modes of behavior, such as those involved in Jewish holiday observance, are either ignored or thwarted by the majority culture which tends to view Judaism as a deviation from the norm.

Finally, Rabbi Levy and those who accepted his basic approach, had the hunch that nature should be an important component of Jewish education. In the first place, a natural setting seemed more suitable for the communication of some usually neglected aspects of Judaism. Many facets of Judaism, for example, bear the stamp of its rural-agricultural origins. Three of its major festivals celebrate harvests, grain as well as fruit, and much of its literature, including complicated legal tractates, grows out of the rural setting and treats issues which derive from the agricultural experience. Secondly, Rabbi Levy had the sense that nature incorporates within itself certain values which are especially relevant to religion in general and to Judaism in particular. For example, Judaism's emphasis upon the need for man to be aware of his dependency upon God and His creation implies if not a return to the idyllic life then periodic contact with nature. Thus he felt that not only should there be a total living situation but that it should be within a natural setting.

In summary, the working hypotheses, which might also be called conceptual hunches, were: a fresh start; a basically Origin-like atmosphere; a total living situation; and contact with nature.

The Initial Vov Class Program, 1969-1970

A great deal of thinking and planning culminated in a program which sought to incorporate these working hypotheses. It was known simply as the Vov Class Program because the Vov Class, which designated the sixth grade of the B'nai Israel Hebrew School, was chosen for the new program.

The choice of the Vov Class, equivalent to the eighth grade in Public School, or age thirteen, was based upon several different kinds of considerations. In the first place, since the Vov Class was the Hebrew School graduating class, whatever the results of the experiment, the effect upon the rest of the school would not be critical. In addition, the choice was related to the extremely important position of the Bar and Bat Mitzva ceremony within the Jewish community.

As a major rite of passage almost universally recognized among traditionally oriented Jews, Bar Mitzva for boys, on or near the thirteenth birthday, and to a lesser extent Bat Mitzva for girls, exercise considerable control over Jewish families. Congregations, including B'nai Israel, quick to recognize this fact stipulate a certain number of years of attendance in the Hebrew School as a prerequisite to the ceremony. Thus, while family and other pressures usually are sufficient to effect attendance up until age 13, once the ceremony is over, most students, 90 — 93% nationally,[5] and about 50% at B'nai Israel, "quit" Hebrew School. Students, therefore, who begin their Hebrew School at the beginning of the third grade of public school, approach their Bar or Bat Mitzva towards the end of their fifth year of Hebrew School or the beginning of the sixth (Vov). A successful program at this level it was thought might have the effect of retaining the students in the Hebrew School and eventually in the Hebrew High School after Bar and Bat Mitzva.

More important, however, than these considerations were the psychological-educational intuitions of Rabbi Levy and the B'nai Israel staff. They viewed this period in the student's life as a kind of rebirth and felt that at no time could the religious school exert greater influence upon the student than at this time. Subsequent study tended to confirm the importance of the thirteenth year and the year or two immediately following in acculturating Jewish youth to the Jewish community.[6] Erikson, for example, spoke of adolescence as a recapitulation of all the earlier stages of development. He therefore pointed to the need for "a psycho-social moratorium during which the young adult through free role experimentation may find a niche in some section of his society."[7] There seems to be as well some affinity between this age group and matters of concern to religion. Kohlberg and Mayer, for example, in their analysis of the development of moral judgment, asserted that "moral maturity at age 13-15 predicts to terminal status maturity" while "at age 9-11 it does not."[8] According to Silberman, it is at this period that "young people gradually gain command over what Piaget calls formal operations — the final 'stage' of cognitive development." In fact, "it is during adolescence, as the philosopher Alfred North Whitehead suggested, that 'the lines of character are graven.' "[9]

In addition to the choice of group, the first year of the program established its essential structure. In place of afternoon Hebrew School classes, the students, of whom there were 24, were asked to give nine weekends during the course of the year, spaced approximately a month apart. They were to meet at a central location after public school on Friday and journey with their teachers to a rented retreat center in Rosefield, some thirty miles from Graceville, where they were to remain until approximately noon on Sunday. Apart from the weekends, the students were asked to come once a week, on Wednesday afternoon, for an hour and a half, in order to plan for the forthcoming weekend, and learn conversational Hebrew to be used on the weekends. An Israeli teacher was engaged to teach the group Hebrew on Wednesdays.

Each weekend had its own theme, chosen with an eye to relevance and personal involvement. All meals were taken together. Services which were held frequently were regarded as experimental in nature. If the students wanted to interrupt services for questions or objections they were encouraged to do so. They were urged to assume responsibility for many of their activities. There was a good deal of conviviality and informal interchange between staff and students. Internal structure was dictated largely by built-in considerations such as meal times and service times. Yet almost everything, from the dynamics of interpersonal relations to traditional ritual forms, was open to question. The group relied heavily on phonograph records and movies to stimulate thought and discussion.

By the end of the third weekend, through an unavoidable circumstance, the Rosefield facility was no longer available. It was necessary, therefore, to search for another. This turned out to be a blessing in disguise because up until that point no such program had been attempted at an in-town location. There being no other choice, the group went to the Jewish Student Center across from the Jefferson University campus. The weekend was just as successful as the previous ones. Students were able to come up with their own recreation and their own games, intimating for the first time that it may be possible to relinquish the emphasis upon nature without damaging the program.

Perhaps the most significant outcome of the initial experiment was the conviction that it might provide a feasible and potentially worthwhile alternative to conventional Hebrew School education at this age level. B'nai Israel's staff, particularly Rabbi Levy, sensed that there were insights contained in the experience which could be developed and perhaps applied more widely to the school. It was decided therefore to repeat the program in the school year 1970-1971 with the next Vov Class.

The Vov Class, 1970-1971

The fifteen families represented in the new Vov Class,[10] although typical of the congregation's families with respect to socio-economic level, enjoyed an even higher educational level, general as well as Jewish. For example, of the twenty-seven parents for whom the information was available, ten held graduate degrees and six held undergraduate degrees. Eight others had completed some college work, while the remaining three had finished high school. Five of the fifteen mothers were either fulltime or substitute public school teachers.

Also, from the point of view of Jewish background and Jewish identification,[11] the Vov Class families represented a very special group in the congregation. With the exception of three of the parents who were born abroad, all were either first or second generation native American. All but three — as it happens, a different three — indicated having received some formal Jewish education in their youth. Yiddish was spoken in eleven of the parental homes. The overwhelming majority claimed membership in one or more Jewish organizations other than B'nai Israel. About half of the mothers and fathers occupied positions of responsibility within the congregation and the Jewish community.

There is reason to believe also that personal religiosity, at least as denoted by the performance of certain ritual acts, was far in excess of the ordinary. Twelve of the fifteen families observed the Jewish dietary regulations in some fashion and almost all gave attention to the celebration of the Sabbath and other Jewish holidays. The families of the new Vov Class, in short, exhibited very positive Jewish identification.

It is safe to assume that parental expectations for their children were similarly above the ordinary. As to what the specific Jewish expectations consisted of, it is rather difficult to say. Some families were concerned with the communication of particular cognitive skills, such as knowledge of Hebrew and the ability to participate in a traditional prayer service. But most were as uncertain as the rest of the Jewish community as to the nature of Jewishness in modern times. In the absence of guide-lines, the families emphasized the development of positive atti-tudes which would be followed, they hoped, by their offspring's willingness to establish Jewish homes, when the time would come. In no case did they want their children's Jewishness, as they themselves interpreted the concept, to be less intense than theirs. Most hoped that it would be more intense although a few hoped that it would be the same. Actual expectations, as dis-tinguished from hope, were modest. The majority of the parents expected their children's Jewishness to be approximately the same as theirs. Of the remainder about half expected the level to be slightly above or slightly below their own.

As the parents represented a special group within the general community and the Jewish community, the nine girls and six boys who comprised the Vov Class did also.[12] Distributed among six suburban Junior High Schools, most were above the general population in intelligence[13] and motivation towards Jew-ish educational goals. Up until they entered the Vov Class, the students had attended the B'nai Israel Sunday School seven or eight years and the Hebrew School five years. Most were among the best students in their classes. The boys, all of whom had had a Bar Mitzva ceremony, and six of the nine girls who had under-gone a Bat Mitzva ceremony, had accepted a degree of participa-tion in the service well above the average and had acquitted themselves admirably.

Most significant, however, is the fact that they had not yielded to the temptation to quit all but Sunday School follow-ing the ceremony. One may assume formidable pressure upon them by parents. Still, other B'nai Israel sons and daughters had succeeded in making their feelings on the subject so clear to their parents that they were allowed to sever their ties with the Hebrew School. If these youngsters had felt as strongly no doubt they would have displayed similar determination. It seems plausible therefore that these young people, coming as they did from homes in which education in general and Jewish education in particular were valued far above the ordinary, had interiorized some of these same values. They may have been sent to the Vov Class; but they were not really forced to come.[14]

The students' attendance however should not be interpreted to imply a fascination with or even an acceptance of their previous religious education. Quite the contrary. If there was one sentiment in the group regarding which there was virtually no dissent it was that religious school until that point had been repetitive, irrelevant, and generally distasteful. Something of the mood was conveyed by one student who described her previous religious school experience in the following succinct but devastating comment: "We sat in rows and an old lady walked around the room." Without presuming to judge whether such a characterization is justified, suffice it to say that its acceptance was well-nigh universal. These students were ripe for something different!

During the year prior to their thirteenth birthday, like everyone else at B'nai Israel, the students had heard reports of the new program designed to replace conventional Hebrew School for post Bar/Bat Mitzva youngsters, which incidentally involved an additional cost to parents of $100.00. Chances are, too, that they had heard about a certain Roger Wilkinson who was associated with the program and who, it was rumored, shared their own critical appraisal of conventional Hebrew School procedures.

Roger and Sara Wilkinson

Roger — as he insisted on being called by the students right from the start — was born in a moderate-sized midwestern community. A second generation American, he grew up in a Jewish family with strong Jewish identification and established close ties with the synagogue and with Judaism generally. During his formative years one of the major Jewish influences upon him was a Conservative Jewish youth organization, which has chapters throughout the country. He was extremely active in his local chapter and eventually rose to the presidency of his region.

In this office, he had occasion many times to be involved in the group process, including camping, within a Jewish framework.

It was not long before the possibility of pursuing a career in Jewish education or the Rabbinate or both occurred to Roger. He investigated the subject and discovered that admission to the Conservative Rabbinical School requires a college diploma as well as a keen familiarity with Jewish texts and the Hebrew language. He applied for admission and was accepted by Jefferson University in Graceville. There he pursued his secular and religious studies, the latter, in part, at Congregation B'nai Israel.[15]

Roger, who had known both Rabbis Levy and Katz from his participation in regional youth activities, approached them for part-time employment. As it happens, there was an opening in the area of Bar and Bat Mitzva instruction. Although just turned eighteen, Roger was engaged to train the approximately forty-five twelve-year-olds who were to undergo the ceremony in 1968-1969.

It was during this same period that Roger was beginning to make contact in his university courses with the work of those educators who advocate what is variously called the "free school" or the "open classroom." Highly syntonic to Roger's own personality, he was very much impressed with this approach to teaching. For Roger himself is well-described as an open, outgoing person who enjoyed being with people and who made friends easily. He also showed the talent of being able to share easily — goods as well as feelings — and in general proved to have an engaging manner. It was apparent that Roger was strongly motivated towards a "free" approach to teaching and felt particularly comfortable doing so in a Jewish context.

Some of the excitement Roger felt as he came to know the satisfactions of such teaching is conveyed in an excerpt from an essay which he wrote at the time:

> Through all the work, the struggling, the worrying, and indeed the tears, comes one of the most rewarding experiences I have had at any time in my life. For the

first time I experienced what a teacher and teaching are all about.

It was because of his success in preparing students for the Bar and Bat Mitzva ceremony that Roger was asked to assist the man chosen to lead the initial Vov Class Program in the fall of 1969.

As the first faltering steps were taken in the program, Roger proved to be more than helpful. He revealed himself to be a complex, highly sensitive individual, mature beyond his years. Particularly on weekends, when there was considerable informal interaction between students and teachers, did Roger demonstrate strengths which were destined to play an important role in the subsequent development of the program. He showed, for example, a prodigious grasp of popular music as well as a knowledge of sports and the popular media. He showed equal familiarity with current events and current hockey standings. He showed, in short, an awareness of what is going on in the world generally, and in the Jewish world.

It was natural that when the head teacher announced that he would not be available for the following year Roger was asked to succeed him as head of the Vov Class Program, 1970-1971. By then he had acquired not only considerable teaching experience but also the growing conviction that the program offered both an alternative to current ineffective and even repugnant educational approaches as well as an opportunity for him personally to make a contribution of value. He warmly agreed to teach the new class and to further develop what he regarded as the program's essentially fine thrust, especially since he was going to have the help of Sara who that very summer, on the eve of the new term, was to become his wife.

Sara was a petite, round-faced young lady, whom Roger had known for several years. Born in Europe, she came to this country as a baby and settled with her parents in Roger's home town. Her family, like Roger's, was steeped in Jewishness although as a result of their recent arrival they were somewhat less active in Jewish communal affairs.

Sara, by nature a rather reticent individual, attended Jewish camps and became a member of several Jewish youth organizations. One of them proved to be the very one in which Roger was active. They met and their love for each other blossomed. When Roger decided to go to college in Graceville, Sara followed. She became an education major at State University and thus increasingly shared Roger's growing interest in teaching. When they were married in the summer of 1970, Sara looked forward to her own involvement in the Vov Class Program, because she agreed with her husband that new winds were blowing in the world of education and that Jewish schools should set their sails to take advantage of them.

Chapter Two

Setting the Climate

Uniting in a Common Cause

The students of the Vov Class, it will be remembered, felt highly critical towards school in general and religious school in particular. They considered the school experiences to which they had been subjected to have been uniformly repressive and irrelevant to their real concerns. Imagine their surprise and puzzlement when their new Hebrew School teacher, Roger, not only agreed with their criticisms, but made his agreement known in clear and unequivocal terms. The very first day, he played Pete Seeger's record, "What Did You Learn in School Today?" after which he conducted a frank discussion on what he considered to be the ills of conventional school practices. Without listing those ills, for they will become evident as the story progresses, suffice it to say that he, Roger, categorically disapproved of many widely accepted school policies and declared to the students his intention of avoiding them with this class.

The fact is that Roger's and the student's common cause, at least from the viewpoint of the students, rested on a somewhat shaky foundation. The reason is that most of these students had been similarly enticed before, by other teachers. Invariably, however, enticement was followed by disappointment as those teachers who gave promise of opposing traditional school practices eventually reverted to the expected role. Several students were fond of telling about one public school teacher in particular who had tried to "identify" with them, to use their word. He had urged them to call him by his first name and had invited them to confide in him their true feelings. Far from appreciating his effort which they regarded as ineffectual, they thought less of him than of those traditional teachers whose traditionalism was sincere. Indeed, they had been deceived many times. Would Roger eventually deceive them, too?

Roger began the year with certain procedures which gave the students hope that perhaps he would be different. For example, he established the practice of not receiving students in his assigned room. Instead, he would seat himself in the lobby of the synagogue and greet his students as they entered the building. As a rule, he would sit or stand, as the case was, and converse with the students. Frequently, it would happen that a small group would gather about him and engage in animated conversation with him and with each other. At the bell, or even a few minutes later, the group would enter the room and the lesson would begin. The observer, in time, came to appreciate that the lesson had in fact begun earlier!

By the time they would enter the room, Roger would have already seen to it that the desks were arranged in a circle rather than in rows. He felt — and so expressed himself to the students — that people should look at one another in a classroom. One of the main concerns of education, he said, is interaction between people — hardly possible when they are forced to look at each

others' backs.[1] By the same token, securing permission to speak
by raising a hand he saw as inhibiting the free interaction that
he was seeking in his room. When, upon occasion, out of habit,
a student would raise his hand, Roger would chide him and
remind him that so long as he accorded to others the same
privilege all he had to do was say what was on his mind.

Very early in the year, Roger took issue with another routine which represented a much more serious departure from the
conventional mode. There would be, said Roger, no grades given
in the Vov Class. Evaluation to the extent that it might prove
valuable would be part of the total classroom experience or, if
preferred, a private matter between the student and Roger. No
one, including Roger, was going to judge a student's performance. The single criterion of success in the Vov Class was
whether or not it was interesting and enjoyable to the student.
The following, excerpted from the typescript of an evaluation
conducted by the class in the middle of December, illustrates
Roger's perception of this criterion. He and the students, in the
presence of Mrs. Cohen, their Hebrew language teacher, were
discussing the apparent lack of interest in the Wednesday Hebrew lessons. Roger is speaking.

> I just wish you'd come with a little more enthusiasm
> about what we are doing . . . We don't want you to be
> bored. We don't want you to waste your time. We want
> you to use your time . . . I wasted too much time when I
> was a youngster in Hebrew School and I don't want to
> see you wasting time . . . Now, we sat here and spent the
> last half hour amid interruptions, granted, but we talked
> out a little bit about a mutual problem that arose last
> week. Some people were really expressing verbal discon-
> tent with what we were doing in Hebrew Class. And I
> keep asking you to give me feedback on what I present
> to you. If you don't like it, we'll change, right then and
> there. We'll do something that's really interesting!
> (12/16)

As to the school-wide practice of report cards, that too would
be dealt with in time. It was not at all clear how it would be

dealt with, but that did not seem to matter. Roger's assumption, which he often shared with the students, was that they were there because they wanted to be there and that it was their prerogative in the final analysis to judge their own success or failure — the success or failure of a particular experience as well as that of the entire experience.

Many educational theorists point out that the informality represented by such approaches as Roger employed, whether sincere or not, after all is said and done are ploys. The reason, simply stated, is that the students attend school, to begin with, as a result of law or some other coercive pressure. They are subject to some form of higher authority usually embodied in the teacher, and no matter how much freedom is given they know and the teacher knows that they are at the mercy of the adult world. While this is true of any class which is part of an organized establishment — and the Vov Class surely was — Roger sought to minimize the implications of this condition by means of what he called the "leave, if you want" rule.[2] Briefly stated, this meant that a student had the prerogative of leaving the room if and when he wanted and to stay away for as long as he wanted. To state that this rule was established by Roger and honored without equivocation would be to stretch the truth. It, like many other rules in the same category, emerged gradually and then in response to certain specific situations. Their promulgation was accompanied always by a great deal of testing on the part of students and by uncertainty on Roger's part. Was this or that rule the right thing to do or not? was a question which was constantly on Roger's mind. The rule or the practice he employed flowed from the logic of Roger's overall concept of education. Still its diametrical opposition to current practices of classroom management caused doubt to become his constant companion.

By way of illustration some students took the "leave if you want" rule quite seriously. They left. In some cases they returned to the room rather quickly; in others they did not. Roger suspected that he had gone too far. He therefore amended the rule to read, "leave if you want, but only if you get my permission." When confronted with a request for permission — and it was not long in coming — he had no choice but to give it. A new formulation of the rule therefore made its appearance, namely, "leave if you want but only if you intend to do something worthwhile while you are gone." It was unclear to the students, and it may be presumed to Roger himself, whether under such conditions permission was also required or whether the student was the sole judge of what was worthwhile.

A student-produced tongue-in-cheek cartoon, which made its appearance on the fourth weekend, lampooned Roger's and the class's confusion on this matter. It pictured the students, Roger and the observer — all easily identified by their caricatures — in typical Vov Class fashion, gathered around a rectangular table. The table top was covered with a series of verbal squibs, the targets of which were also easily identified. One read as follows: " '. . . if you don't want to be here then leave!' 'Let's leave!' 'Are you kidding!' 'Of course!' " It should be added that Roger was not beyond expressing displeasure when a student did elect to leave the room, although one had the feeling that in so doing he was faulting himself more than the student for the inadequacy represented by the departure. In any case, the rule was promulgated and led a very uneven and at times uncertain existence.

Right from the start, Roger evinced a great deal of personal interest in the students. One early expression of this interest was a long series of questionnaires designed to give him information, some of it quite intimate. He wanted to know who his students were, what they were thinking, and what they wanted to learn about. He felt, intuitively, that such information would enable him to relate to his students more effectively.

The students did not always take the questionnaires seriously nor did they always answer honestly. They had a deep-seated fear of reprisal from teachers or, at the very least, a fear to expose feelings and attitudes which long experience had taught them to keep to themselves. Roger had considered this, too. Thus he established another rule in the classroom. One was not required to fill out questionnaires, unless he so desired. "The right to say no," as the observer termed this practice, was soon extended to every aspect of classroom activity. If a student was called on for his opinion or invited to answer a question, he could decline to do so without receiving more than a gentle prod from Roger. Upon occasion, Roger would register pique, but in general, just as the student had the right to leave at will and reject, as it were, the entire experience, he also had the right — exercised by some students with considerable regularity — to reject each particular item.

Closely related to the "right to say no" was the "right to privacy." When questionnaires or other written work were distributed, students were informed that they were not required to sign their names. Some students did sign their names, depending upon the paper, although some, from the beginning of the year to its end, did not. In these latter cases, it was the observer's impression that, for the most part, Roger honored the implied guarantee to privacy by not identifying the authors, even though soon after the start of the year he was able to match each student with his handwriting. It was the observer's further impression, however, that when Roger felt the need for a particular bit of information about a particular student, he did identify unsigned papers.[3]

The "right to say no" and the "right to privacy" thus were not carried to undue lengths. There were circumstances, for example, which required the division of the class into two or more smaller groups. Roger let it be known that he expected his assignments to the groups to be honored. By and large, they were. There were times when work had to be done and volunteers were lacking.[4] Roger unhesitatingly appointed students to the tasks, and by and large secured their cooperation. Also, preference sheets regarding possible Independent Study Projects, for obvious reasons, had to be signed. The exceptions notwithstanding, it was the individual student, rather than the subject or the class, who was the locus of decision. The individual student was firmly ensconsed, right from the start, as the principal arbiter of his own involvement, or lack of it.

From the conceptual standpoint, this fact implied the right

of each student to take issue with the teacher. Roger was a man of strong conviction and often took strong stands on a host of different subjects. The content of the convictions aside, students were made to feel that it was legitimate for them to differ and to voice their differences. Many were the times that Roger would ask the class if it liked a particular exercise and would be showered with rather descriptive one-word appraisals such as "stupid," "ridiculous," "worthless." Many were the times too that he invited and received criticism of aspects of the experience that would be considered by some teachers as coming dangerously close to their persons. Bruce, for example, virtually accosted Roger on the ubiquitous "leave if you want" rule. "You don't really mean it," he said to Roger, "because if we do, you yell, 'Get back here and sit down.' " Roger's response in this case was typical. "I'm sorry if I've done that; I don't mean to do it and you catch me when I do." He added as an afterthought, "But, I don't think I've done that too much!" Roger, if he was anything, was human!

There were occasions, too, when students took issue with their teacher on matters of judgment and even on matters of fact. At times, the students were mistaken or misinformed. But, there were also times when Roger was wrong and was declared so in full view of the class. When this happened, he would freely admit his error, attempt to rectify it in some fashion and then proceed with the matter at hand. As this was Roger's stance in situations after the fact, it was also his stance in situations before the fact. One frequently heard him offer a simple "I don't know" or "That I'll have to look up." It is not hard to guess why there came to be a growing regard on the part of the students for that which Roger did know and for that which he did not have to look up.

Roger's willingness to let students hold to their own views — which they did sometimes with great tenacity — was not limited to situations in which he was wrong and they were right. It included situations in which the students adopted positions clearly in opposition to his. An excellent example is the impromptu student-initiated discussion held the February weekend as the group was gathering in the makeshift synagogue for a Saturday morning prayer service. The observer's notes describe what happened as follows:

> George and Bernice got to talking about Hitler and his genius and Sylvia objected . . . . They made the point that what Hitler achieved was very smart. He used the Jews as scapegoats, and organized the whole country in opposition to them. This took a degree of genius unparalleled in history. Both students supported their point of view by referring to readings they had done . . . . The point that Sylvia made was that the processes were really very simple and that no particular smartness was required in order to do what he did. He was just insane. He was a madman. (2/12-2/14).

Roger, who was present the entire time, must have been tempted to enter the discussion on Sylvia's side, for there was no doubt in his or in anyone else's mind about where his sentiments lay or about the strength of the conviction which supported those sentiments. Yet, when he did enter the discussion, Roger's purpose was not to push his view, as the continuation of the notes indicates:

> Roger picked up the theme and turned it in a Jewish direction by pointing out how the Jews were treated in Germany. He said that this was one of the things that he hoped to deal with on future weekends . . . . (2/12-2/14).

Roger, in other words, attempted to influence, but only up to a point — up to the point of usurping the students' right to decide. Whether he adopted this practice because he appreciated the need that adolescents have to "try on" new ideas — even incorrect ones — or whether he did not consider the game "worth the candle," he always gave the impression that he felt there was more at stake than truth in any abstract sense. People were at stake and with people one cannot rush. If the students were wrong no great purpose was to be served by forcing an admission. Given time and a bit more maturity the students would think more deeply about the subject and would arrive at the truth.

The effect of this approach of Roger was that when students differed with him they did not thereby sacrifice their relationship with him. They were objects, or better, subjects of near ultimate respect and differed by right rather than by sufferance. As such they were always welcome back into Roger's good graces if indeed they had ever fallen from them.

In general, it may be said that Roger related to the students with uncommon honesty. He told them what he thought and listened to them as they did likewise. In such a classroom it is not surprising that the students felt themselves to be junior partners in the class's decision-making process. Taught by Roger's behavior towards them that they had the right to make up their minds on any issue, it was only natural that this right should have been exercised in matters affecting the conduct of the class. And if the "right to say no" may be viewed as the negative side, participation in the decision-making process may be viewed as the positive side of the same coin. At first the students' participation applied to matters of little moment, such as how to spend a particular Saturday evening of a weekend. As time went on, however, students participated in matters of greater substance. It is not that Roger withheld the substantive decisions until the students proved their mettle. There was a rather natural progression on their part from the simple to the more complex. Nor did they ever reach the point where they either wanted or were able to assume full responsibility for the class. They were junior partners and rather liked it that way.[5]

The Influence of the Weekends

One aspect of the Vov Class structure which contributed mightily to the building of the relationship between Roger and the class was the weekends.[6] Nine in all, Roger and the students lived together in relative equality for more than forty consecutive hours, from Friday evening until Sunday noon, once each month. They ate the same food, used the same facilities, and in general lived under the same conditions. That Roger was willing to do so was sufficient in itself to make an impression upon the young people. But more important than the impression upon them was the opportunity provided Roger to extend and intensify the atmosphere that he was after.

A residential or total living situation seems to possess a built-in faculty for locating the responsibility for decisions within the individual. At the same time, it seems to be able to influence those decisions in the direction of involvement both with the program and with other people. On the most rudimentary level, because the settings were relatively self-contained, there was no place really to escape to and little else to do other than to participate in the program and otherwise interact with the people who were there. A student could wander away, physically or mentally, just so long. Eventually he was drawn back. Even more important is the fact that much, if not most, of what happens over a weekend cannot be — and in the case of the Vov Class was not — planned precisely by the teacher, or even by the class. The individual was literally forced to assume responsibility for much of what he did and how he did it. To cite but one example, all students ate and slept on the weekends and did so obviously in their own unique ways. To that extent, at least, students were involved and at a level largely of their own choosing.

Perhaps the most critical quality of the total living situation, however, was the opportunity it afforded not only to live the principle of individual responsibility under novel and unexpected circumstances but also to test it under such circumstances. It is one thing to tout a principle and even to adhere to it in a classroom for an hour; it is quite another to act upon it in a long, sometimes grueling total living situation. Roger, however, did just that, although again with something less than total consistency. There was no raising of hands, of course. Students decided whether or not to participate in particular activities and left if they desired. In general, the inherent demands of the total

living situation, combined with Roger's dedication to the prin- ✗
ciple of student self-determination, yielded an atmosphere which
was essentially warm and informal. The effect on the overall
program was both reactive and circular — reactive in the sense
that both Roger's and the students' rejection of traditional educational forms became even more irrevocable, and circular in the
sense that their mutual commitment to a new path fed into
subsequent class sessions and back again into the weekends.

One particular outcome which seems to have derived in significant measure from the weekend experiences was Roger's
total accessibility to his students. The sheet of particulars
handed out in advance of the very first weekend ended with
"Questions??? Call Roger anytime — 318 5731." Each subsequent sheet ended with one or another variation of this same
theme: Roger was available any time the students wanted him or
needed him. On weekends there were of course no artificial
barriers, whether oversized desks or teachers' lounges, to thwart
free communication between him and the students. It is not
surprising that between weekends students felt free to approach
Roger before, after, and even during class. By about a third of
the way through the term they began to make telephone calls to
his home. At one time or another during the year all but two
students found it necessary to call, more to bridge the traditional teacher-student gulf, one suspects, than for any other
reason. Again, it was the individual student who decided if he
needed Roger and Roger, for his part, felt obligated to honor
the judgment.

In certain cases, telephone contact developed into actual
home visits. Roger rather encouraged the process by declaring to
the class that "the Wilkinson home is always open." In time, he
and Sara arranged an "official" visit to their home after a Saturday night excursion to a school play. Soon the students recipro-
cated and Roger received and accepted invitations to visit several
of the students' homes.

If the growing relationship between Roger and the students
extended beyond class time it was the class and its concerns
which formed the major content of their interaction. It was not

thought presumptuous therefore when several of the students solicited rides with Roger to and from school. Roger let it be known that he did not mind chauffering students to class or home. It is not likely either that when he offered to do so he anticipated just how important a function these rides would eventually assume. For it was during car trips with one or more students in tow that he gleaned some of his important information on overall class progress and on a number of individual problems. Several youngsters for example confided to him to a degree which would not have been possible for them perhaps in any other setting. In one particular case, a student became embroiled in a conflict situation which but for the car rides would surely have resulted in her leaving the class. Her dropping out, apart from everything else, would have robbed the class of one of its most important learning experiences.

The burgeoning and broad-based interaction between Roger and the students led gradually to a deep awareness[7] on his part of each individual student's needs and interests. On the simplest level, Roger was aware of birthdays which he never failed to mention, as well as discrepancies in students' vacation schedules which threatened to affect his programming. But beyond this, he became aware of such matters as Rich's film making and theological interests, George's knowledge of cameras, Dorothy's talent for drawing, Bernice's love for books and Sylvia's preoccupation with camp — to cite but a few of the myriad of facts which he would store in his retentive mind and call forth later, in order to enrich the experience both of the individual and of the class. He found many occasions for example to refer to Rich's views about God and at one time considered combining Rich's and George's talents into a major class project. Dorothy helped with the graphics on class worksheets. Bernice received ample opportunity to tell about what she had read and even Sylvia was obliged by having the cords of her camp nostalgia plucked periodically. It was the individual about whom Roger was concerned — not the class nor the subject — but the individual student. It was he who was the focus of Roger's sensitive concern. For Roger was determined to know each student as intimately as that student's willingness and Roger's own ability would permit.

Moments of Stress

In truth more was involved than the student's willingness or Roger's ability. People are complicated and their actions seldom follow straight and therefore predictable paths. A student who is willing some of the time may not be willing the rest of the time. A teacher too who may show fine ability in ordinary interactional situations may be completely inadequate during moments of stress. For this reason it is important to examine Roger's behavior under conditions in which his students were uncooperative or misbehaved. When, for example, a lesson was disturbed by a student calling out or by mischief of one kind or another, Roger tended to ignore the incident, if he could. He showed high selectivity regarding those incidents worthy of being pursued. Frequently, as a result, an incident would pass by and soon be forgotten in the sweep of whatever was happening. The observer was constantly amazed at the tolerance shown by students for other students who disrupted situations with which they themselves were deeply concerned. The tolerance was extended to include even injury inflicted upon fellow students. Once, for example, Rich threw a cue stick and hit Claudia in the side. Proper concern was shown by everyone for Claudia who, though she had a nasty bruise, was not seriously hurt. Rich, however, was not punished in any way. He walked around aimlessly for a while and finally ended up at the foot of Claudia's bed where he joined a discussion in progress among a few of the students who had been looking after her. The point is that they expected similar tolerance from Roger and got it.

Roger endured quite a bit of good-natured kidding and some which was not good-natured. In all cases he would avoid a confrontation if that was possible. Even if students, usually male, violated his person by picking his pocket or throwing things at him, he would attempt to defang the incident by ignoring it or by making a casual comment. At times, he would light upon the incident but use it primarily as an object lesson in an essentially impersonal way. This is not to say that Roger was anyone's "whipping boy." He was quite capable of returning tit for tat and did frequently.

One Wednesday afternoon, for example, Roger was helping the students organize their notebooks. He distributed, according to number, duplicate copies of dittoed sheets that students were lacking. Roger's post-situational summary notes describing Bob's late arrival to class, following the break, accurately reflect what happened:

> Bob did not come back until the end of the period — for what reason I do not know. When he did come in, he was kind of caught off guard and tried to make like he was a good boy. He made some kind of wisecrack like "Oh, is the break over?" I just ignored it .... We kept handing out sheets and he was not accepting any. I said, "What's the matter with you? Do you have these sheets?" And he said, "I don't know. I don't know where we are." I said, "I've been calling out numbers; you could be looking for it!" I got kind of stern with him. And I said, "You know, if you want to help me out, I'll help you out. It's that kind of ballgame!" Finally, he found his place and got back in the groove of things. (5/19)

Roger was capable, too, of considerable anger, though by and large he was rather much in control of himself.

Try as he might, however, there were times when ignoring misbehavior or diverting it simply did not work. Roger would then employ a number of techniques from the arsenal of conventional tactics. He would regroup[8] students or seat himself or his wife strategically between them. Rather than handle the matter antiseptically though, as some manuals suggest, he would usually wait for an offense to be committed and then respond in this or a similar fashion. Sometimes he would confiscate a cap gun or other weapon. Upon occasion, he went so far as to ask one or several students to leave the room. This punishment, if it

can be called such, never involved higher authority, such as the
Principal or the Rabbi. The student who was removed knew why
he had been removed and knew also that he could return whenever he was willing to end his offensive behavior. Usually he
would stand around the door of the room and slink back when
he thought no one was watching. In no case was Roger's
response to an offense more than that which was necessary to
bring the situation under control, despite occasional threats to
the contrary. It was never retaliatory in any sense. In fact, it
often happened that Roger would review what an offender had
missed upon his return to the room.

Note should be taken too of the approach to misbehavior
directed against material objects. When a thing would be misused
or broken, as would happen upon occasion, even through the
neglect or the conscious intent of a particular student, the offender was not penalized. Once, for example, during a weekend,
the only record player there was left on all night, probably
intentionally by a particular student, whose identity was known
to everyone. As the group gathered the next morning and discovered that the record player had burned out during the night,
Roger and the students merely registered disappointment and
went on without the record player. Material objects, with the
possible exception of food — and that for reasons yet to be
discussed — were simply not regarded as important.

Teaching Strategies

No serious attempt has been made thus far to delineate the
more usual teaching strategies employed by Roger both in class
and on weekends, nor will there be. Not that these were unimportant in creating the atmosphere which was beginning to
develop in the Vov Class. It is just that Roger, as the reader has
no doubt already presumed, was an able teacher. For this reason, certain teaching behaviors should be taken almost for granted. Most of the time, for example, Roger prepared well. Except
for a few occasions towards the end of the year, he invariably
went to a great deal of trouble to think out the purposes of a

particular lesson and to find resource material related to those purposes. He did not hesitate to do the research necessary to gain a grasp of a particular subject nor did he hesitate to bring in resource people when needed. He took pains to couch the material in forms which made it suitable for the class. He himself typed and ran off no fewer than 175 sheets containing such material. He paid careful attention to detail, seeing to it that looseleaf-type holes were punched in the sheets and that there was ample music available for breaks during weekends. In addition, he repeatedly anticipated contingencies[9] by providing rainy-day alternatives and extra supplies.

By the same token, Roger's classroom presentations usually were interestingly done. He searched for and often found imaginative ways of gaining the students' attention. He employed role playing, games, quizzes and other such techniques in his effort to involve the students and to keep them involved. In general, whatever he did was done with enthusiasm and even drama. Roger had participated in dramatic performances as a teenager and had developed as a result a keen sense of the dramatic. When he firmly grasped his own purpose in a particular lesson, usually he could build in sufficient dramatic ideas to highlight the purpose. One example comes to mind from an early weekend, the theme of which was the Sabbath or Shabbat as the day is known in Hebrew. Roger composed and dittoed an invitation which he addressed to each student personally by name. The invitation written in his own hand, stated, "Sara and I would like to invite you to become a part of our family for this weekend. Most importantly, we would like you to join with us in celebrating a traditional Shabbat, just like we would if you were a guest in our home." The enthusiasm and dramatic affect of the invitation are even more apparent in the closing paragraph: "Forget about school work, classes (sic!), and the everyday world you are used to — Have a *Completely Unique Experience — Shabbat!*" One student expressly said that it was word of Roger's enthusiasm which had brought him to the Vov Class in the first instance and its confirmation in real life, he implied, was what kept him there.

Roger also had the teaching skill to make the most of chance occurrences within his planned lessons. By way of example, Jeanne had found a book on "Sexology," in her basement at home. She brought it to the weekend the theme of which was "love." Small groups gathered around her and took naughty delight in the contents of the book. At one point, Roger happened by. Jeanne hid the book coyly behind her back. As Roger stood uneasily for a moment, Jeanne asked if he wanted to see what she had. He did and it was not long before he and the girls were pointing out sections of special interest. When they had done this for a few minutes, Roger turned to the group and asked about the sex education they were receiving in school. This question led to a full-blown treatment of sex in relation to love and the inadequate sources from which many students receive their information on the subject.

This same kind of thing happened often, partially because of the relationship between Roger and the students and also because Roger had the ability to alter his plan and create a new one on the spot if the new one gave promise of being more natural or better in some other way than the original.[10]

Roger was perceptive enough also to realize when the students needed to ventilate or to release pent-up feelings. He provided outlets in the form of games and the acceptance of profanity, within limits. Without belaboring the point any further by adducing additional teaching behaviors of this kind, suffice it to say that Roger succeeded in providing his students with experiences related to their interests and his purposes.

At this point it would be well to insert a caveat which applies to all of the foregoing and to much of what will follow. Roger's behaviors should not be thought of as the product of a studied and therefore essentially linear effort on his part to create certain specific outcomes. In the early stages especially, Roger approached the class with certain passionately-held but vaguely understood perceptions regarding people and education — perceptions which coincided with the needs and the perceptions, if they can be termed so, of the students. One of these perceptions was that people are essentially good and hence worthy of respect. According to Roger, the basic nature of his students and indeed of all people, is goodness, in the sense that the term is used by the Bible in the creation story. It is not that people do not incorporate evil within their makeups or upon occasion do not stray from the circuitous and broad path which leads to messianic perfection. They do. But the evil and the straying do not represent people's natural and most fundamental quality. They are rather aberrations of their true self; deviations from their essential beauty.

One must acknowledge that Roger's identification of the reasons for the aberrations or the deviations bordered on the naive. Often he would express the belief that ugliness of character was really not the fault of its host. If ugliness, in any form, were present in an individual, it was other people, that is, the immediate group or society at large, who were to blame. By the same token, all that was required for the removal of the ugliness was for people "to react to each other as human beings and to accept each other's individuality." If that were to happen, wrote Roger, people would not find it necessary "to goof around and show off for each other. They wouldn't have to impress each other; they wouldn't have to pick scapegoats; they wouldn't have to alienate people; they wouldn't have to create cliques. If everybody accepted everybody else on an equal basis, then everything else would fall into place . . . the problems, the discipline would be gone. All the things in the world that we would want to happen would happen!"

Now, naiveté may not necessarily be a fault. Whatever truths it may cause to be obscured, it may also, not unlike the self-fulfilling prophecy, reveal or lead to certain others. Naiveté, for example, may be responsible for a person, especially if that person happens to be a teacher, underplaying and depressing thereby certain tendencies in his students. At the same time, it may cause other desirable tendencies to be highlighted. Much the same as a parent — and the epithet is not idly chosen — sees his child through lenses colored with love, so a teacher, who views his students in like fashion, may be inclined to inspire those students to otherwise unattainable achievement.

Under no circumstances did Roger think of students as raw material to be refined and moulded and certainly not by him. It was his responsibility as he saw it to perhaps locate the causes of the imperfections which marred character and then to love his students back to psychic or emotional health. And he did so in a thousand different ways. From simple effusions such as conferring a bear-hug upon one student who had been away for some time to the perceptive compassion shown the smaller boys when Roger would assure them that suddenly one day they would spurt up to the height of the others, Roger accepted his students unconditionally[11] and loved them deeply.

Another incident culled from the field notes, though subtle, will be recognized by the sensitive teacher as perhaps one of the most difficult expressions of love a teacher can give. The lesson in question dealt with a subject that Roger was anxious to get on with. He distributed several mimeographed sheets and had individual students read them aloud, paragraph by paragraph. He then called upon a girl, one of the poorer readers in the class, to read.

> She constantly trips. She mutilates word after word and pays no heed to punctuation. Bob says, "You skip all the commas" (which she does). She, looking at Roger: "Shall I go on?" (by which she means, "Do you want me to keep up with this punishment I am inflicting upon you or not?") Roger, "Sure we want you to go on." She does and he helps her in a warm and kindly way to get through. (1/13)

On many occasions, too, Roger demonstrated his compassion and concern for the individual by protecting those students who were put upon or persecuted by their classmates. If a student's statement would elicit a disparaging comment from a fellow student, Roger would protect the student and urge him to hold to his view. In a scuffle over a seat, Roger would protect the weaker student. In general Roger avoided favorites although if and when he took sides it was invariably to support the underdog.[12]

Beyond repeated incidents of this kind Roger trusted his

students implicitly. For example, he would state certain rules for weekends, such as not to leave the premises, and then not check for compliance. Students were on their own, for he, Roger, was not going to be a "policeman." Even when confronted with clear-cut evidence that his rules were broken, he refused to believe that there were not extenuating circumstances. He was offered many times and refused just as many times assistance from parents on weekends to help maintain so-called discipline. Again, Roger did this not because he calculated behavior of this sort to produce what he considered certain desirable results. The behavior rather flowed from his vague but firmly entrenched faith in his students — a faith which he maintained even when he did not understand what was motivating his students as well as when they showed signs of rejecting both him and his efforts. If, as Gibb and Gibb said, "the deepest needs of man are to trust and be trusted,"[13] Roger had found the secret of meeting those needs.

Mutual Self-Disclosure

It was only in an atmosphere of this kind that self-disclosure on the part of both the students and Roger could begin to occur. The tone was set perhaps at the beginning of the year when Roger instituted the practice of himself filling out questionnaires that the students were asked to fill out and then offering to let the students read his responses if they were interested. It is not known to the observer whether or not students actually asked for and reviewed his papers. But there was really little need to do so. All a student had to do was ask and Roger freely divulged information about himself, not just his views on various subjects, but details of his personal life that one would normally regard as privileged. At only the second session of the class, for example, he told the students about his draft status, what he was studying in school, and something of his career hopes. At various times he shared information about his childhood — how he used to travel with "The Crew," as well as some of the pranks the group performed; how, at first, he was afraid to go out on dates, and how he had met, courted, and then married Sara. He talked about his parents and especially his grandfather in connection with a celebration for which he had to cancel a class. He discussed his personal religious problems in a straightforward, matter-of-fact way. Frequently he voiced other areas of personal doubt, especially regarding Jewish education and his own role in it.

Although the example of Roger's self-disclosure probably influenced the students to respond in kind and reveal portions of themselves not usually shared in a Hebrew School situation, this one behavior, perhaps more than any other in the Vov Class, Roger consciously and carefully attempted to elicit. He did so by means of sensitivity-type exercises. While "sensitivity" may embrace a variety of exercises, serving related but different purposes, what is referred to here is the type of exercise which seeks to encourage self-disclosure primarily for the purpose of self-awareness. One exercise, which Roger called "focusing," involved a series of open-ended sentences such as "I feel good about myself when people . . . I feel bad about myself when people . . . My greatest strengths are . . . My greatest weaknesses are . . ." The instruction paragraph at the beginning stated the purpose quite clearly: to provide each student with "a list of things others do which make (him) feel good or bad about (him)self; a list of things (he) think(s) are (his) strong and weak points; a list of things (he) care(s) about; a list of things that make(s) (him) angry or glad." When the exercise was completed, Roger invited students to read their answers aloud. Karen was first. She stated that in her opinion her greatest weakness was criticizing too much. The statement brought a question from George as to whether her criticism was of the constructive kind. Brad divulged how he liked to go to baseball games, buy general admission seats and then when no one was watching occupy box seats. It is for that reason, he added, that he preferred to go to games without his parents. Some students declined to share their answers nor did it seem important at this stage that they should. Even though self-disclosure ideally may come to serve social purpose, the first step, certainly in the Vov Class, was the habit of self-disclosure to *one's self*. Again, it was the individual student to whom Roger related at the beginning. It was for the individual primarily and through him that the atmosphere of the Vov Class began to take shape.

This sensitivity exercise was followed by many others like it. Students came to express themselves about themselves quite freely, in writing at first and then verbally. They did so before long in the presence of fellow students, Roger, and the observer. Soon students began to voice their opinions on topics which in most school situations they would avoid. It was the Saturday afternoon of the second weekend, for example, that the students shared a view of their school and teachers that was a source of illuminating shock, particularly to the observer. The following excerpt from the field notes is presented not only because it illustrates student self-disclosure, but because it paints with such vivid strokes the students' whole relationship with school and teachers.

> We began to talk and we had an interesting, to say the least, thirty-minute session during which the kids shared impressions of certain of their teachers, in Hebrew School, Sunday School, and Public School. They talked individually and together and showed a great deal of excitement in their description of the foibles as well as the gross inadequacies of their teachers. Story followed story — they could hardly contain themselves — and most of them were funny in a sad sort of way. I laughed so hard at a certain point that tears came to my eyes.
>
> They described teachers who are self-centered, authoritarian demigod types. They attempt to impose situations upon the kids that are of no interest and in some cases cruel. Some teachers, for example, employ corporal punishment. This came as a complete surprise. Several teachers are described as having students bend over and hold their ankles in order to be whacked. This goes on in Graceville schools today! In one particular school the kids said a paddle is used, though it is light and does not hurt much. When I evinced interest in this subject, one

student pointed out that the purpose was really not to hurt physically as much as to embarrass! Then followed a whole group of episodes involving placing students in other embarrassing situations. For example, students who are caught chewing gum — the gum is put on the board with a big circle around it and the offender is required to stand up near it. In other cases, students have the gum placed on their noses and are required to walk around all day long that way.

At the same time as the kids described their teachers, they also described their own efforts to get back at them and generally to make them miserable. And from their description they seem to be quite successful. One teacher, for example, has hand lotion which she uses every day before lunch. Seldom does she find the lotion where she left it the previous day. Many incidents of this kind were told in which the students, who seem to be very perceptive of their teachers' areas of vulnerability, show how assiduously they dedicate themselves to making their teachers uncomfortable.

As I sat and listened to the stories, amidst peals of laughter, my mind wandered back to Dewey's description of the classrooms of the early 1900's. I am amazed that so little has changed .... It is not that teachers hit children, but that there is the necessity for hitting because there is so little identity between the students' real interests and what goes on in school. (10/30).

Eventually the willingness to share was not limited just to information about the self or even opinions on off-limit subjects. Students began to express their deepest feelings and concerns to Roger and to each other. One girl, for example, suffered greatly from what she considered another's rejection of her, and said so; a boy wondered why he seemed to have the need to act, as he put it, and upon occasion to steal. A girl's confused responses one afternoon led her to admit, "I don't know my real self at all!" Another could never understand why she was "mad at everybody, but her sister." This kind of frank disclosure soon was extended to include almost every subject of concern to young people, from prayer experiences, to evolution, to menstruation. Mutual self-disclosure of both teacher and students was a fact of the Vov Class experience.

The effect of the foregoing was the creation within the Vov Class of an atmosphere which had a peculiarly human quality. Despite uneven pressure systems within the atmosphere and periodic turbulence surrounding it, individual human beings found in it warm acceptance and love.[14] The tone was set largely by Roger, who, whatever else he did or did not do, showed himself to be a person free and unthreatened enough by other persons to be able to invite them to enter an empathetic relationship with him and that for which he stood.

For the moment, the relationship between him and the students and among the students themselves was merely that of somewhat reserved friendship. There was yet a long road to travel before the students could permit themselves a more demanding involvement with Roger and with each other. Yet, unbeknown to them and perhaps even to Roger, the major lines of a much deeper interaction had already been set even as the foundation for a whole new experience in Jewish living had already been constructed.

Chapter Three

The Curriculum Content[1]

Introduction

Two important problems which engaged Roger from the outset were: What should be taught the students; and, By what methods? Although the experience of the previous year, when he had been an assistant in the Vov Class, provided Roger with some curriculum ideas and materials, neither before the term began nor during it did any authority inform him of a particular body of subject matter which was to be "covered" in the course of the year. In this matter, as in many, Roger was quite on his own.

Yet, the fact is that the Vov Class did deal with a considerable body of subject matter both Jewish and general. Students acquired information on a variety of subjects and made contact with ideas which were new and challenging to them. Many learned new skills, religious and general, and all found ample opportunity to practice old ones. While it may not be possible to distinguish between the two, it may be presumed that the students' cognitive acquisitions were accompanied by affective acquisitions and that the latter were no less important than the former. The students of the Vov Class, in short, learned, as the term is used usually, a great deal about Judaism and other subjects in the course of their experience together.

The difficulty involved in identifying precisely what the learning, both cognitive and affective, consisted of is a function, among others, of the highly unconventional approach employed by Roger in subject matter selection and presentation. If, as was pointed out in the preceding chapter, Roger's approach to classroom management was non-traditional, his approach to the curriculum was equally so. Just as the school authorities, for whatever reasons, refrained from stipulating curriculum goals and materials in advance, so did Roger. In response perhaps to necessity as much as to principle, Roger and the students developed the curriculum as the year unfolded. They pursued what in effect was an evolving curriculum.[2] From week to week neither Roger nor the students were sure what it was they would study or if indeed they would study at all in the accepted sense. Plans for a forthcoming lesson would be formulated after the experience of the previous lesson. Nor was it unusual for Roger and the class to lay plans and then have them overturned or at least altered greatly by a development whether within or without the class which was not anticipated previously.

That which motivated the choice of particular subject matter and the methods of its presentation was first and foremost Roger's and the students' interests as they developed over time. Roger had certain personal allegiances and needs which expressed themselves in certain emphases. And the students did likewise. To assert that the allegiances and needs, especially those of the students, were fluid, is to assert the obvious. Yet, many were constant in the sense that they made their appearance at the beginning of the year and persisted throughout.

Young people's tastes by age thirteen are highly developed. In the trustful atmosphere of the Vov Class they were openly and forcefully expressed.

A second motivation for the choice of subject matter and methods was the nature of the Jewishness within the orbit of which the Vov Class experience was lived. Jewishness is far more than a religion in the accepted sense of the term. It is a highly developed, sophisticated religio-cultural entity which incorporates a land, a language, a literature, and all those manifestations which are normally associated with a culture. The specifically religious component of Jewishness is unique also. It relies heavily upon action symbols as distinct from verbal means of expressing religious conviction. This unique character of Jewishness, if it did not provide the specific subject matter of each lesson, certainly set its parameters.

One of the dangers inherent in an evolving curriculum of this kind is that the participants' interests and the nature of the subject notwithstanding, class activity comes to be dictated largely by the whimsical gratification of desire rather than by thoughtful concern with more substantive considerations. That this did not happen in the Vov Class is a function of three factors each of which interacted with the other two in such a fashion as to produce a curriculum which had considerable substance. The three factors were the teacher, the students and the character of the B'nai Israel synagogue under which auspices they came together.

As has been noted, Roger was not only a warmly identified Jew but a Jew who was possessed of a rich store of Jewish and general knowledge. His whole background and future orientation, including his career expectations, implied a commitment to Jewish subject matter. Though Jewish education was closer to his heart than the pulpit his resolve to spend a minimum of five years in Rabbinical School was motivated in part by his desire to deepen his knowledge of classical Jewish sources.

That Roger could think in terms of bringing his students into contact with authentic Jewish subject matter and that he could entertain some hope of success in the endeavor derives in part from the nature of his students. Like Roger, the students also felt that their Jewishness was dependent in some fashion upon their knowledge of Judaism. Their parents believed and they to a greater or lesser extent shared the belief that in order to be Jewish in a meaningful way they had to be conversant with the ideas and forms of Judaism. The desire to achieve this ability may be presumed to have been one of the reasons they had decided to continue their Jewish schooling after Bar and Bat Mitzva. Though the curious Vov Class program, which involved them in weekends away as well as regular sessions overseen by a person who resembled a camp counselor more than a Religious School teacher, left them more than a little uncertain as to what direction the effort would take that year, long association with Jewish schooling combined with their own perceptions of Jewishness led them to expect that it would involve exposure to a body of ideational and ritual content.

The third factor which assured an emphasis within the evolving curriculum upon Jewish content was the character of B'nai Israel and its religious school. Long regarded in Graceville as an upholder and protector of Jewish tradition, the very name B'nai Israel implied that a program conducted under its auspices would involve some concentration upon substantive material. B'nai Israel and its educational system were venerable and highly respected institutions. That which would be done under their aegis would be as solid as they.

These three factors then — Roger, the students, and the B'nai Israel auspices — interacting in a relatively free and protected environment combined to form a highly flexible but substantive curriculum for the Vov Class. A Sunday or Wednesday lesson ranged from a critical analysis of a classical text in which, it might be added, the teacher filled a prominent role, to individual student projects in which the teacher exercised little if any direct supervision. What applied to Sunday and Wednesday sessions applied to the nine weekends. Though students were expected to come at the beginning of a weekend and stay until its end, the time in between was spent in diverse activity ranging from carefully structured discussions, centered about authoritative reference material, to carefree walks in the park, the latter for no reason other than it seemed the right thing to do at the moment.

The foregoing should not be construed to mean that the curriculum inputs of the Vov Class were limited to the outgrowth of what occurred from lesson to lesson. Some items of curriculum, particularly those of a structural nature, made their appearance at the beginning of the term and remained with the class throughout. These intertwined with the occasional inputs and that which derived from particular lessons to form an extremely varied, highly eclectic curriculum. While the curriculum which emerged was responsive to the needs of the hour, it had considerable constancy and stability. One of the major structural forms which was responsible was the weekend themes.

Weekend Themes[3]

In addition to the standard items of content derived from routine, it was intended that each of the nine monthly weekends of the Vov Class have a central topic around which programmatic materials and techniques would be organized. It was Roger's responsibility to choose the themes and to develop specific means for their treatment. The hope was expressed that he would involve the students in theme selection and development.

Prior to the first weekend, held in September, the class had had only three sessions, one of which was the orientation. Thus there was little opportunity for either Roger or the class to involve themselves in the preparation of a theme. Nor was this of particular concern to Roger. It was his view that the first weekend should be devoted primarily to conviviality and to the casting of the musical, "Fiddler on the Roof," which the class, at the orientation session, had decided to produce. He and the students would pray and eat, listen to records, watch films and enjoy each other's company which would be theme enough.

As it turns out, this is precisely what happened. The group did all of these things and established thereby an overall pattern for future weekends including the main lines of their social interaction. Later in the year, when an attempt was made to recall the weekend themes, Roger attached the designations Awareness and Sensitivity to the first. The fact is, however, that the weekend had no theme, unless the fellowship which was fostered during it can be characterized as such.

October was the first weekend to have a theme in the sense in which it was conceived originally. Though Sabbath observance was to be a major ingredient of every weekend, in order to provide an opportunity, at the outset, for a more thorough treatment of its qualities, Roger decided to make it the theme of the second weekend.

It was on Friday, shortly after the arrival at Mary Grove, as the students were arranging their sleeping bags, that Roger handed personalized invitations to the students, from him and Sara, to join them in a traditional Sabbath. The purpose, said Roger, was to have them experience a *bona fide* Sabbath such as he and Sara would observe when they would have children of their own. All of the students were invited to what he described as Sara's and his Sabbath table. Under Sara's direction, the girls lit the Sabbath candles. Everyone gathered around the table which had been set in typical Sabbath style. Roger, as the head of the household, blessed the assembled, first the boys, then the girls, and finally his wife. He led the group in the Sanctification Prayer over the wine. Then, after first explaining its significance, he had the students line up in front of two large basins filled with water. Each individual washed his hands to the accompaniment of the appropriate blessing and returned to the table for the blessing over the Sabbath bread. There was considerable interest in the procedure which, though not strange to the students, had seldom been done with such meticulous attention to detail. The meal consisted of typical Sabbath foods. It was followed by the singing of the traditional songs. At one point Roger interrupted the singing to pass out and read a dittoed sheet entitled, "Some Thoughts for the Sabbath Table," the flavor of which is conveyed by the first of the three selections:

Said Rabbi Yaakov Yosef of Polonoyve: "If this Shabbat[4] day is wholly a day of the spirit, why is it a custom to eat a special meal on Shabbat eve?"

He was answered: "The young son of a lord, while at school, received a splendid gift, which he had long desired, from his father. No one else at school had anything like it. He would have danced for joy, but he felt sorry for his best friend at school, who had received nothing. He therefore prepared a special banquet, and invited his friend to celebrate and feast with him, and there they danced joyfully together."

So, too, the soul of the Jew receives from his Father a priceless gift — the spirit of the Shabbat. It desires to express its delight in prayer and in song — but it feels sorry for the body, who has been given nothing. We therefore are told to eat a special meal and wear special clothes on Shabbat — so that the body too can join in the soul's delight.

When the readings were completed, Grace was recited and the students dispersed. The remainder of the evening consisted of a brief service and relaxed game playing. Just before bedtime, Roger gathered a few of the students together and read them a short story with a Sabbath-like theme.

The next morning was spent in typical Sabbath observance. After a light breakfast, the group participated in two prayer services and reviewed the weekly Bible portion, which happened that week to deal with Noah. Later in the afternoon they listened to Roger read a nostalgic description of the Sabbath as it was observed in the Shtetl.[5] The notes describe the response when Roger invited the students to talk about their own Sabbath experiences:

Two types of experiences emerged. One was home experiences and the other was camp. In all cases, the kids expressed warmth and nostalgia. . . There was quite a bit of emphasis upon food — chicken and chicken soup are the standard fare for Friday night. Many pointed to a changed atmosphere in their homes. A number pointed out that this is a family evening, when relatives gather.

One little girl, in particular, recalled that her grandfather used to sip tea out of a glass Friday night. Another, that her father would not yell at them as much on Friday night. Those that recalled camp experiences, described typical Shabbat observances such as one finds in Jewish camps. On Friday night the children wear whites. There is dancing. Saturday morning, breakfast is later than usual and they do not have to be there at any particular time. The day is a relaxed day. One young man described a very observant Boy Scout chum of his who refused to do any work whatsoever on Shabbat. Roger suggested that since they would be having seven more Sabbaths together during the course of this program they think about how to observe it in a more satisfying manner. (10/29-11/1)

Several hours later both the theme and the Sabbath were rounded out with the Havdala,[6] for which Roger had prepared a brief dittoed service. As the group stood in a friendship circle, the twisted candle was lighted, the spices passed and the prayers intoned. The Sabbath had ended and the group could now go to the recreation hall for its "Fiddler" rehearsal. From that moment on, and by means of the Sabbath, the concept of a weekend theme was firmly established in the Vov Class.

The theme of the third weekend, which was the Cycle of Life, had about it a degree of integration not duplicated with the other themes. Roger played several current records and showed several films which treated aspects of the subject of growth and the aging process. With the help of a guest, the teacher of the first Vov Class, the group read portions of and discussed the weekly Pentateuchal Reading which dealt with the death of the matriarch Sarah and Abraham's effort to find a suitable burial plot for her. The song, "Sunrise, Sunset," from "Fiddler's" wedding scene, describing the feelings of parents as they witness their children marry, was highlighted also. The Saturday evening program consisted of the movie "2001" which depicts man's evolution from the apes to the space age. The picture's meaning and significance occupied the group in animated discussion late into the night. As that weekend came to a close, it was clear that in addition to the intrinsic value of the subject matter, Roger had established the weekend theme as being concerned with matters of serious moment to the students and to himself.

Because of a social crisis which developed in the class during the third weekend, Roger decided that the theme of the fourth should be Friendship. Two of the three Wednesday sessions leading up to the weekend were devoted to sensitivity exercises which pointed up aspects of the general topic. At these same sessions Roger also saw to it that the friendship-inhibiting cliques were broken up. Simultaneously, he searched for materials and techniques which would enable him to deal with the problem effectively on the weekend itself. As the weekend approached, both Roger and the class sensed that they were about to engage in an important experience, important to them individually and important to the group as a whole.

The fourth weekend treated the friendship theme by means of a number of excellent films, records and dittoed sheets, all of which underscored the same basic point; namely, that people should open themselves up to other people to the end that they might all enter into more satisfying and cordial relationships. The first sheet Roger handed out depicted stylized human forms standing in a circle with hands clasped. The text in the circle's middle read:

> PERSON EQUALS COMMUNITY:
> If each person is really a community of persons someone who is made real by being affirmed or loved as a person by other people, then wouldn't you say we find out who we are by needing other persons and having meaning-full relationships with them?
> Songwriters tell us that people who need
> PEOPLE
> are the luckiest people in the world.
> Do you see it that way?

From the start, it was hoped that weekend theme choices would reflect the thinking of the students of the Vov Class as well as that of the teacher. In pursuance of this hope, in early December, Roger distributed a list of sixteen "problem areas that might be relevant to . . . Jewish teenagers." Students were asked to choose those which were of most interest to them. Roger implied that decisions on future weekend themes would follow student preference. The tally, which Roger made after class, revealed the top three choices to be The Drug Scene, Is Judaism Relevant? and War and Peace, in that order. Later, however, when Roger referred to the results, he erroneously reported that War and Peace had been first. It should not be supposed that Roger intentionally misrepresented the facts. Concern for War and Peace was first on his personal agenda and hence first on the agenda of his class.

Like many people his age, Roger was highly critical of United States involvement in the Vietnam War. Even though he had a pre-Rabbinic deferment, he suffered constant anxiety that it would be revoked. There was no doubt in his mind that, if this were to occur, he would resort to almost any means, including voluntary exile, in order to avoid conscription. Most of the students, particularly the boys, at one time or another, indicated that they agreed with Roger's position. The theme of the December weekend, having been set already, Roger felt that War and Peace would be ideal for the fifth, that is, the January weekend.

Because of winter vacation and the especially early date of the weekend, only three class sessions, one Sunday and two Wednesdays, separated the January from the December weekend. The first of these sessions Roger began with the record, "The Eastern World, it is explodin!" The lyrics, which the class followed by means of a dittoed sheet Roger had prepared, conveyed the message that the world is on the eve of destruction and that nothing can be done to avert the disaster. Upon completion of the record, Roger solicited one word reactions from the students. Bomb, annihilation, boom, and end were some. Thereupon followed a discussion on the relative merits of pacifism and preventative war, as applied both to America and to Israel. The discussion turned to anti-war demonstrations, including those on behalf of Soviet Jewry. The fatal shooting of four college students a short time before came under discussion as did the question of how much authority young people in this society possess. American war atrocities were also considered as was the question of the extent to which a person is justified in disobeying orders when he considers the effects of obeying to be immoral. Roger emphasized the connection between all of this and respect for people which had been the burden of the friendship theme the previous weekend.

At the second of the three sessions preceding the January weekend, the theme of War and Peace was kept alive in the minds of the students by means of a class-executed collage on the subject. Actually, the collage ended up as a potpourri of many subjects. But its employment demonstrated to the students Roger's desire to have them think about War and Peace in advance of the weekend.

The last of the three preweekend sessions focused on the divergent views of three imaginary college students regarding the Vietnam War issue. As he distributed the two dittoed sheets containing the views which he stated had been copied out of a book on Judaism and social issues, Roger pointed out that the subject was far from theoretical. It affected many young men personally, himself included. He added wistfully, "Please God, it will not affect you."

Roger had individual students read the material, after which, with the help of the board, he attempted to summarize each view in relation to the other two. Students were invited to state their own positions. Even though he did not say so explicitly, Roger's preference for the pacifist position was apparent. The session ended with Roger suggesting that students write original prayers on the subject, which would be used at the services on the weekend, scheduled to begin that Friday night.

The fifth weekend, devoted to the theme of War and Peace, was the richest to that point with respect to the quantity and the quality of the material used. This is so in part because the

Jewish tradition, as reflected in its prayers and music, is engrossed with a longing for peace. It is so additionally because the youth culture, with which Roger and the students were intimately acquainted, was replete with concern for the subject. By actual count, the weekend incorporated five songs, thirteen individual readings, three films, one transparency and three traditional prayers on either the beauty of peace or the horror of war. In addition, Roger included three original prayer-poems which had been submitted to him by Claudia, George and Jeanne. Jeanne's read:

> I'm a soldier, isn't it fun!
> To have, attached to you, a gun.
> I'm a soldier don't you know!
> My guns are friends, my brothers, foes.
> I'm a soldier, don't you see!
> The whole wide world destroyed by me.
> I'm a soldier, nothing new!
> Someday they will get you too.
> I'm a soldier, in my place!
> Who'll die first, it's all a race.
> I'm a soldier, don't ask why!
> THEY HAVE CHOSEN ME TO DIE!

The fact is that the weekend turned into a virtual peace rally with Roger as its promoter and organizer. Somewhat in the nature of a revival for the already committed, the immorality of the Vietnam War and the legitimacy of avoiding military service were underscored time and time again. It should have come as no surprise to anyone that on Sunday, as the students dispersed to the waiting cars, Roger handed each a present — a Hebrew peace button! Not only had Roger's and what he regarded as Judaism's view of War and Peace been forcefully presented, but the weekend theme as an educational tool had come of age in the Vov Class.

Following closely upon the heels of War and Peace in the December preference sheet, the students had indicated their interest in the subject of Love and Sex. Obviously not comfortable with treating what had been the students' first choice, namely, The Drug Scene, Roger decided that Love and Sex would be the theme of the sixth weekend, to be held in February. At the first session following the fifth weekend, Roger informed the class of his decision. He then conducted a "sing down" of the word love. In the space of about twenty minutes, the class, which had been divided into two teams, thought of forty-two individual songs, which incorporated the word love in their titles. Roger read the list aloud and reminded the class that love was the direct opposite of what they had been studying, namely war. He closed the lesson with the statement, "What I'd like you to do for Sunday — I know some of you have record collections — is bring one of your favorite records which deals with love."

Though Brad and Bruce did bring records to the Sunday session, it was not until later in the week, at the Wednesday session, that Roger picked up the love theme by means of a commercially produced educational tape he had acquired. The tape described a man who was so desperately alone that he literally bought a telephone service which permitted him periodically to dial an expression of love. In the discussion which followed, Roger related love to loneliness and the need that every person has to be loved. At the same session, he called attention to the happy calendar circumstance that the sixth weekend would fall on Valentine's day. He suggested that since the Monday following the weekend was a holiday, the group might want to stay together through Sunday in order to see the film, "Love Story," at a local theater.

During February, the subject of love was dealt with twice more. Once, Roger had the group perform a sensitivity exercise in which it formed a circle and physically excluded one of its members. The purpose was to show how painful it is to be rejected by others. Another time, Roger played a tape entitled "Barrage of Sound" which treated problems of communication and which he promptly related to love. By the time the February weekend arrived, the Vov Class had had formal contact with the subject of love at no fewer than five sessions.

As the weekend began, Roger quickly established the theme and his own competence for dealing with it. He did so in response to a question from Karen:

> Karen asked the question, "Who will be our guest this week?" Roger said, "We are all the guests this week and particularly Sara and I . . . because the theme is Love, and Love leads to marriage and Sara and I are married." (2/12-14)

During the ensuing forty-eight hours, Roger and Sara and the Vov Class immersed themselves in a perusal of the theme of love from numerous vantage points and by means of a variety of materials. Hebrew and English songs about love, some from the record player and some from the throats of the students, reverberated through the corridors of the Community Center. Services highlighted those traditional prayers which speak of love — man's love for God and God's love for man — as well as readings which Roger had prepared. The readings, of which there were twenty-three in number, ranged from one sentence aphorisms to a somewhat involved statement by Erich Fromm on modern misconceptions of love. Included too was a description of the Biblical love affair of Jacob and Rachel and its Rabbinic counterpart, that of Rabbi Akiba and the daughter of Kalba. Both relationships were analyzed and contrasted to the typical romantic approach to love found in current media. At one meal, a newspaper article which urged people to spend as much effort developing friendships as they do choosing valentines, was read and discussed.

Whereas Roger felt confident in dealing with the subject of love, the subject of sex was a different matter. Discussing sex with his students caused him uneasiness and he frankly shared this feeling with them. Nor was there much overt desire on their part to have the subject dealt with. Apart from Brad and George and occasionally Bob and Bruce, student concern for sex seems to have been minimal. Thus, when Roger previewed the three films on sex he had brought along, he decided to limit himself to the one he regarded as the most suitable. In animated cartoon form, it portrayed a father's embarrassment in discussing sex with his son. Roger made the point that students should attempt to acquire their information on sex from reliable sources. As to the relationship between love and sex, Roger offered a terse verdict, "Sex without love is zilch!"

Throughout the weekend, Roger made repeated reference to his courtship of Sara and to their marriage which had been solemnized the previous summer. On several occasions he held up marriage as the logical outcome of the love relationship, even as he considered love to be the logical outcome of friendship. This particular emphasis led to a critical observation by the observer:

> I question the effectiveness of this approach with this age group. This is the beginning of the adolescent period and I am not quite sure that the students should be expected to relate to the whole subject of marriage. Not that the groundwork should not be laid at this point and even earlier, but I believe that it may be more worthwhile to deal with friendship relationship — the peer relationship — the boy/girl relationship. (2/12-14)

Apparently Roger's hesitancy to deal with all of the ramifications of the boy/girl relationship caused him to opt for the safer alternative.

Though some of the students had seen it already, the weekend ended with an excursion to the theater to see "Love Story." The movie proved to be a fitting close to what had been a touching weekend experience, both for the class and for the young couple which led it.

With the sixth weekend behind him, Roger reached two significant conclusions. One was that the students were now ready to assume a more prominent role in the planning of weekend themes and, two, that the time had come to concentrate more heavily on themes of specific Jewish content. The first step in following the implications of these conclusions Roger took one

Wednesday afternoon when he asked the students to see if they could recall the themes of the first six weekends. To his satisfaction and to the observer's surprise, the students reeled off the names of all the themes as well as the weekends on which they had been treated. Listing them on the board as they did so, Roger drew a heavy chalk line below the sixth. He stated that the year's three remaining themes, corresponding to the three remaining weekends, would honor what had been the class's second choice on the December preference sheet, namely, Is Judaism Relevant? Roger asked the group to think about those aspects of Judaism which were of special interest to them in preparation for the following Wednesday's lesson when the final decisions would be made.

As they entered Roger's room that Wednesday, the students were greeted with the question, "WHAT DO I WANT TO KNOW ABOUT JUDAISM?" written across the board in capital letters. Distributing blank sheets of paper, Roger directed them to write out their answers to the question and to sign their names. When everyone had finished, each student was requested individually to state the "one major thing" that he, the student, considered to be the "most relevant." The responses, written on the board beneath the question, were as follows:

1) Discrimination of Jews in sports
2) Israel — Kibbutz — Mid East situation — Army
3) Jewish attitudes and how they affect religion.
4) Israeli government.
5) Inter-religious relationships — inter-dating.
6) Death and reincarnation
7) Is Judaism worth it? Why be Jewish?
8) What's true story of Jesus?
9) What is the Messiah?
10) What's unique about Judaism as opposed to others?
11) Holocaust.
12) How can I keep myself close to Judaism?
13) Is there a possibility of a God for the Jewish people?
14) Jewish customs and traditions.

15) Jewish mysticism.
16) What do we do about our Jewish education, personally, after the Vov Class? (3/3)

Continuing the discussion, Roger and the students boiled the sixteen items down to the following three composite topics: Messiah — Life After Death, Israel, and Jewish Way of Life. Roger gave the impression that the three topics would constitute the themes of the last three weekends.

His good intentions notwithstanding, it was not until three weeks later, just three days before the seventh weekend, that Roger brought the class back to a consideration of the composite topics. As he wrote them on the board, the observer noted several changes in the original list. "God" was now first on the list. "Israel" and "Jewish Way of Life" having been deleted entirely, "The Messiah" and "Life After Death" had been separated and assigned the second and third spots, respectively. Roger also added a fourth topic, "Freedom" which he referred to as his contribution in anticipation of the forthcoming Festival of Freedom. Students were invited to form themselves into three committees — one for each topic. The job of the committees was to formulate provocative questions which would guide the group's future consideration of these subjects. By the end of the session three pages of questions emerged. Unbeknown to the students, however, Roger had decided that instead of distributing them over the remaining weekends, all three topics, together with their questions, would be concentrated into the upcoming, that is the seventh, weekend.

Roger introduced the subject of the Messiah at the opening meal on Friday evening by teaching a Hebrew song which expresses the hope that the advent of the Messiah will not be long delayed. He returned to the subject at the Friday evening worship service, this time relating the Messiah theme to the concept of freedom as symbolized by the Exodus from Egypt. But it was not until very late in the evening that what turned out to be the most prominent curriculum item of the entire weekend made its appearance. Earlier in the week, Bruce had brought a new record album acquisition of his to Roger's attention. Its name was "Jesus Christ Superstar," a rock opera which at that time was well on its way to becoming one of the country's most famous expressions of current culture. Roger immediately perceived the relevance of the opera to the Messiah theme and resolved to use it on the weekend. Additionally, he saw the opera as one means of approaching the subject of Christian persecution of Jews which he had wanted to treat before the end of the year. He therefore borrowed the album from Bruce and taped it.

Announcing "Jesus Christ Superstar" as the late Friday evening program, Roger and the students gathered around the tape recorder. As many as could followed the lyrics in the one copy of the libretto which was present. The opera was an immediate success. Rich appeared to be transfixed by it. Bob became so excited that he suggested the possibility of using "Superstar" for the class's graduation program. Everyone, without exception, expressed his admiration for the opera and his eagerness to listen to it again. From that time until the end of the weekend there was hardly a moment when the opera was not being played. During free time and during structured time, unless Roger intervened, students huddled about the tape recorder and listened with rapt attention. Though the students could not help but be impressed by the degree of curriculum eclecticism, if not ecumenism, represented by the composition's employment, it is doubtful that they were rewarded as Roger had hoped they would be with a greater understanding of either the Messiah concept or Christian persecution of Jews.

Saturday morning's service concentrated on God. Seven sheets of readings of a total of twenty-seven prepared by Roger augmented the traditional prayers. Roger repeatedly underscored what he rightly claimed to be the normative Jewish view of man's posture in relation to God. That posture briefly stated is one of near equality and partnership rather than subservience. Thus the Jew is encouraged to question the ways of God and even to dispute with Him if he feels that some injustice is being perpetrated. The childish, grandfather-type, God-conception was contrasted to what was identified as the more mature, adult conception. The very same theme was picked up again late in the day by means of a Havdala Service based upon Leonard Bernstein's "Kaddish Symphony," which Roger had dittoed and given to a small volunteer committee to present.

Saturday afternoon, Roger led the group in two discussions, separated from one another by a long walk in the woods. The first was concerned with Life After Death and the second with God. Both were guided by the questions the committees had prepared as well as by the extensive and in some cases highly sophisticated study material which Roger had brought. Sprawled about the room in relaxed fashion, students entered into the discussions eagerly. They expressed themselves on both subjects quite freely and were given a more or less authoritative view of the normative Jewish positions. In reaction to the discussions as well as to this first and in a sense only attempt by Roger to devote a weekend theme to Jewish ideational material unrelated to the specific conditions of the weekend, the observer made the following comment:

> One has to be very much impressed by the fact that there have been so many discussions on serious questions and that there has been such wide participation . . . . It should not be forgotten that these are eighth-graders. Yet, the material has not been couched in childish terms in any sense . . . . There have been today alone more than four hours of concentrated cerebral exercise on religious questions. I think that this may be something of a record for this age group. (3/26-28).

With the one possible exception of the founding of the State of Israel, the extermination of six million European Jews by the Nazis during World War II constitutes the single most traumatic event in modern Jewish history. The Holocaust, as it is called frequently, is never far from the consciousness of Jews who, though they may not have been involved in the carnage personally, bear its scars with sadness and not a little bitterness.

Like the rest of the Jewish community, the families of the Vov Class were deeply influenced by the Holocaust. Many had lost blood relatives to its slaughter; all had been bereaved of coreligionists whom they considered relatives. Sylvia's father himself had been an inmate in a concentration camp. Once, she shared with the group how even then, thirty years later, he would awaken at night screaming. Bob's mother worked professionally with victims of the Holocaust. It is no wonder that for his Independent Study Project Bob chose to read a book on the Holocaust, and that when asked to offer suggestions for weekend themes he suggested the Holocaust.

Roger too had more than a casual interest in the Holocaust. For a college course that year he had written a term paper on the Warsaw Ghetto uprising which he submitted with the impassioned assertion that more should be known and felt regarding what he considered to be one of the cataclysmic events of Jewish and world history. He responded to Bob's curiosity by giving him the paper and advising him to report on it to the class. It came as no surprise to anyone when Roger announced that the Holocaust would constitute the theme of the next, the April weekend.

Preweekend preparation on the theme was confined to the session before the weekend began. Overriding Rich's objection that the subject of God had not been dealt with sufficiently at the previous weekend and therefore should be continued as the theme of the present weekend, Roger reviewed the "facts of the Holocaust," as he termed them. He taught the Hebrew term for Holocaust and read a lengthy and rather moving section from one of the nine books on the subject that he brought with him to class. As he read the description of the deportation and the eventual destruction of a group of Jews at Auschwitz, he found himself overcome with emotion. He caressed his cheeks with his palms and exclaimed, "Boy, this is hard to read!"

Because of the rapid approach of warm weather and the lengthened period of daylight on Friday before the onset of the Sabbath, the April weekend, like its March predecessor, was held at Mary Grove. The spirit on the bus during the hour-long ride to the camp was so exuberant that the need to retrace more than half the distance in order to collect forgotten supplies depressed it hardly at all. When towards evening, however, Roger asked them to gather around a table in the dining room the group sobered up considerably. On the table Sara had set out, in addition to the Sabbath candles, six Yahrzeit or memorial candles, one for each million Jews killed in the Holocaust. Explaining that this weekend was devoted to the memory of the six million, Roger designated Bernice to light the candles. He then distributed copies of, and had the group join him in reading, this free verse poem by Natalie Precker:

> It's been years since your uncles stoked their ovens with my uncles.
> Since my aunts' and sisters' skins protected your lamps from glare.
> I do not hate you anymore — I hate no more than I understand.
> But bitterness sits deep in me, and rises when I recall.
> "Forgive and forget" is blasphemy to those whose hair made uniforms.
> If we forget what Dachau was, we will see Dachau rise again.
> So I will not forgive, I say, until you light my Yahrzeit lamps,
> Until you say my Yizkor prayers,
> Until you light, for those you killed,
> > Six million lights,
> > For sixty years,
> > On the anniversaries of the deaths
> > of our bodies
> > and your souls.

Silence enveloped the room as the girls proceeded to light the Sabbath candles. Nor was it much interrupted as everyone dispersed to haul in his gear and prepare his bunk. Vov Class students had embarked upon a weekend of collective remembrance designed to acquaint them with one of the stark realities of being Jewish in the modern world.

The service that Friday evening consisted of seven of the

twenty special readings on the Holocaust which Roger had prepared. Several of the readings offered graphic descriptions of extermination procedures in the death camps. Some were poems of protest; some were heart-rending, effusive reactions of survivors. One raised the problem of the world's silent assent to the destruction of European Jewry and speculated on the causes. The last described the ninety-three maidens of Warsaw who chose to die as martyrs rather than defile themselves for the Germans. Roger took the occasion to tell the students about the first time he became aware of the Holocaust and the physical illness he experienced when he did. He also told them how much he appreciated the full day fast of Yom Kippur because of the opportunity it afforded him to identify with the starvation of the Holocaust era. The evening program consisted of thumbing through the numerous books on the Holocaust which Roger had strewn about the room and the reading aloud of selections from his term paper.

Although it was alluded to at the morning service, it was not until the middle of Saturday afternoon that Roger returned to the theme. He did so by means of three hypothetical situations which he invited the students to role play. The first situation consisted of a debate among members of Israel's Knesset (Parliament) as to whether or not it should sell Israel-produced grenade launchers to West Germany. The second presented the problem of whether an American Jewish family should purchase a Volkswagen. The third concerned itself with the reactions of a Jewish college student who was informed that he would be rooming with an exchange student from Germany. To Roger's disappointment, only a few of the students volunteered to act out the situations.

After almost two hours of free time the group gathered once again, this time to consider three different conceptual views of the Holocaust. Perhaps the most striking was the one written by a German lady who said that if people remember they should remember also the thousands of innocent Germans who were killed during the war. Beyond the half-hour discussion that the class held on the relative merits of the three views, the theme was referred to only once more during the weekend, at the Sunday morning service, by means of a poem written by a child victim of the Holocaust.

As the April weekend drew to a close, Roger shared with the students the news that, though not yet definitely decided, he and the school authorities were inclined to grant their request to have the Vov Class continue into the next year. Under those circumstances, a graduation would not be necessary. Since, however, Shavuot[7] services, in connection with which a graduation would have been held, coincided with the date of the ninth weekend and since the weekend site was the Jewish Student Center, within walking distance of the synagogue, both Roger and Rabbi Katz felt that the class should come to the synagogue that day. Instead of their presenting a program to the congregation, they and their parents would be honored at the service. Roger took the occasion to apprise the group of the fact that Shavuot fell on Sunday and Monday, and that Monday was a day-off-from-school legal holiday. The lengthened weekend would afford the group ample time for the visit to B'nai Israel as well as anything else they might want to do. As to theme, its choice and content would be up to the students, though Roger did express his opinion that Shavuot would be most appropriate. He advised the students to give the matter thought. Plans would begin to be formulated at the next regular session of the class.

The assumption by the students of responsibility for the final weekend, including a decision on its theme, was seen by Roger as something of a test of the effectiveness of what he had come to regard as the new approach to Jewish education represented by the Vov Class. Roger had tried to motivate his students, especially in the previous two months, to greater responsibility for weekends but had had little success. He reasoned now that if the Vov Class approach, at least as carried out by him, were valid, students should be capable of deciding on a theme for the weekend and work out the details with his help. Thus it was that the second Sunday after the April weekend, Roger opened class by placing on the board a skeleton time schedule for the ninth weekend. The visit to B'nai Israel was fixed, as were meal times. Listed also were two regular services and the traditional all-night study session in honor of Shavuot, scheduled to be held Friday night. It was the class's job to decide the nature and number of discussions to be planned, the type and number of films to be shown, the kind of recreational activities to be conducted and generally how the time of the weekend would be spent. After a brief excursion into the differences between Sabbath and Shavuot work restrictions, Roger and the class engaged the task. The following excerpt from the notes describes in part what happened:

> Roger explains how he goes about planning a weekend. First, he decides on a subject. Then he tries to find relevant materials. (Arnold flicks Rich's ear. Rich takes it nicely.)
> Finally, he arranges prayer services around the subject. Roger: "Then we have to arrange social activities. But, we must first come up with a subject."

Sylvia: "Let's talk about Hebrew School."

Karen: "Let's talk about Pete[8] and he can talk about us."

Karen: "Let's talk about each other."

Bob: "Let's have a rap session."

Someone says: "Let's talk about George" (who was not present — Observer).

Roger: "We have a policy not to do that."

> Roger goes around the room soliciting topics.

Arnold: "Nothing."

Rich: "God."

Bruce: "The God thing or . . . sex."

Brad: "Nothing."

Sylvia: "I gave one already."

Bernice: "Marriage."

Ruth: "Intermarriage."

9:37 Roger: "How many are interested in planning the weekend?"

Bob says he wants to go to Jefferson University alone. Says there are burial tunnels under the quad. He asks Roger if he knows it.

Sylvia and Eve: "We have a discussion we want to do but we can't tell you."

Roger: "All right, plan it in."

Sylvia: "It is already planned."

Roger points out that he has never given out a time schedule for weekends. Disadvantage: hard to go off it. Suggests loose time schedule.
Kids are quite restless and not focused at all.

Roger: "I hate to get angry and throw you out."

Bruce: "You're a nice guy."

9:42 Roger: "But we've got nothing done. If I have to be a bitch, I will." . . .

Roger threatens to plan the weekend himself. (5/9)

Throughout the remainder of May, Roger reiterated, from time to time, his hope that the class would reach a decision on a theme. Once Bernice suggested ecology as the theme. Bruce joined Rich in reminding anyone who would listen that the class had yet to complete its discussion on God. Roger himself abandoned the thought of using Shavuot as the theme and suggested an evaluation of the year's Vov Class experience instead. But the effort to decide on a theme ended in failure, as Roger's notes recorded on the eve of the weekend reveal:

> My preliminary plans, very briefly, for the weekend are to follow the kids' desires for most of the weekend, to have a great deal of free time, to bring in a lot of games and things that we had played and experienced during the year . . . . Also to run the services basically on a format of informality, stressing the important parts of the looseleaf Siddur that we had compiled, and generally to observe Shabbat and Shavuot in a leisurely, fun kind of way. (5/28-31)

As it developed, the ninth weekend was indeed a leisurely, informal experience. The group took long walks on the campus of Jefferson University and in Woodland Park. It had equally long conversations on the experience of the Vov Class and its hopes for the coming year. Discussion spilled over into individual student career intentions. Services, other than the one attended at the Synagogue, consisted of rereading dittoed sheets from the looseleaf prayer book. The all-night study session turned into a viewing of a full-length feature "thriller," frontwards and backwards, and a playing of "Jesus Christ Superstar."

If the ninth weekend can be said to have had a theme, it was the joy of Roger and the Vov Class students being in each other's company, heightened by the knowledge that their relationship would continue beyond the school term, albeit in a fashion yet to be determined. While the observer was himself not unaffected by the joy, his summary comment, recorded during the weekend, reveals his disappointment that this was as far as it went:

> One must wonder at the advisability of such a very long weekend with such very little content. Would it not be better for these kids to be at home with their families? Why are they together over this weekend with such meager offerings in terms of Jewish or cultural experience? The Biblical portion was not so much as mentioned today. The fact is that the students have not had

contact, other than through the meal ceremony, with a single word of Hebrew. The fact is that there has not been hardly any meaningful interchange on a high level at all. One therefore questions what the value of the experience is. One might contend, and perhaps Roger does, . . . that there is definite social value in terms of creating a homogeneous group. And indeed this may be the case. But if that were the case, perhaps it has already been achieved, or at least achieved to the point where it can be built upon, where real ideas can be dealt with and real questions posed. (5/28-31)

The employment of themes in connection with Vov Class weekends proved to be a significant determinant of the character of those weekends. When used, the themes provided Roger with central cores around which he was able to organize discussion and curriculum materials. Additionally, through the themes he was able to bring his students into contact with new information and ideas as well as with emotions with which they had had scant experience previously. An example is the April weekend, the theme of which was the Holocaust. Midway through the weekend, the observer noted a certain disquietude abroad among the participants, including Roger and Sara. There was in evidence an uneasiness bordering on depression which seemed to become more intense as the weekend progressed. Students lolled about aimlessly and indulged in mildly antisocial pursuits. Although he was not sure what or why, the observer felt that something was awry. Searching for an explanation, he thought first of the bothersome boil on Roger's neck which gave him no rest throughout the weekend and shortened his temper somewhat. He thought too of the denouement of one of the class's major social struggles which occurred over the weekend and which will be described below. Still, after all was said and done, the observer could not escape the impression that the discomfort and temporary depression exhibited by the students were a response to the theme with its emphasis upon the destruction of six million Jews. While there may be legitimate question concerning the wisdom of tapping such emotions at this age, this was Roger's purpose and he realized it by means of the theme.

Weekend themes also provided Roger with a tool for dealing with occasional situations which arose in the class. Prior to the December weekend, for example, another social crisis threatened to engulf the class. The result was a weekend theme which enabled Roger to fend off the threat and then turn it in constructive directions.

The foregoing should not be construed to mean that the themes were allowed to tyrannize the weekend proceedings. When the group happened upon a topic of greater or more immediate concern, it had the freedom to abandon the designated subject and deal with the new subject. Though weekends by their very nature implied a certain body of content, in most cases it was the themes which provided the ideational centers of the experience.

In addition to their influence on weekends, the themes influenced Vov Class sessions before and after weekends. Particularly when designated early in the month, themes inspired specific curriculum content as well as calendar goals for its mastery. Thus most of the classes from mid-January to mid-February, were tied in some fashion to Love and Sex, the theme of the February weekend. By the same token when a weekend passed, it together with its theme, became part of the living history of the class and was resurrected often for reference and review. In short, monthly weekends constituted an important feature of the Vov Class program and in seven out of the nine of them, themes were an integral and highly influential curriculum component.

"Fiddler on the Roof"

The first Sunday session of the new term was to be an all-day orientation at Woodland Park. Students were to bring their lunches and meet Roger at the Zoo entrance. When, however, Roger awoke that morning, a persistent downpour convinced him that he had best call the students and transfer the orientation to B'nai Israel. Upon their arrival there, the single unoccupied spot that they could find was the synagogue sanctuary. Nor could there have been a more fitting location, in view of the orientation to the work of the Vov Class which Roger was about to present to his students.

All tradition-based groups, including the Jewish group, constantly face the challenge of keeping abreast of changing conditions and at the same time maintaining continuity with the past. The challenge, frequently referred to as the challenge of Tradition and Change,[9] is particularly acute in modern times. It engages the attentions of all serious-minded Jews, especially those, such as Roger, who concern themselves with the task of helping young Jews establish a relationship with their heritage. That it was central to Roger's thinking at this orientation is indicated by his use of two recordings, the first of which was "Tradition" from the prologue to the musical, "Fiddler on the Roof."

"Fiddler on the Roof," known by its admirers simply as "Fiddler," was enjoying great popularity during this period. Striking a responsive chord in the hearts of Jews, the play is set within the Shtetl of eastern Europe at the beginning of the century. By means of sentimental songs and moving dramatic situations, the dissolution of the Jewish world of that time, under the twin impact of persecution and modernity, is depicted. The play closes with a portrayal of the beginning of the painful transition to the twentieth century and to its geographical centers, Israel and the United States.

Most Jews in the United States, including Roger and his students, trace their origins to the Shtetl. Memories of it and its culture still persist in aging grandparents and in some cases even in parents. The memories are consciously fostered by many Jewish institutions, among them synagogues, who look back upon the Shtetl as the symbol of Jewish cultural and religious innocence. It is no accident that B'nai Israel sponsored a benefit performance of "Fiddler" which was attended by many of the parents of the Vov Class together with their children.

Now, as the students sat under the high-vaulted, virtually

empty sanctuary in which they had sat so many times before, Roger played "Tradition." Its point was clearly conveyed in the words of Tevya, the play's leading character, "Because of our traditions, we've kept our balance . . ."

The students followed the words to the song by means of two dittoed sheets Roger had prepared. When the song was finished, Roger questioned the students about their adherence to tradition, general tradition and specifically that of the Shtetl. More than a third of the students volunteered that they were in the habit of having Sabbath dinner with grandparents each Friday night.

It was then that Roger suggested that the class might want to consider staging "Fiddler" as a year-long project and perhaps even film it. General excitement greeted the suggestion. Losing no time, Roger and the class formally accepted the idea and decided to begin work that very weekend, the first of the nine to be held during the year.

There remained, from Roger's point of view, a second element which needed to be highlighted at the orientation. After a brief luncheon break, he treated the class to another recording, this one also accompanied by a sheet of lyrics. It was the song "Revolution" by the Beatles, known to most of the students, but never before associated in their minds with the synagogue sanctuary or the religious school. The song's basic message, designed to augment and counter-balance the theme they had just heard, is contained in the opening stanza:

> You say you want revolution . . .
> We all want to change the world . . .
> You tell me that it's evolution . . .
> But when you talk about destruction . . .
> Then you can count me out.

Not only had Roger put his finger on one of the, if not the essential tension in modern Jewish life, he had already taken a position with the Vov Class firmly astride both its poles. Tradition was to be respected in the Vov Class Program and so was Revolution — of the non-destructive variety, to be sure.

It was after dinner on the Saturday night of the first, that is the September weekend, that Roger, in pursuance of the decision reached at the orientation, conducted tryouts for "Fiddler." Everyone but Dorothy tried out. Roger and Sara put their heads together and awarded parts. Bob was disappointed that the lead went to Bruce instead of to him but in general everyone was satisfied with the choices. The group proceeded to block and rehearse the prologue. When it came time to disband and to prepare for bed, one student commented to Roger, "Congratulations for getting something we are all interested in."

From that moment forward, "Fiddler" became the single most prevalent and time-consuming curriculum component of the Vov Class. It occupied all or a portion of more than half of the Sunday sessions and more than a third of the Wednesday sessions. It was a major ingredient of each and every weekend with the exception of the last and it was the subject of at least one special event. The group was involved constantly with rehearsals or with preparations for rehearsals. It was involved constantly too with discussion as to how the play would be performed and before whom, what the impediments were to its being brought to a performance level and how they could be circumvented, as well as what was the value, if any, of the entire enterprise.

To his credit, Roger never permitted the class to become, as it might easily have become, a class in dramatics. Though he devoted the flower of his ingenuity and pre-class preparation to ways and means of advancing the production of "Fiddler," educational purposes, especially Jewish educational purposes, were uppermost in Roger's mind. At the same time, it must be acknowledged that his deep personal involvement with the dramatic aspect of the activity, upon occasion, obscured from Roger's memory the circumstances of its institution:

10:10 . . . Roger: "Today, we're going to talk about 'Fiddler.' Sometimes people play roles. Sometimes I'll be playing a role. When we work on a play, I'll have the role of Director and you have to listen to me . . . A good actor will sink his teeth into the part. Any good actor has to know his part well and know what he is doing. This is the 'Shabbas Prayer' from 'Fiddler.' Everybody is in this. So I want to go over this prayer — the words and the music — so we can do it right. I want to make sure we know what we are saying. I'll play the record, you follow the words carefully."

. . . Rather good attention. Roger puts on record.

Roger: "Sh . . . Sh. Now listen carefully."

Introductory music. He explains that though Tevya and Golde start it off, "we'll all do it unless we don't want to do it that way."

10:20 Finishes record. Begins to analyze words. Roger asks who is praying for whom. Bob helps elicit thought that Tevya and Golde are praying for their daughters.

Sylvia: "My father blesses us every Friday night. This sounds like a take-off on that."

Roger: "Most of you have — you beat me to the punch — a Prayer Book at home."

He takes the Hertz Prayer Book in hand and quotes the portion which describes and prescribes parents blessing their children on Friday night. First boys and then girls, followed by Priestly Benediction, which they know well, because it ends each of the services.

Roger: "What things are they praying for? What is Tevya trying to do in the whole play?"

Claudia: "They are poor."

Roger: "The song before this is, 'If I Were a Rich Man.' "

Roger acts out the words of that song.

Roger: "All during the play Tevya addresses God in the epitome of private prayer. Then here, public prayer. Everybody sings this one. Let's go over words first."

Reads words in cadence.

Roger: "Are you with me? The whole group is singing this."

Arnold is sleeping on his hand. Brad and Bob exchanging comments. Eve is conversing.

Roger: "I'll wait. This isn't even my idea. This was your idea!" (10/25)

A number of the students became almost as deeply involved in the production as Roger. Sylvia, Jeanne and Karen, for example, decided to make their own costumes. They, as well as Claudia, Bob, Bruce, Brad and Arnold, often stayed after class on Sundays or utilized free time on weekends to rehearse on their own. Rich returned to the suggestion that the production be filmed. Bob, whose interest had been lukewarm until that time, became deeply enthused with Rich's idea. He called Roger at home and volunteered himself to head the filming effort. He also secured a book on how to film home movies which he intended to use as a guide if he would be awarded the job. Even Mrs. Cohen contributed to the growing enthusiasm by devoting a Wednesday afternoon lesson to a recording of "Fiddler" in Hebrew.

During the first part of the year, Roger had employed dittoed sheets for the words to the songs and oral directions for staging. Loss of sheets and occasional absence from rehearsals convinced him, however, that each student should have a personal copy of the play. He ordered a paperback volume of the play for each. When the books were distributed at the January weekend, the students were surprised and pleased to see that each had his name affixed to the fly leaf of his copy and that his lines had been designated with checkmarks.

For reasons largely unrelated to "Fiddler" or to the class's relationship to "Fiddler," the Saturday night rehearsal at the January weekend was by far the most successful of the year. It involved the willing participation of each and every one of the fourteen students present and lasted for a full three and a half hours.

> For the last hour the group has been gathered in the auditorium, going through "Fiddler on the Roof," with the books that Roger ordered. Nobody gives any signs of being bored with what is happening at this time. Students are simply sitting in front of the stage, reading through the scenes and singing the songs. The people who are really coming alive in this experience are Arnold and Bob who incidentally is very quick to point up all of the boy/girl and sexual references in the play.
>
> Bruce is doing a fantastic job as Tevya and everybody is having a blast. Those who are really not participating but who are still finding interest in what is happening are Susan and perhaps one or two others. This is a really fine, enjoyable experience. I am laughing a great deal and everyone else is. (1/15-17)

By midyear, "Fiddler" had become far more than a project. It had become an integral and significant part of the culture of the Vov Class. One Wednesday, for example, the class was divided into two teams for a "sing down" of the word love. At one point, Bruce arose and with arms extended in mock dramatic fanfare, sang "Do You Love Me?", one of "Fiddler's" songs which, as Tevya, he was to sing. As he did, an approving cheer went up from both teams. On another occasion, the class considered whether or not to invite guests to its Sabbath table on weekends. The example of "Fiddler" provided the precedent for doing so. More significant, "Fiddler" role names came to be used by the class almost as readily as real names.

"Fiddler's" fortunes, however, changed abruptly in February after Roger was reminded that the Vov year was the final year in the B'nai Israel elementary Hebrew School. Completion of the Vov year was marked traditionally by a May graduation, the program for which the class itself was responsible. When Roger presented the problem of the program to the class, naturally "Fiddler" occurred to them as the ideal solution. The tacit acceptance of the idea was followed quickly by Roger's compilation and distribution of a call sheet of characters and a schedule of rehearsals for the remainder of the year, with a production quota for each rehearsal. Henceforth, Sundays would be devoted exclusively to "Fiddler." Roger instructed all students to memorize their lines straightaway. He was eager to see the project through to a successful completion in time for the graduation. He was confident that his students would cooperate.

The fact is, however, that "Fiddler," with its intricate songs, dialogue and choreography, is very difficult to stage, especially by young people whose interest in dramatics, not to speak of skill, leaves something to be desired. Roger had participated in dramatic productions as a high school student and was rather adept at the art. His students, on the other hand, were totally without sophistication in this area. Nor could the class even afford the luxury of allowing those with marginal interest to withdraw. If all the characters in the play were to be portrayed, every student, other than perhaps those who had lead parts, would have to assume the burden of several roles.

The Sunday morning rehearsal following the decision to stage "Fiddler" for graduation suggested that serious difficulties lay ahead. It should be noted that by this time Dorothy had accepted a part:

> 10:12 Roger, trying to get attention, "Do you people want to be in this or not? I'm not going to spend our time on this if you are not interested." Reminds group that each person must cooperate. Group sobers up. "I can't say to one of you, get out. I can only say it to the whole group. We are dependent on each person."
>
> Group lines up in two sections behind blackboards for prologue. Bruce stands out front. He begins and he knows his lines.
>
> 10:17 A teacher enters and I believe is informing Roger

that she and her group are scheduled to be in this room. They converse and seem to work it out. She leaves and Roger calls after her, "Thank you very much!" Roger tries to get order again. The Tradition dance begins. Peters out.

Roger: "Let's try it one more time." He asks group just to sing, not move out. They sing (not very good) . . . Then Roger demonstrates the walk to accompany the singing.

10:25 This is only the opening minute and it has been rehearsed at least a half dozen times. How are they going to learn the rest? I still don't know.

Brad does not cooperate. Instead of raising his hands, as the others, he throws a paper wad. Next time, he does what he is supposed to do but without enthusiasm. Brad, on the next try, attempts to pick the wallet out of Roger's pocket . . .

10:52 Roger suggests that from now on he will call the disturbers out by name and if "public embarrassment" (his phrase) doesn't help, they will have to cancel it. (2/28)

Following this less than successful rehearsal, Roger decided to put the matter squarely before the class. He opened the subject by emphasizing the need for each and every student to have what he called a personal commitment to the production of "Fiddler." In the absence of such a commitment, there was no hope that the play could be produced; in its presence, all of the problems, from casting to sufficient rehearsal time, would melt away. The result would be the finest graduation program anyone at B'nai Israel had ever seen. Roger invited suggestions from the students as to how the effort might be facilitated. George voiced concern on the subject of scenery. He and his family had gone behind the set at a professional production of "Fiddler" and he could testify that scenery would prove to be "quite difficult." Arnold countered that scenery was not even necessary. Bob thought that realistically it might be well to consider doing selections from the play rather than the whole play. George thought that if the play could be "adapted to modern times" it would command greater interest among the students. The lesson ended with Roger asking each student to declare his commitment or lack of it before the entire class. All of the girls present, as well as Arnold and Rich, volunteered a positive "commitment" to the production. When Brad was called on, however, the first chink appeared in what had been, until then, the class's united front. Seeing his hesitation, Roger assured him that he was under no compulsion to agree. Brad then said that he had no commitment to "Fiddler" and cast his vote in opposition to its production. George joined him. Bob who at this time was still closely allied with both boys, abstained. Sylvia commented wryly, "Everybody who says we can't do it, hasn't even tried."

After class, Roger took Sylvia and Claudia aside and suggested that they find a way of exerting subtle pressure upon George, who was in his view the "real problem." They concluded that the best approach would be to speak to Bob who, deep down, they felt, wanted to do the play. They would ask him to speak to George and if he were won over, Brad certainly would follow.

The following Sunday, which was the second in March, "Fiddler" came up for discussion again. The subtle pressure upon George, if indeed it had been attempted at all, in no way altered his and Brad's opposition. They stoutly maintained that it would be impossible for the class to do the play. And what is more, they felt qualified to speak on behalf of Bob who happened not to be present that day. Throwing up her hands in disgust, Bernice offered her perception of the cause of the impasse, "Brad really wants to do it and so does Bob, but Mr. Logic over there (George) has convinced everybody that they shouldn't." The class ended with the announcement that Roger had purchased tickets for a performance of "Fiddler" to be presented that Saturday night at a local high school.[10] Everyone was required to come. The purpose, in addition to spending a pleasant evening which would be capped with a visit to Roger's home, was to help the class decide on whether "Fiddler" could or could not be done in time for graduation.

All but Ruth attended the performance that Saturday evening. It was time well spent, from everyone's point of view. Yet, seeing a finished performance by carefully selected and rehearsed young people had the opposite effect from the one Roger had intended. Not only were George and Brad confirmed in their opposition, but even the play's most ardent supporters for the first time began to question the class's ability to stage such an elaborate production. Perhaps the idea of excerpts or at the very most Act I only would be a more realistic goal.

A rather successful rehearsal at the March weekend served to renew the class's hope that some part of "Fiddler" could be readied by May. But the hope was only temporary. For each successful rehearsal held during the ensuing weeks, there were at least two which failed. Only Bruce knew his lines and even he did not know them well enough to present them before an audience. "Fiddler" was well on its way to becoming a curriculum relic rather than a subject of current concern.

Fortunately, however, "Fiddler" was rather much spared this indignity. At the very time that the Vov Class was coming to realize that the production of "Fiddler" was beyond its ken, it also was in the process of deciding to continue its association in some form the following year. Under such circumstances, a graduation exercise, if it were held at all, would be quite meaningless.

By the end of April, the decision to continue the Vov Class into the next year was made final and the graduation program was cancelled. Though one more rehearsal of sorts was held, for all intent and purpose "Fiddler" had come to an end in the Vov Class. At that final rehearsal the students sat in leisurely fashion with their "Fiddler" books open before them. With obvious enjoyment they read through the play, which by then had become like an old and dear friend who perhaps once did but no longer made demands on their time and energy.

The notes contain one more reference to "Fiddler." In the

middle of May at a Wednesday session, Roger offered a brief explanation of what had happened:

> Roger: "When I suggested the possibility of doing 'Fiddler' (Bruce: "The first day we met!") I did so because it is a fun thing to take a play and work through it."
>
> Tells about how he used to be with a group which analyzed plays. Says that it is worthwhile and enjoyable experience by itself without producing it.
>
> He continues: "What has happened is mostly my fault. We never sat down to say that we are going to do it on such and such a day, for such and such people." . . .
>
> Bob: "Let's do it for graduation for the Tet Class."[11]
>
> Sylvia suggests doing it next year.
>
> 5:08 Roger apologizes to those who are disappointed that they never finished it. Invites comment.
>
> Sylvia: "If we don't reach a decision now we'll end up doing the same thing next year as this." (5/12)

Although one may question the emphasis upon "Fiddler" from the standpoint of the efficient use of precious time, the play did confer certain benefits upon the Vov Class. First, it provided a springboard for Roger's treatment of many topics of Jewish and general interest which he deemed important. From the significance of a father's blessing his children on Friday night to the role playing opportunities provided by the marriage scene, "Fiddler" was a rich mine of Jewish ideas and associations which Roger could and did work at will. By the same token, it helped the students to appreciate the similarities between the Jewish group and other groups. At the last weekend, for example, Roger showed a film called "Good Night Socrates" which depicts the consequences of the destruction of a Greek neighborhood in a typical urban center. The students immediately identified the neighborhood with Anatevka, the mythical setting of "Fiddler," and in the ensuing exchange expressed commiseration for the displaced inhabitants.

Second, "Fiddler" helped to awaken the Jewish pride of the Vov Class students. Whatever one's view of such popular forms of Jewish culture, it cannot be denied that "Fiddler" succeeds in presenting the Jewish experience of several generations ago with warmth and some beauty. While Vov Class students should not and probably do not require the authentication of their Jewish antecedents by means of a Broadway musical, to have those antecedents portrayed so openly and received so positively by the non-Jewish as well as by the Jewish world could not but enhance their pride. Some of these same thoughts occurred to the researcher as he sat once and watched a "Fiddler" rehearsal:

> Granted that "Fiddler" may not be *haute culture*, Jewishly, it is perhaps a way station to more authentic Jewish culture in the same way that the Vov Class altogether may be such a way station. Once a love relationship to life and to Judaism is developed all kinds of things can be attempted. "On the other hand" (the Fiddler influence) it may well be that this is as far as it will go. How do you know? One thing is for sure: if their Jewish level is "Fiddler," it will not be lower than that of their parents, which in this society may be an achievement in itself. Yet, agreed, we ought to shoot higher. (3/31)

Possibly "Fiddler's" most important benefit was the sense of cohesiveness that working on it helped to engender in the class. While the group formation process as it occurred in the Vov Class constitutes the subject of the next chapter, suffice it to say that "Fiddler" was the first and, in some ways, an important vehicle for moulding the class into a homogeneous unit.

Worship Services

Ideally, observant Jews join a prayer service each and every morning of the week, including Sunday. On Sunday, however, because the worshippers are less rushed than on weekdays and because some drive their children to Sunday School and have almost two hours to wait until the closing bell, the service tends to be more leisurely. This was true of the B'nai Israel Sunday service especially from the time that the Men's Club assumed responsibility for it. Called a Full Participation Service and Breakfast, the Men's Club instituted what in its terms was an innovative service. Though the traditional prayer book was used, it was marked with explicit directions, and though the tradition-al service was followed in the main, more lay participation[12] than was the rule was encouraged. Three men — one facing the Ark and the other two facing the Congregation — led the ser-vice. The man facing the Ark intoned some of the prayers in the usual manner whereas the other two led the Congregation in either responsive or unison recitations. The service was followed by a Bagels and Lox Breakfast, restricted to those who par-ticipated, and a program, once a month, usually a speaker.

One Wednesday early in September Roger announced to the class that from then on each Sunday session would begin with participation in the Men's Club Service. The class would have breakfast but would not stay for the program afterwards. He reminded the boys to bring their Talis and Tfillin[13] from home that Sunday and to come on time.

Sunday morning arrived and at the appointed hour Roger could be seen at the entrance of the Chapel waiting to greet his charges. One by one they straggled in — hardly on time — and sat quietly as a group in the first several rows. The congregation, which numbered some thirty-five adult men,[14] seemed proud that their ranks had been augmented by representatives of the younger generation. Those in charge invited several of the stu-dents, including several girls, to lead English readings and one boy to lead a Hebrew prayer. The students so designated par-ticipated and all followed the service dutifully. When, however, at the close of the service, the students were apprised of the fact that preparations for the forthcoming holidays prevented break-fast from being served, they registered keen disappointment. They were assured that the situation would be rectified the following Sunday, if they would return. They did return the following Sunday but again there was no breakfast. It probably is not coincidental that it was at that point, for the first time, that the students began to question the wisdom of their participation in the service. Apparently Roger shared their question, at least in part, as his summary notes of that Sunday reveal:

> As there are no Wednesdays (because of the holidays — Observer), save one, until the October weekend and in order to do several exercises which I want done before the weekend, I thought that we should not go to services this (past) Sunday . . . there was no breakfast served in any case. (10/11)

It was not until two weeks later, that is on the fourth attempt, that the class joined in a Full Participation Service with benefit of breakfast. The summary notes on that day convey something of the spirit which was to characterize the class's involvement in this activity during most of the first half of the year.

> 9:20 The kids are rather attentive to what is happening. Brad is invited to lead a Hebrew prayer. Evidently, there is no advance notice; they are simply invited up. He does very well and his schoolmates are participating. Part of the reason has to be their knowledge of the Ashrei, one of those prayers which all of these kids can recite very easily. Bernice is next for an English reading. She receives similar cooperation and approving smiles from Jeanne when she sits down. Next is a song from the Prayer Book, poorly sung but a good change of pace. Every form of response is being employed in this service. One good thing is that the books are clearly marked with directions which makes for ease of participation. Yet, there is very little participation in the Hebrew sections for the simple reason that they are not fluent in Hebrew. During these Hebrew responsive sections (there has been no silent Hebrew praying thus far) the children are quiet, but largely uninvolved.

9:30 They come to the Shema, one of the most important portions of the service and there is a regular cacophony of sound. The kids are *not* involved. Some silent prayer. The preponderance seems to be Hebrew responses said aloud. Bob tries to join in. Rich likewise, although only with his eyes. Most are not with it.

It occurs to me to look at the adults. What is the level of participation among them? Much higher, of course. Most of these men are regulars to the daily service. Those who are present on a once-a-month basis seem to be trying but not participating very much.

9:37 Now the Amidah — the most important part of the service. Everybody rises and begins to go through it. Claudia invited to read English. She passes Roger who pats her on the back and says, "Sock it to 'em." She does well. They seem to have little hesitation to participate and little or no stage fright. When Claudia sits down, Roger turns back to her and says, "Very good!" . . .

9:45 I feel that we have had almost enough. Whether it is because I am tired or I feel they are, I don't know.

Mr. Shamash looks for another girl. Points to Jeanne who, in turn, points to Sylvia, who agrees to come up. Does well.

Roger turns to Claudia and the two of them join in singing a portion of one prayer quietly and it gives them pleasure.

9:50 Services end and Mr. Gross thanks and invites everyone to breakfast in auditorium . . . .

Bob to Roger: "You should have seen the breakfast I had today, but don't worry, I'll eat three breakfasts." (10/25)

Though the Vov Class went on to participate in ten more Men's Club Services during the year, the level of participation at that particular service represented the high point. Whether because of increased exposure or because of the growing influence of their own Vov Class modes of operation, neither their interest nor their involvement in all but the breakfast portion of the experience were greater than they were that day. At subsequent services, the girls especially began to exhibit a decline in interest.

> 9:15 Service continues with responsive readings in Hebrew and English. Girls, by and large, are conversing; boys seem much more attentive to the actual progress of the service. Perhaps they have a greater stake in it, having put on their Tfillin. It is also possible that the tradition of male participation in the service is still operative despite the attempt of Conservative Judaism to equalize the role of the woman. In truth, a real attempt has never been made. Cultural lags are nothing by comparison to religious lags. (11/15)

At subsequent services, as inattention among the boys, too, increased, Roger searched for a solution. A city-wide rally on behalf of Soviet Jewry in the middle of December gave him a solution of sorts. He summarily withdrew the class from the Sunday service preceding the rally and spent the time discussing the condition of the Jews in the Soviet Union.

Yet, flight was not Roger's way. He had the habit of facing issues squarely and trying in the best way he knew to deal with them. Thus when the students returned the Sunday following the rally, he ushered them into the service. He let them know however that henceforth, instead of relying on the inspiration of the moment, they would receive assignment cards carrying the names of the prayers, the method by which each was to be recited and the name of the student who was to lead it. The cards, which in time came to include cumulative records of individual student participation in the service, were handed to the students as they entered the Chapel and returned after their participation. One effect of the cards was that their participation went more smoothly than before. Students knew their parts in advance and responded more or less willingly. One further effect seems to have been a sense on the part of the students of their ability to influence the service.

Included in the service, for example, are a number of prayers which usually are sung. While earlier in the year there had been an attempt by the Cantor to standardize melodies, everyone — students and adults alike — eventually reverted to the melodies he knew best, with the adults for the most part determining which were sung aloud. The same service which saw the institution of the assignment cards also saw a new assertiveness by the youngsters in the music area. One group, in particular, which had been together at camp, insisted upon its own melodies and won the point by singing loudly and in concert at the appropriate spots in the service.

What might be considered this new surge of interest and involvement was short-lived, however. Two Sundays later, which was the last in January, after breakfast, Roger said to the class: "What I'd like to do today is discuss with you the possibility of altering our plan of action on Sunday morning." Roger then went on to describe his feeling that the Sunday morning service was failing despite his best efforts to the contrary. He ended by inviting the students to react with suggestions of their own for improvement. The following excerpt from the notes of that day shows how the discussion developed:

10:18 . . .

Sylvia: "Services are not bad. Just there are no tunes. Everyone mumbles." She makes fun of the adults' accents . . .

George: Doesn't want to go to those services. "Have our own."

Bruce: "Like we do on weekends."

Dorothy: "They should have others participate instead of us."

Sylvia: "Why can't we write prayers of our own?"

Ruth: "If we knew more prayers to sing, it wouldn't be so boring."

Roger: "Mr. Gross asked if our group wouldn't teach the adults new tunes."

Bernice suggests more tunes to "add color."

Sylvia: "Aren't those services just for mourners?"

Roger: "Sad thing about Jewish life is that the morning service has come to be just for mourners, unless they are very Orthodox Jews."

Sylvia says she doesn't know whether to stand during Kaddish (Mourner's Prayer — Observer).

Roger: "Reform Jews stand up for Kaddish."
    Reason?

Sylvia: "Everybody has someone to mourn for."

Bruce: "It is really not a mourner's Kaddish. All it does is glorify God."

Sylvia: "I thought you (Bruce) didn't believe in God."

George: "He swears to God he is an atheist!" Tells about Jesus and God changing water to wine . . .

Roger points out that they are having a good discussion without his leading it.

Bernice tells about her uncle who goes to services every morning since her grandmother died.

10:30 She tells about her cousins beginning Sunday School as a result, which is "really great" because "they are getting more religion now."

George tells about certain kids going to Sunday School and hating it.

Sylvia: People embarrass her when she uses God. "Why

shouldn't I? I am going to write a 'Dear Rabbi' letter. I say God all the time."

Roger brings group back to Sunday morning problem. Suggests that they combine their service with the regular book and do their own service. Sylvia protests she would not like to miss service.

Bernice: "I feel grown up there."

Group: "We'll miss breakfast!"

Roger: "Is that the reason you go?"

Sylvia: "I go to Sabbath Services and don't understand everything," in response to Roger's "How many understand what's going on?"

Sylvia: "Can't we lead the service completely?"

Some disruption.

Roger: "If we do so, we have to get together and work on it." Suggests that kids take Prayer Book home. "See if you know any of the tunes. Next Sunday we won't go to that service but we'll work on a service. Then after the weekend we'll lead the service." (1/31)

It is doubtful that any of the students worked with the Prayer Books at home. Nonetheless, when the group gathered the following Sunday, they went to their room instead of to the Chapel and proceeded to conduct their own service with Roger as leader. More accurately, they proceeded to conduct an analysis of the Men's Club Service. And they did so by contrasting it with the services they had been conducting on weekends.

In stark contrast to the straight pews of the B'nai Israel Chapel and the bound prayer books which greeted the worshippers as they arrived for the Sunday service, the five services held each weekend were the epitome of informality. Roger did designate a prayer and study area at all weekend sites — a full

room at the Community Center and several tables pushed together at Mary Grove and at the Jewish Student Center. But the
formality usually associated with a Chapel or other such prayer
place was nowhere in evidence. Students sat in a circle or
around a table. They frequently cupped their chins in their
palms or rested their heads on the table, although Roger drew
the line at outright lounging. There may have been some consideration given to the type of clothing worn but in general students dressed for services as for all other weekend activities. As
leader of the services, Roger encouraged students to speak out
on any point, at any point, so long as the comment or question
was relevant.

Beyond the informal atmosphere, perhaps the clearest departure from the Sunday morning format was the presence of
the looseleaf prayer book, prepared by Roger and the class
especially for use on weekends. Bound prayer books, Roger felt,
had a stultifying effect upon prayer, especially for young people,
whose needs and interests are in constant flux. Required, he
thought, was a prayer manual which would allow a supple response to the dictates of the hour. Using as a model a looseleaf
prayer book from a Jewish summer camp, Roger had duplicated
forty-five pages of those Hebrew prayers he considered to be the
most important. To these he added, periodically, dittoed sheets
— as many as a dozen on a particular weekend — of songs,
prayers, graphics, readings, or whatever he thought relevant. The
combination of the Hebrew prayers, placed in the front of a
binder supplied by the student, and the dittoed sheets, which by
the end of the year amounted to 135, was the Vov Class's very
own, highly distinctive prayer book. Although the concept of
the looseleaf prayer book was introduced prior to the second
weekend, it was not until the third, held in November, that the
book was used in a service.

Collaterally with the looseleaf prayer book, Roger employed
a traditional prayer book — similar to, but not exactly the same,
as the one used at the Men's Club service — and the Pentateuch,
the latter for the Saturday morning Scriptural Reading. In addition he made extensive use of transparencies, records, and tapes,

as well as whatever he regarded as helpful to the service he was conducting.

The choice of particular prayers from either the looseleaf prayer book or the traditional prayer book, much the same as the choice of the supportive material, was determined by what in Roger's mind were the desires of his students. That student desire regarding religious services was not always easy to ascertain, however, Roger discovered on the first weekend, as his post-situational notes testify.

> On purpose, I had very liberal services because of my experience last year with a group that rebelled completely against traditional services in every way. The only materials that seemed to reach them were modern English readings, based on contemporary themes and audiovisual material . . . To set a tone for services as open to experimentation, I concentrated heavily on the kinds of materials we used the previous year. I was surprised, to say the least, when these materials were welcomed with relatively little warmth and excitement. Most of the kids expected and/or wanted traditional services . . . (9/18-20)

The reliance of the students upon traditional services, so-called, must not be understood as applying to anything other than the content, that is the recital of particular prayers in the traditional mode. While students were perfectly comfortable around their prayer table, for example, wearing the most informal of clothes, when it came to the actual prayers, they were accustomed to the traditional ones and preferred them. Thus student reaction to the first sheet Roger handed out on the third weekend — the same one which saw the introduction of the looseleaf prayer book — while sympathetic, was not quite as uniform as Roger might have expected. The sheet consisted of a reading entitled, "The Ultimate Bore . . . Services!"

> The sheet conveys the idea that services are dull, unimaginative and cold. Roger read through it once and had others read it with him. He then invited discussion . . .

As with so many of these exercises in criticism of the status quo, once the criticism is voiced there is not much that can be added. As a matter of fact, it seemed that Roger was eager to get unanimity of opinion regarding the criticism. He kept asking for shows of hands to indicate whether or not the people agreed that services were boring. Most, of course, did agree, although one or two people, mainly Sylvia, Bernice and to an extent Bob, were not satisfied with the critique. They made the point that the reason people do not find the service interesting is that they are not familiar with what the service means and the solution to the problem is not to provide new prayers, or colorful ideas, but merely to learn what the service is trying to convey. Sylvia made the statement that she was rather forced to come to services when she was very young but she is very happy about it now because she is beginning to understand what it is that is being done there and each week the services prove to be a little less boring. This was somewhat disconcerting to Roger and he kept recapturing the point, namely, that services are boring, and that something significant ought to be done. He suggested that the intelligent way to handle the problem would be to try to change the situation. All of which, of course, was leading up to the value of the looseleaf notebook which had been prepared. (11/20-22)

Despite the stated preference for the traditional service and the students' familiarity with it, as each weekend came and went, the Vov Class's services incorporated fewer and fewer traditional prayers and practices. It soon reached the point where most of the services were little more than informal meetings, in which spiritual or aesthetic themes were portrayed by means of various materials among which, upon occasion, traditional prayers and/or Scriptural readings were included. For example, one of the key elements of the traditional Saturday morning service is the public reading of the Pentateuchal portion. In fact, it is this reading which constitutes the chief distinguishing feature of a community service on Saturday as against a private service. Yet, on the fifth weekend, the one held in January, Roger dispensed with the reading altogether. There was not so much as a reference to it by Roger or by the students. The actual services held that weekend included only a sampling of the traditional prayers. Paradoxically, the sheets Roger distributed, more copious than at any other weekend, included one on the structure of the traditional service. Included also was an original prayer-poem by George and another by Jeanne, written in response to a suggestion by Roger, and related in content to the overall theme of the weekend.

It is difficult to ascertain the reasons for the disintegration of fidelity to the traditional service on weekends. One possibility is the growing sense of cohesiveness among the participants of the Vov Class[15] and the corresponding disinclination to be bound by rules of behavior not of their own making. A more likely possibility is the progressive weakening of the Sunday morning entente between the Vov Class and the Men's Club.

It was, for example, on the Sunday following the January weekend that the camp group attempted to impose its own melodies at the Men's Club Service. It was at that same service, incidentally, that one of the most vocal supporters of the traditional approach to services, Bob, for the first time failed to don his Tfillin. It was shortly thereafter that the class engaged in the discussion on the value of continuing with the Men's Club on Sundays and reached the decision to work on the service in order, eventually, to lead it themselves.

Separated from the Chapel in which the Men's Club Service was in progress by not more than thirty feet, Roger stood before his class that Sunday and articulated what he considered to be their goal:

> (Roger:) What we are going to do today is . . . more or less have services of our own . . . We are going to start with their book, with the services the Men's Club has and we are going to compare them with the services we have. And, hopefully, we can come up with some things that we can teach them so we can make the service a

little more exciting and a little more meaningful . . . . We are going to try and help them." (2/7)

Each student had in hand both the traditional prayer book and his own looseleaf prayer book. Roger asked the students to turn alternately to the appropriate prayer in each, pointing out along the way which prayers were missing from their looseleaf book and why. Volunteers were called upon to lead particular prayers and instruction was given in the "correct" melodies. Roger also offered suggestions as to the best way "to do" certain prayers when they would return to lead the Men's Club Service in future weeks.

After approximately a half hour, some difficulty with pagination in the looseleaf prayer book combined with a decline in interest led to general confusion. Roger castigated the class in such a way as to reveal the frustrations he felt in teaching prayer:

> You know the thing that bothers me most is that when people try to explain to you things that go on in the service, and then are rebuked like I'm being rebuked this morning, and then turn around and say, 'The services are so damn boring and we can't understand it, we don't want it, they're worthless, they're so boring and we don't know what's going on, it's a lousy experience, why should we ever come again?' And then when they're twenty years old, they say, 'We never learned this and no one ever gave us the opportunity to understand the service.' Yet the same people today, who are sitting and talking now and are not paying any attention, and who are saying on one hand that they want to learn about it and on the other hand fool around, they're being hypocritical — and I'm sick and tired already. You know, it's sickening. You try to do things. I am trying to get you out of there where I think most of you are sleeping, or just getting through it so you can go to breakfast, which is a lousy excuse to pray. You know, we might as well not do it. We're wasting our time. Is this a worthwhile thing to do? To go through the service and try and

understand a little bit more? If you don't think so, we'll
do something else... (Pause) No, really, I'm tired.
You're supposed to be kids who want to study and learn
a little bit. And obviously, it's not happening... Either
I'm doing something wrong, or it's just not working.
Something is wrong some place. (2/7)

The service analysis was discontinued at that point. In its
place, Roger conducted a discussion on what prayer is "all
about." Although there was some involvement by the students,
Roger was far more concerned about the subject than they. No
doubt he would have insisted that the discussion continue had
not the clock revealed that the Men's Club Service was over and
that it was time to join the adults in the auditorium for breakfast.

Despite this initial setback, Roger remained committed to
the task he had taken upon himself to work out, with the help
of the students, a rapprochement between the traditional service,
as represented by the Men's Club Service and the non-traditional, as represented by the class's weekend efforts. As the
students gathered for the sixth weekend at the Jewish Student
Center, Roger invited volunteers to come forward and work with
him on a new and better service for the Men's Club on Sundays.
Five students volunteered. To the best of the observer's knowledge, however, that is where the matter ended. The volunteers
and Roger never met. In fact, between the February weekend
and the end of the year, the class managed to find its way back
to the Men's Club Service only four times. At the first of these,
there was a feeble attempt by Roger and the adult leaders of the
service, whom Roger had alerted earlier, to join the students in
the melodies they preferred. At the next to the last, only one
out of the four boys present wore Tfillin. At the last, which was
in the middle of May, the Vov Class participated rather much as
they had at the first held in September. The service was exactly
the same as it had been and the students exhibited now as then
what might be called a distant attachment, which neither they
nor their teacher understood fully.

As to weekend services, they gradually became even less traditional and even more eclectic from the point of view of the material which Roger employed. He showed no hesitation in including as part of a service anything he deemed worthwhile, irrespective of the source. From a comedy satire of a Biblical story to a rock opera inspired by a non-Jewish tradition, almost anything qualified as a replacement for the traditional prayers.

Roger and the class for a time did employ a rather novel technique which had the effect of postponing the complete demise of the traditional service on weekends. In one of the periodic discussions of the traditional *vs.* the non-traditional service, it was decided that, instead of trying to mix the two, henceforth different services would be conducted differently — traditional or non-traditional — as the case was. On the sixth weekend, for example, the Saturday Morning Service was traditional, which meant that a selection of Hebrew prayers only was recited in the accepted fashion. However, the Additional Service, held later that same morning, was non-traditional, to the extent that a spontaneous discussion, sparked by a student comment, constituted the service.

It was not long, however, before even this solution fell by the wayside, as the traditional service became little more than a memory. On the final weekend of the year, other than at the service the class attended at B'nai Israel, there was not a single Hebrew prayer uttered as part of any weekend service. Beyond the Grace After Meals, which was never neglected, whatever worship there was resulted from a nostalgic rereading of the dittoed sheets found in the rear section of the looseleaf prayer book. It was apparent that the group had developed some genuine affection for these sheets, which they reviewed and discussed with considerable eagerness. Roger's favorite, as he reminded the class on that occasion, was "The Ultimate Bore . . . Services!"

Roger and the Vov Class never really admitted that they had given up on traditional services. Until the very end of the year, Roger clung to the hope that the Vov Class one day would find its way back to regular participation in a reformed Men's Club Service. In some mysterious fashion, which he never defined, the class would serve as the instrument for making that service relevant without, at the same time, disrupting its traditional character. The students continued to express fealty to the traditional service, although in point of fact they opted for traditional services only when they or their teacher could not find something which interested them more. Prayer in the traditional mode, in the course of the year, had come to be honored in the Vov Class, as the saying goes, more in the breach than in the observance.

Any thoughtful Jew living in modern times, especially one who teaches Judaism, faces a conflict, the implications of which touch the very essence of Jewish religious education. Roger, for example, had deep respect for the traditional service and correspondingly deep appreciation for the importance of inspiring his students to regular and comfortable involvement with it. At the same time, it was his opinion that his religious needs and those of his students, manifest and latent, dictated a much freer approach than that which was found within the traditional service. Nor was the conflict restricted to Roger. Many of the students themselves were conversant with the issues involved in traditional *vs.* non-traditional worship. They had heard or participated in discussion of its elements at home or in Religious School. They had listened to sermons which espoused one point of view or another. Most important, they were children of an age which forced concern, albeit at different levels, with the problem.

In some Jewish educational establishments this issue becomes a dilemma on the horns of which students and teachers are impaled. This did not happen with the Vov Class. One reason is that the structure of the class and its relationship to the congregation permitted grasping both horns, more or less simultaneously — the traditional in the form of the Sunday Morning Men's Club Service and the non-traditional in the form of weekend services. By means of the former, the Jewish past and its present protagonists, the parents and the congregation, were treated with regard; by means of the latter, the youthful search for meaning within the students' own idiom, which included to be sure significant elements of that same past, received its due.

This is not to say that the dilemma ever disappeared. It was present whenever and wherever the class was engaged in a service — either their own or one conducted by adults. It was present, for that matter, whenever or wherever the class was engaged in the performance of any religious exercise. Yet, the fact is that participation in both types of services, despite all the attendant difficulties, prevented the issue from becoming a rock on which the Vov Class program might have been dashed.

More significantly, participation in both gave rise, at times, to a creative interplay which may not have been possible had one path only been followed. Note in the following lengthy excerpt from the March notes of what is well-described as a nontraditional service, how the tradition, particularly as represented by the Men's Club Service, and the students, interact creatively with one another.

> 9:13 Roger starts with page 3 in the Hebrew section of the looseleaf prayer book. Will do it twice. Last two weekends Bob has done it. He would like to see who else can learn it. "It would be good if we could come out of this experience with some knowledge of prayer. At some time or other you will be standing in front of a group and this will help." There is perfect quiet. Participation by everybody with eyes and most with mouth . . . . Roger translates the first part of a blessing and has Brad put it in his own words.

> 9:22 Cousins enter. Continues the translation of remainder of first blessing. Karen gets לשכוי because it says תרנגול on bottom.

> 9:23 Rich enters. Roger works on להבדיל and ties it up with הבדלה. Eve is examining Dorothy's pants suit. She is not with it yet. Rich is putting on his Tfillin. Roger goes to second blessing . . . .

> Roger: "Would anyone like to try it? Does anyone care enough to try it? We have been friends long enough to say honestly. My purpose: when we return to Men's Club

Service I'd like some others to participate." He pauses. There are no takers. He says, "O.K." and goes on to Ashrei. Kids point out that they know the content of the Ashrei. Rabbi Katz took all last year to explain it.

Bruce: "It says that God is great and good. He does everything."

Roger detects some questioning in his reply. Sylvia disagrees. Bruce admits that he feels some doubt. Brad makes disruptive comments.

Roger: "You can leave if you want to." Roger asks group for examples of prayer which is not praise.

George: "Isn't there a prayer for rain in the dry season in Israel? The whole thing is 'buttering up' God."

Roger: "We all have the idea that God is high in the sky and we are down here and He has a big book." Characterizes such views as naive and childlike.

Bernice: "As you get older it may not be a big book but it is the same thing basically — like a guilt complex. An escape. Some people if they do something wrong, they use Yom Kippur as an escape."

Roger: "Like free psychiatrist help. The beauty about praying to God is that He never talks back."

George asks about Christian practice of confession.

Roger: "Each of you should think about what you feel about what kind of Person or Thing or Being God is." Relates it to their expressed interest in the Messiah, etc. "Think about this for two minutes. Think about what God is to you."

Brad rocks chair and makes noise.

9:37 Claudia: "I know there's no right answer. It is like

your good conscience. I don't think of Him as being a Being."

George: "He created the earth. He created a big ball of fire and it exploded and it evolved and stuff."

Roger: "What do you learn in science class?" . . .

Noise.

George makes point that knowing a little about science leads you to think that everything has a logical explanation. But real geniuses can see all the "untied ends."

Karen (called on) identifies idea of God with "myth." . . .

9:42 Roger: "Maybe God doesn't matter for 13-year-olds." (Class corrects to '14-year-olds'). When he was thirteen God meant nothing to him. Ties up his awareness of God with his marriage, when his mother will die, when he will have a child, on Yom Kippur, and at "certain moments."

Bruce: "Why not every day?"

Roger: "Yes, every day, but there are occasions when He is more real."

George: "I wonder if some day people will look back on us, like with the Greeks, and say we were primitive." God is an attempt to explain unexplained phenomena.

Brad: "The ancients used God as a causal explanation for 'mysterious things.' "

George: "Maybe when science finds more answers we won't need God. The only time we turn to God is in time of tragedy."

Roger asks for example. Tries to lead group to

Kaddish-sayers at Men's Club Service. Group does not get it.

Roger: "Where do we see tragedy or the reflection of people in tragedy?"

Rich gets answer: Kaddish at the Men's Club Service.

Bruce: "It is during Kaddish that these people have God — not the rest of the service."

Roger: "If there were not Kaddish how many people would attend daily services? Nobody would come. We would outnumber the men in there."

Bernice: "It is a farce."

Roger: "No, it isn't." Question: is it important to say Kaddish for someone who has died? "It is something you've got to think about." . . .

Sylvia: "When people cry at the death of someone, it is not for them but for the people who are left behind . . . ."

9:43 Bernice directly to Roger: "Do you believe in the Messiah?"

Roger: "I don't know. Important thing is not the answers but the questions which prove that you care." Says he will play Bernstein's Kaddish: a conversation — talking back to God.

Bruce: "But He doesn't talk back."

Roger: "Maybe He does. We'll talk about it."

9:45 "Let's go to breakfast." Girls exit and boys remove Tfillin.

Bruce: "I'd like to discuss this further, Roger."

Roger: "We will. It's important. I see kids in the school

leaving the synagogue and Judaism until someone dies. Come back for crisis moments, birth, death. I've seen the most unreligious people come back in time of death."

Rich: "That's what happened to me." (3/14)

If the nontraditional format was important in terms of providing the forum and the incentive for the kind of exploration represented in the above, confrontation with traditional worship seems to have been equally important, but in a different way. This is the point of the following two interpretive comments by the observer, the first of which derives from a Men's Club Service experience and the second from a weekend service experience.

> Such a service has value to the extent that ritual, i.e., the mindless repetition of familiar forms which eventually become habitual, have value. Thought, inspiration, and that sort of thing are concepts foreign to this approach. Heschel and others can talk all they want about surprise and excitement in prayers, but where is it here, and how, in the name of heaven, literally, do you engender it? Maybe it's like creative, subjective scholarship which seems to follow only upon a strong foundation of familiarity with others' creations and the knowledge of facts. Similarly, the stuff of creative religious expression also requires this kind of grounding. (2/28)
> Should one wait for some spontaneous expression of wonderment or thanksgiving or whatever, or does one induce this and, if so, how? There is no question in my mind that if there were not some structure, if it were not statutory to have a service on Saturday morning, there would be no inclination on the part of anybody to indulge in this type of activity. Assuming that the activity is valuable, the tradition serves to call it forth. This, after all, is the function of ritual. Ritual serves to remind the person periodically, ritually, if you will, of certain emotions or events or feelings that should be reviewed on a regular basis because of their importance to the individual or to the group. Internally to the prayer ser-

vice, I am not quite sure that there would have been any content had it not been for the traditional ritualized form. It is true that the group did just one or two of the prayers from the traditional service, but even these were sufficient to relate what it was they were doing to the tradition. The fact that the Ashrei was recited, and the Barchu, seemed to have the effect of reminding them that they are part of an overall Jewish sweep. (11/20-22)

Important or not, the fact is that in the course of time the traditional service all but disappeared in the Vov Class. One reason seems to be that the traditional service, both on Sundays and on weekends, was out of character with the thrust of the Vov Class program and perhaps with the life style of the young people in general. This is the judgment of the following effusion recorded by the observer at a Men's Club Service early in the year.

This is the only place in the program where the kids are consumers — consumers from leaders, from a book, from a tradition. This is not to say that there is no participation. There is indeed some, but it is of a different character from what they are involved in during the rest of the program. (11/15)

Another reason that the traditional service may have fallen by the wayside is that after a certain time it ceased to be useful to Roger and the class. Just as both showed the need to rebel against traditional educational practices, so they showed the need to rebel against traditional worship practices. The one difference is that with traditional educational practices there was a spirit of outright rejection; with traditional worship it was rejection set within a framework of qualified respect and veneration. But, the point is that once the rebellion was underway and legitimized by the program, a major function of the traditional service was lost. It had done its work of providing a cause for Roger and the class. It had even provided a point of departure for the creation of some new religio-cultural forms peculiar to this group. After it did so, it was no longer needed. As to the vacuum which resulted from its passing — principally the appointed service times on weekends — it was filled by free-flowing, highly informal worship sessions, the contents of which were compounded of Roger's ingenuity, student interest, and only bits and pieces of the two millenia Jewish prayer tradition.

Hebrew Language

The major literary treasures of Judaism, chiefly the Bible and the Prayer Book, are written in Hebrew. The study of Hebrew, therefore, has long constituted the focus of the curriculum in Jewish schools, particularly during the early childhood years. So significant a place did Hebrew language instruction occupy that one whole class of schools — the weekday afternoon schools — came to be known as Hebrew School. The establishment of the State of Israel gave added impetus to the study of Hebrew. As the language of daily communication in the Jewish state and as a symbol of the renaissance of Jewish culture in modern times, conversational Hebrew came to be viewed alongside literary Hebrew as a vehicle for establishing and maintaining contact with the worldwide fellowship of Jews.

It was out of concern that their children continue the study of Hebrew — literary or conversation or both — that the parents of the original Vov Class requested a weekday afternoon session in addition to Sundays and weekends. Whatever else the fledgling program might accomplish or might fail to accomplish, the children would acquire at least this. The suggestion was accepted and Wednesday was chosen as the day. By the end of the year, when plans were being formulated for the new Vov Class program — the one which is the subject of the present investigation — the Wednesday afternoon session, devoted to the study of modern conversational Hebrew, had become an accepted part of the program.

The most respected teacher of modern conversational Hebrew on the B'nai Israel faculty was Mrs. Cohen, an Israeli Jew, who had lived in Graceville some ten years. She was engaged to teach the class on Wednesdays, presumably under Roger's overall direction. In consultation with him and chiefly out of concern for the different levels of Hebrew knowledge represented among the students, it was decided to divide the class into two more or less equally sized groups. One would study Hebrew with Mrs. Cohen for the first forty minutes while the other would be with Roger. Following a ten-minute break, the groups would exchange places for the remainder of the session. Thus each individual student would receive a total of forty minutes of Hebrew language instruction weekly in the company of six or seven of his classmates. Roger expressed his intention of augmenting the admittedly short class time by using functional Hebrew words and phrases, especially on weekends.

When the students went to Mrs. Cohen's room for their first Hebrew lesson, approximately a month after the start of the term, no doubt they noticed significant differences between the lesson she conducted and those Roger had been conducting. Mrs. Cohen tended to relate to them cordially but with considerable more formality than Roger. Especially at the beginning, seating arrangements as well as the canons of teacher-pupil relationships usually associated with traditional classrooms were followed. Mrs. Cohen expected the students to be quiet, to speak when spoken to and generally to apply themselves to the lessons she set before them, according to methods which she stipulated. She also made it clear that her sole function was to teach Hebrew so that beyond her forty minute stint she expected little contact with the students.

Mrs. Cohen's lessons relied heavily on direct Hebrew conversation between her and the students, centered around, although not limited to, particular themes which she selected. By means of expressive gestures, contrived situations, some board work and above all her insistence on oral repetition, Mrs. Cohen attempted to induce students to speak Hebrew. The general tenor of the approach may be seen from the notes of the first session:

4:25 Mrs. Cohen starts Hebrew conversation on the

forthcoming Holiday. Rather good attention, but kids having difficulty in getting the drift. She moves alternately into Hebrew and English and the dawn eventually comes.

Brad first and then others give Hebrew names of seasons. Rather eager participation. Full conversational approach. Movable blackboard in room but no move to use it. Teacher quite expressive. To illustrate that leaves fall she drops pencil . . . .

4:32 She gets kids, even those with the least facility in the language, to speak in Hebrew. Brad answers correctly and looks very surprised. Method: question followed by student's attempt to answer. Mrs. Cohen admits not knowing names since she had not seen the group but once. They review their names in Hebrew. She asks for ages in Hebrew, too. Ruth and Jeanne talk as the repetition of the age moves to the other side of the room.

Mrs. Cohen: "Who remembers what we talked about last time?" After a few hints they recall they did "table Hebrew." (10/7)

While this first lesson began, as can be seen, in a promising fashion, its continuation, as documented in the notes, indicates that all was not well, even at that early date. Traditional emphasis upon Hebrew and parental and faculty wishes notwithstanding, the study of Hebrew in the Vov Class was not running smoothly.

4:40 First insistence by Mrs. Cohen for more order. Advises George and Brad that they are disturbing. Continues same process and those two are attentive. Questioning continues on tableware: "What do you eat with?" "Do they have ham in Israel?" Giggles.

Bob seems to be out of it. Chews and plays with hair. Brad lost something, looks for it, settles back down.

4:45 . . . Brad is reprimanded, mildly, for talking with George. Mrs. Cohen reviews conversation from beginning of session . . . .

4:50 George and Arnold are hand wrestling. George starts same game with Brad. Mrs. Cohen moves into all English conversation. Children seem to be aware of what the High Holy Days are all about.

Main problem which is now being considered is why did the New Year move from Pesach to Rosh Hashana. Brad and George duel with pencils.

4:55 Mrs. Cohen sends Brad out. "When you feel you can pay attention, come back." Continues conversation on the seasons. Introduces several new words. Eve seems completely uninterested. . . .

5:00 Break . . . (10/7)

The latter scene of inattention turning into disruption, for reasons yet to be explored, was repeated with growing intensity at virtually every subsequent session of the class. After only fifteen or twenty minutes of halfhearted participation in the lesson, students invariably busied themselves with other things. This was so irrespective of the group division on a particular Wednesday. The few who were interested, like Rich and Sylvia, had little chance of learning and soon gave up trying.

By mid November signs of a total breakdown in the Hebrew program were clearly evident. Every effort by Mrs. Cohen to maintain discipline and interest, from admonishment to the institution of new techniques, ended in failure. Apart from brief periods and then only with one or two of the students, the study of Hebrew in the Vov Class had become an unpleasant, distasteful experience for all concerned.

One Wednesday, early in December, when the students reached the classroom and waited to be told by Roger what the class division for Hebrew would be that day, they were informed that they would be taught as a unit by Mrs. Cohen during the first half of the session, with Roger present. Unbeknown to the students, Roger and Mrs. Cohen had conferred on the Hebrew problem and had decided that Roger would observe a typical lesson. Perhaps he could be of help.

If his purpose was to witness the disruption first hand, he

was not disappointed. Due to the influence of his presence, class discipline held up perhaps a bit longer than usual. But some fifteen minutes before the scheduled break, near bedlam broke loose. A stern reprimand by both Roger and Mrs. Cohen enabled the class to stumble through to the break, but only barely. It was time, agreed Roger and Mrs. Cohen, for an open confrontation with the class on the subject of Hebrew.

The confrontation — held at the very next session — provided Roger with an opportunity to express his attitude on the place of Hebrew in the Vov Class program. He described the "original conception" of the role of the Wednesday session in the following manner:

> We felt that it would be useful to spend some time, number one, for myself to talk to you about things that you are interested in, things that we can relate to the weekends ... The second part of Wednesdays — and here's where Mrs. Cohen comes in — would be working on Hebrew. This is, after all, Hebrew School and we felt that it's important not to lose contact with Hebrew language and to follow up on some of the work you've done in the past five/six years of Hebrew School. (12/16)

It is apparent that in Roger's view the study of Hebrew was far from being the purpose of the Vov Class Program, even on Wednesdays. Like worship services, Hebrew was respected by Roger, but only in relation to other goals which had not yet been defined.

Mrs. Cohen's perspective, revealed at that same session, was of a somewhat different character. To her Hebrew was number one on the agenda of the Wednesday class. Yet it mattered not at all to her what the Hebrew conveyed. In a masterful understatement, Mrs. Cohen said:

> My feeling is that ... some of you were resisting what we've been doing in class and I thought perhaps you have better ideas as to what you want to study. To me it doesn't make any difference, as long as it is in

Hebrew. I am open to suggestions, and if one subject doesn't interest you, I can teach you another subject in Hebrew. You see, I want to give you the tools — and the tool is Hebrew — to use it whatever way you want. (12/16)

The fact is that there was no confrontation that day simply because the students refused to be confronted. All they could suggest, after their repeated but unsuccessful attempts to change the subject, was that, if they were going to study Hebrew, conversational Hebrew made more sense to them than any other kind.

When the students assembled at the first session following the winter break, Roger told them that, in accordance with their expressed desire, they would continue the study of conversational Hebrew with Mrs. Cohen. Henceforth, however, instead of dividing the group into two parts, the class would remain a unit. The first half of the session Mrs. Cohen would teach Hebrew, in Roger's presence, and the second half they would study with him. As it turned out, the lesson that particular day was, if anything, more disorderly than previous lessons. Mrs. Cohen attempted to incite a conversation in Hebrew on what the students had done over the holiday, but with no success. It was not surprising that during the break Mrs. Cohen informed Roger that she was going to resign. She had done everything she knew but nothing seemed to work. This class was, in her opinion, another instance proving the generally low estate of Jewish education. Needed were professional teachers, supervision by educators rather than Rabbis, and a return to conventional classroom regimen.

Following the break, Roger continued his half of the lesson. Although the lesson was far from orderly, the contrast between it and the one they had just experienced with Mrs. Cohen was deafening. At the end of the lesson, in the presence of Mrs. Cohen, the most ambitious attack upon the Hebrew problem until that time was communicated to the class in Roger's following directive:

Next Wednesday, for those who are interested in studying Hebrew, Mrs. Cohen will be here. Those who are not interested go directly to the Library and do your Independent Study Project. (1/6)

Returning to his former practice, Roger began the session that Wednesday by dividing the class into two groups. He asked the first to go to Mrs. Cohen who, in the interim, had reconsidered her decision to resign. Roger, it seems, had not forgotten his offer of the previous week but he hoped that his students had. His post-situational notes of that day read:

> Under the groupings I had written a note that read as follows: "If you do not wish to attend either session for some reason, you may use the Library to work on your Independent Study Projects." I did not announce this note at the time of splitting up, as I didn't want to emphasize the fact that the kids could leave. I wanted to play that down. (1/13)

Subsequent Hebrew lessons tended to be alternately poor and not-quite-so-poor. Mrs. Cohen valiantly sought to employ new approaches with which to engage the imaginations of the students. Roger, with ritual-like regularity, conducted evaluations with the students on the Hebrew problem. These did little more than provide an opportunity for the venting of frustrations. Class division on Wednesdays, when resorted to, ceased to reflect levels of Hebrew knowledge, as was intended originally. It became simply a means of separating potential troublemakers. Even so, the students who were the object of the effort knew it and frequently disregarded the assignments in order to be with their friends.

At first, Roger's offer to miss Hebrew class, if desired, was taken up only by the more mischievous among the students. Most simply did not believe that the offer was a serious offer. One day, however, Dorothy who had never constituted a discipline problem declared that she was not going to attend Mrs.

Cohen's class. In a moment of rare assertiveness, she voiced biting criticism of the entire Hebrew portion of the program. Soon Bruce informed Roger that it was his intention to absent himself from Hebrew. Roger had no choice but to stand by his earlier commitment. He did it, however, in such a way as to make clear, for the first time, that students could miss Hebrew class, without fear of retaliation or stigma. They would no longer be forced or even urged to attend Hebrew class. It was up to them to decide.

When the students entered Roger's room one Wednesday in mid-March, they found the class division for the day written on the board. Group A was to remain with Roger and Group B was to go to Mrs. Cohen's room. The latter, however, were reminded that they did not have to leave if they did not want to. Four out of the seven students in Group B decided to leave. Their decision seemed to be in accord with Dorothy's who, as she left, commented, "I think I'll give it one more try." After the break not a single student from Group A went to Mrs. Cohen's room. All those who had started the session with Roger returned to him. They were joined by the four who had spent the first part of the session with Mrs. Cohen and the class finished the day with Roger, as a unit. As for Mrs. Cohen, she gathered her things together and went home early. From that moment forward, the study of Hebrew in the Vov Class was voluntary. Never more than five students availed themselves of Mrs. Cohen's Hebrew class at any one time. By the end of the year, only two were attending with some regularity. Hebrew, which had begun as a formal and apparently important part of the curriculum of the Vov Class, had been jettisoned.

The failure of Hebrew to maintain itself as a subject of study in the Vov Class may be laid at the feet of several causes. First of all, forty minutes of language instruction weekly, particularly in the absence of contact between lessons, is insufficient to impart a sense of mastery or even a sense of progress. This may be presumed to be so even where there is strong motivation to learn, which was not the case with most of the students of the class. The students simply did not learn enough to make the effort on Wednesdays worthwhile.[16]

Secondly, the differences in the teaching methods of Roger and Mrs. Cohen doomed the latter's attempt to win the allegiance of the group. As alluded to above, one of the working hunches on which the Vov Class Program was constructed was the need to have participants, particularly the students, view themselves as Origins. Roger was inducted into the original program because he accepted the validity of this approach. He was chosen to lead the program the following year because he demonstrated his ability to practice it.

By contrast, Mrs. Cohen was chosen solely because she knew Hebrew. Though she was a veteran teacher, her entire conception of teaching was that students were to be moved, like Pawns, in certain directions for the attainment of certain goals which she and the school deemed important. That the students themselves had not chosen the goal of learning Hebrew was not related in her mind to their rejection of her efforts. She consistently looked elsewhere for the causes.

It should be added that Roger too, when he finally gave students the option of choosing or rejecting Hebrew, did so as a result of their pressure rather than his conviction. It is true that the atmosphere he had created in the class and the character of his relationship with the students precluded his dealing with the issue in any other way. But there was no clear understanding on his part, especially during the first part of the year, of the basic dislocation represented by his approach to the class and that of Mrs. Cohen. Yet, the students felt the difference and reacted to it by rejecting Mrs. Cohen's subject out of hand.[17]

Perhaps the most important reason for the failure of the Hebrew portion of the Vov program, however, is that Hebrew related only peripherally to what came to be the purpose of the Vov Class. Roger and the students simply had a different agenda. Hebrew and the lady who taught it may have been on the agenda, but they were nowhere near its top.

General Jewish Content

The curriculum content of the Vov Class was augmented by a body of material not intimated in the curriculum inputs described above. The reference is to material and activities which were occasional in the sense that they entered the curriculum as a result of specific but unanticipated stimuli; and casual in the sense that they stood by themselves and received as much or as little attention as Roger thought necessary. One example is the march and rally on behalf of Soviet Jewry. Early in December, word reached the Graceville Jewish community that thirty-four Soviet Jews were being brought to trial for attempting to emigrate to Israel. In line with the Soviet Union's long-standing policy of persecution of Jews, the trial was calculated to stem the growing militancy of the Jews of the Soviet Union. Spurred on by youth criticism, Jewish communities in America decided to abandon their traditional reticence on this issue and mount a campaign of support for Soviet Jews. In Graceville, the resolve took the form of a protest march, scheduled to begin at the Jewish Student Center of Jefferson University and to culminate in a rally at a local synagogue.

Less than a week before the march and rally occurred Roger opened a Wednesday class with a vivid description of the manner in which the thirty-four Jews had been arrested at night, arraigned and incarcerated. Relating his description to the pogrom episode in "Fiddler," he pointed out that the Soviet policy of cultural genocide against Jews appeared to be turning into outright physical persecution. Roger handed out circulars containing the details of the march and rally, and urged all of the students to come. "Our presence," said Roger, "will prove we care." Class was dismissed after Roger admonished the students to think about what else might be done on behalf of the Soviet Jews and to make the necessary arrangements to attend the march and rally.

Before class on Sunday, Roger stood at the door of the Chapel and informed arriving students that they would not join the Men's Club Service that day. It was necessary for them, he said, to concern themselves with matters of greater importance. Reviewing the "facts of the situation" by means of a four-page mimeographed "Fact Sheet on Soviet Jewry" which he had students read aloud, Roger played part of a recording in which a well-known survivor of the Holocaust narrated a description of the condition of Soviet Jewry. Roger followed with a selection from the narrator's book on the same subject and distributed additional flyers. Then, bringing himself up to his full height, he said, "O.K., class, what should we do about it?"

The truth be known, a number of the students had had contact with the Soviet Jewry issue previously, either at camp or at home. Some already had written letters of protest and had distributed handbills. They reacted to Roger's question by suggesting that the Vov Class undertake to do the same kind of thing. Other students, however, reacted with incredulity that anything could be done on behalf of Soviet Jews, and surely not by them. Opposing this view, for which Rich was the chief protagonist, was Bob whose exuberant self-confidence bespoke the conviction that with sufficient effort all problems, including this one, are amenable to solution. "We must," said he, "organize everybody in the United States."

Riding the crest of Bob's enthusiasm, Roger directed students to divide themselves into four committees: one to put up posters around the synagogue building; a second to prepare petition forms to be distributed to B'nai Israel's teachers with the request that they secure student signatures; a third to compose letters to Senators and Congressmen urging that pressure be brought to bear upon the Soviet Union on behalf of the Jews; and a fourth to "dip into (the students' own) pockets a little bit" in order to purchase and send Hanuka greeting cards to the families of the accused Jews, demonstrating thereby the Vov Class's moral support of their cause. Quickly effecting the division, the class worked feverishly during the remaining forty-five minutes of the session. Despite one short detour to the Men's Club breakfast by Claudia and three others, posters were put up throughout the school building; cards were bought and addressed; petitions were written out and letters composed.

A tremendous downpour the evening of the march and rally discouraged attendance. Yet, four students, three parents, and one guest joined Roger for the evening. It was the unanimous judgment of all that the time was well spent, which judgment was communicated to the class in a formal report at the next session.

By means of participation in this community-sponsored event, Roger accomplished at least two purposes. First, he informed his students about the situation of their coreligionists in the Soviet Union. Second, he demonstrated his and the school's desire to have the Vov Class become part of the Jewish community. Nor was either point lost on the students. During the year, the group found occasion to return to the subject of Soviet Jewry many times. Students took part in another march held later in the term, by which time, incidentally, there appeared to be a thawing in Soviet intransigence. Roger was quick to bestow part of the credit upon the efforts of the Vov Class.

Another example of an occasional curriculum input of Jewish content is Roger's lecture the Sunday the class met in the Men's Club Lounge to watch a television program. Roger's post-situational notes described what happened:

> While we were watching the TV show, several of the kids — mostly girls — were huddled around the TV set. Some of the boys were further back and were joking and laughing during the show. One of the Men's Club members who had joined us to watch, asked the kids to be quiet .... I became a little distressed because of the rudeness displayed by the kids .... Therefore, I gave about a ten-minute lecture on ארץ דרך, literally, 'the way of the land' concerning practical respect for others. (10/14)

Thereafter the term דרך ארץ and the value it connotes became part of the Vov Class culture. Roger returned to it frequently to remind the students of the kind of consideration for others which becomes a Jew.

In general, the nature of the Vov Class Program made it inevitable that Roger and his students should have had considerable contact under conditions which encouraged informal communication. Late at night on weekends or at breakfast on Sunday mornings there were numerous exchanges between them and often lengthy conversations. Sometimes, a single student was involved; at other times, several or all of the students were involved. During these periods, Roger was on the lookout for opportunities to impart information of a specifically Jewish character. One brief but telling example is drawn from the notes of the October weekend:

> Roger was joshing with Jeanne. He suggested that what she ought to do during free time is take the B'nai Israel Sisterhood Cookbook and make all of the recipes so that he could taste them. She smiled a warm knowing smile. He replied that it wasn't a joke at all because there is Jewishness in cooking. He gave the example of "cholent," which is a typically Jewish dish prepared for the Sabbath. It occurs to me that perhaps the informal instruction is the most important instruction going on at such a weekend experience. (10/30-11/1)

In similar fashion, the class came to deal with other subjects including the Jewish view of capital punishment, the concept of Jewish interdependence, and the value of study in Judaism, as well as the proper method of donning a prayer shawl and the etiquette connected with leading the Grace After Meals.

It should not be thought that the initiative for these exchanges always emanated from Roger. Frequently the students themselves were responsible for contributing subject matter to the curriculum. One Saturday afternoon, for example, four students, three girls and one boy, happened to be at the Public Library located two blocks from B'nai Israel. After finishing their work, they decided to attend Havdala Services at the synagogue. The regular worshippers were pleased to see them and included them in the service. The next day, in class, the differences between the Vov Class Havdala Service and the one performed by the adult congregation was the subject of a short but spirited lesson.

As important as were these occasional inputs, Roger was eager to structure contact with Jewish content on a more regular basis and in ways which would satisfy the needs of individual students. The beginning of his most ambitious attempt to do this is conveyed in his preliminary notes of an early session:

> I have been reading part of Carl Roger's *Freedom to Learn*[18] and agree wholeheartedly with everything he says. Yet, I wonder if contract methods, goal books, and weekly reaction sheets are the key to individual self-motivated learning. The question is, Should I include a series of projects or reaction sheets to work on? But first, I feel that I must make the kids aware of the broad variety of study that could be personally undertaken within the area of Judaism. (10/18)

In order to accomplish the latter, Roger compiled and dittoed a list of fifty topics which he entitled Independent Study Project Topics. The topics, ranging from Jewish Mysticism to Jewish food and sex ethics, represented an extensive listing of areas of possible inquiry on Judaism. In case there were areas which had been overlooked, item number fifty stated, "Any topic mutually agreed upon during consultations."

Before distributing the list of topics, Roger led the class in a discussion on the question of how people learn. He concentrated primarily on the effects of school-imposed subject matter and expressed his conviction that if people study what they are interested in they retain the material for a much longer time. It was Roger's plan, therefore, to provide students with a list from which they would choose for themselves what specifically they wanted to study. In private appointments with him, choices would be discussed and finalized. Students would pursue their topics on Sundays, during free time on weekends, and on their own. It was Roger's further intention to have students keep track of their own progress by means of "Reaction-thought" sheets, which he would give them at a later date.

Following this introduction, Roger handed out the list of topics and read through it quickly. He made appropriate comments as he went along. The mention of the word death in "Jewish birth, marriage and death" evoked reaction from several students. In general, however, there seemed to be little interest either in the topics or, for that matter, in the idea of Independent Study Projects. When questioned as to why, several students claimed that they simply were not used to doing things in such a fashion.

It was not until a Sunday session more than three weeks later that Roger followed up his initial presentation with an effort to have all the students choose topics. In the interim, though no system of private appointments had been organized, several of the students had discussed possible choices with Roger. Ruth, for example, had mentioned that she might want to do an art project on her Bube and Zade.[19] Claudia expressed an interest in Hassidism and the Yiddish language. When Bernice expressed a similar interest, Roger suggested that the two might work together. Yet, most of the students gave little or no thought to the subject. George, in fact, was still not clear on what was meant by Independent Study Projects. Roger cited for him Claudia's example and strongly urged every student who had not yet done so to come to a decision, then and there.

Bob thought that he might like to go to the Library and read about the Holocaust. Sylvia thought that she would like to work on the background of "Fiddler on the Roof" which by then had become a class project. Claudia reconsidered her earlier decision and said that she might like to join Sylvia. Bruce decided to explore the topic, "Is God just an excuse for everything inexplicable?" When Bob heard Bruce's idea, he considered joining him. Roger approached Dorothy to help with the art work on the dittoed sheets. He closed the session by announcing that everyone would have to come to a final decision soon because the following Sunday the class would embark upon the Independent Study Projects in earnest.

After services the following Sunday Roger secured order and announced that he had brought materials along for those students who had decided on their topics. Bruce was handed two books, both standard adult works, which contained sections on God. Bob received three books dealing with the Holocaust. Sylvia was provided with a book about Sholom Aleichem, the author upon whose work "Fiddler on the Roof" was based, plus a record. Claudia and Bernice received a book of Yiddish phrases translated into English, together with the suggestion that they arrange to teach the class a new Yiddish phrase each week. Dorothy received ditto masters with which to make graphics for use on forthcoming weekends.

The distribution of materials provoked considerable interest. Those who had received materials, as well as those whose topics had not yet been chosen, seemed eager to get underway. Roger, however, had other business which he felt he had to transact first. He discussed preferences for the Saturday night program on the upcoming weekend and also distributed various dittoed sheets for the looseleaf prayer book. By the time these matters were completed, only eight minutes of the session remained. Still the group dispersed, both inside and outside the classroom, and a number of the students began their independent work. Roger's evaluation of the effort that day, as revealed in his post-situational notes, shows that all in all he was rather pleased with what had been accomplished:

> Generally, there was pretty good activity. I couldn't tell exactly what was going on in all quarters because I was running from kid to kid. I was kind of nervous because this was my first attempt at self-directed learning . . . . We only had about really fifteen minutes in which the kids had time to work on their projects, which really wasn't enough time to make any concrete observations, but I felt that these kids enjoyed the change of pace and some of the kids were really interested in using the time to work on their projects. (11/15)

Originally, it was Roger's intent to devote that part of each Sunday session which remained after services to Independent Study. However, when the difficulty with Hebrew began to be apparent, it occurred to Roger that these individual projects could serve a useful purpose on Wednesdays, too. It was necessary, therefore, for him to push the projects along. Unfortunately, because of his absence from the city one Sunday and because of a weekend another, he could not return to the projects until the first week in December. It was on that occasion that he distributed the long-awaited Reaction-Thought forms. Dittoed at the top of a blank sheet of paper was a title, followed by spaces for name, project, date, and "Reactions and Thoughts: (New Things I've Learned)." Roger expressed the hope that these sheets would constitute a diary of individual progress on the projects. He advised students to get busy on their projects and before leaving to be sure to make their entries on the forms.

For some reason — perhaps it was the growing oppressiveness of the Men's Club Service — the students were especially restless that day. Many still had not settled on their projects. Those who had, floundered. A few of the students eventually got down to work, but most engaged in conversation or walked about the building. Only one or two jotted their progress on the Reaction-Thought forms. Soon, the bell mercifully brought to a halt this third effort to launch the Independent Study Projects.

The next session devoted to the Independent Study Projects, due to the winter holidays and a number of other matters which had come to concern Roger and the class, occurred more than a month later. The thirty minute lesson that day took the form of individual work on dittoed sheets for use on the January weekend which was to begin later that week. In some cases the subjects of the ditto sheets were related to the topics students had chosen for their independent work; in most cases, they were not. In all cases, little was accomplished because the supply of ditto masters gave out before the end of the session.

After that session in January, Independent Study ceased to exist as an identifiable unit within the Vov Class Program. It was destined to be resurrected at one more session before the end of the year, in March, but as a result of two totally different trains of events. One involved the failing Wednesday Hebrew program, and the other the weekend themes.

Roger himself had chosen and worked out the themes of the first six weekends of the year. As described above, the themes he used were rather general in nature. With the March, April and May weekends remaining, he considered ways of focusing on more specifically Jewish themes and at the same time involving the students in the choice. At the first Wednesday session held in March, Roger handed out sheets of paper and had each student write his answer to the question, "What I want to know about Judaism." He then listed the answers on the board and ended up with no fewer than sixteen foci of student interest in Judaism. By means of discussion, which Roger led, the sixteen were grouped into three general categories: Messiah — Life after Death; Israel; and Jewish Way of Life. These three categories, declared Roger, would comprise the themes of the forthcoming three weekends. Roger collected the Reaction-Thought sheets and the class was dismissed.

Two weeks later, which happened to be the first Wednesday on which Hebrew was totally voluntary, Roger handed back the Reaction-Thought sheets. Upon each, underneath the student's answer to the question, What I want to know about Judaism, he had written extensive comment, including suggested readings and projects designed to guide students in the pursuit of their interest. After soliciting and securing his permission, Roger used Bob's paper to illustrate to the class what he had in mind. Bob's statement had been, "I want to know about the Second World War. I want to know about Jewish views on reincarnation, spirits, etc. I also want to know about Israel." Below, under three separate headings, Roger had listed no fewer than thirteen books and their authors. If Bob would read these books, he would find out what he wanted to know. And so would the other students whose papers carried similar listings.

Roger then walked to the teacher's cabinet, threw open its doors and revealed a neatly arranged shelf of books which he had brought from his personal library so that the students could get started immediately. All he asked of them was that they put their names on the index cards which carried the books' titles. They were free to keep the books as long as they wished. The whole of that session was to be devoted to Independent Study.

On a signal from Roger, the class dispersed for Independent Study. Some remained in the room; some left. Karen and Eve teamed up on a discussion of the question, Is Judaism worth it? Arnold began to thumb through a book on the Israel army which Roger had recommended to him. Brad used the opportunity to beat on Rich. Ruth had a guest with her that day and took the time to show her around the building.

The observer, too, scouted the building, but his object was to find students and to see what they were doing. Happening upon Mrs. Cohen's now teacherless room — that was the day she left for lack of students — the observer peeked through the peephole in the door. He saw three students — Rich, Bruce and Arnold — involved in animated discussion. Entering together with Roger who happened by at the same moment, he witnessed an unusual discussion:

5:05 . . . There is a discussion in progress, between Rich and Bruce — the same one as before. Rich is questioning where the soul comes from. Rich has written a diagram of God, who he says may be a composite of all the souls. Roger asks Arnold what he thinks. He says that he believes in a Supreme Being. Rich who is quite worked up continues to expound on the subject of God. General idea is that unless there is a God who cares, "who would there be to cry?"

5:18 Roger asks Bruce's opinion of Rich's statement. He says his approach is "scientific." God was used because people didn't understand the world. Rich says maybe animals think and have spirits, too. He continues to pursue argument of the design of the universe. Roger asks how the universe got there.

Bruce: "How did God get there?"

Roger: "Maybe God is the ultimate existence."

Roger: "Do you really need God?"

Rich draws line on board: Science can explain one level — the physical. But how do you explain why you are here?

Roger injects birth of child idea as being much more than mere physical. Roger ties point in with Judaism as having decided that there is only one God. Injects central thesis of Rubenstein's *After Auschwitz.*[20] Bruce says, "Do you think there is a God up there who cares about us?"

Rich and Bruce talk about the "up" concept. Arnold looks more alive and more interested than I have seen him. Roger rises, talks about the possibility of other inhabited worlds and they speculate as to whether they believe in God.

Rich: "The world is kind of ridiculous without God. Why we are all alive. Does it make any difference that we live and die. We might as well be dead. God makes it all worthwhile."

Bruce: "People remember Einstein!"

Rich: "People live and die and are remembered by other people, but they die, too, and are forgotten. There is need for an Eternal Rememberer!"

5:28 Arnold is now describing his diagram to Rich. . . . The explanation is that there may be a counterpart of the atomic system in the universe. There is a center and galaxies revolve around it. He says that the center may be God.

Rich and Roger continue to speculate on the part of the person that may be considered God.

5:32 Roger advises Bruce to keep an open mind. God may come alive for him in the future. Describes how difficult it is to say positive things about God. Like Maimonides said only negative things. It registers with Rich . . . . Roger ties up the discussion with Rabbi Green's speech and the Hassidic approach to continually searching after God. Bruce and Arnold exit, Rich and Roger continue . . .

Rich alludes to the possibility of his own death. Roger mentions custom of naming kids after the deceased. That's a kind of rebirth. Rich says that that is insufficient.

Roger admits he is not sure about life after death and discusses the immortality of influence.

5:35 Mentions the contribution a person can make to mankind. Cites Abe Lincoln. The important thing is the contribution you make to other people.

Rich says he doesn't like the idea of the finality of death. Heaven and hell enter the discussion and Rich makes no move to leave. Rich asks to take book, *The Zohar*, home. (3/17)

Following this session, the record contains only one more reference to Independent Study. A week later, Roger received a telephone call from Claudia. In addition to telling him that she would not be able to be at class that day, she wanted to clarify Roger's suggestion for her Independent Study project, namely surveying student attitudes towards Judaism by means of a questionnaire. Apart from this brief conversation, Independent Study in the Vov Class was heard from no more. It had engaged Roger's and the class's attentions during part of only five sessions the entire year.

The technique of the Independent Study Projects, despite its limited employment in the Vov Class, performed several functions. In the first place, used as it was in connection with Jewish topics, it helped to establish in the minds of the students

Roger's commitment to Jewish content for the class. His list of fifty topics, to cite but one example, demonstrated Roger's awareness of the range of Jewish knowledge. It demonstrated too Roger's conviction that the study of Judaism, as distinct from the experience, was in some way connected with the work of the class.

The second achievement of the Independent Study Projects was the legitimization of whatever means of relating to Judaism or Jewishness that students chose, including some not commonly considered to be within the purview of religion and the synagogue. Judaism, as a variegated system of beliefs, rituals, cultural forms and attitudes, has long provided almost as many means of identifying with it as there have been Jews. Continuing this tradition, the Independent Study Projects encouraged students to begin to think of their own means of identifying and implied at least Roger's acceptance of their choice.

Thirdly, the Independent Study Project technique provided Roger with a convenient stop-gap curriculum alternative which helped him to deal with a number of crises that arose in the class. It enabled him, for example, to withdraw the class with honor, as it were, from the Men's Club Service when he deemed it necessary. The transfer of Independent Study to Wednesday, if only at the single session in March, also helped to rescue him and the class from the Hebrew dilemma. It is questionable whether the transition to voluntary Hebrew could have been accomplished quite so smoothly had this technique not been available.

All in all, the Independent Study Projects, like the other components of the evolving curriculum of the Vov Class, brought the students into contact with many of the concepts and forms of Judaism. Curriculum content, as such, however, was not viewed either by Roger or by the students as the essential purpose of their association. What it was they did view as the purpose forms the subject of the next chapter.

Chapter Four

From Aggregate to Group

The Social Structure

The fifteen students and the teacher who comprised the Vov Class had had little contact before the term started. It is true that all of the students knew one another from having been in the same classes at religious school and in a few cases from having attended the same public schools. Two of the students were cousins. Three of the girls had been together in one Jewishly oriented camp the previous summer and two in another camp. Several of the parents were friends or neighbors and their children, as a result, had had some carpool contact over the years. Yet, as a whole, the Vov Class formed an aggregate of disjointed individuals whose relationships, at the start, were based primarily, if not entirely, on the accident of their Vov Class association.

As might be expected, it was in the form of dyadic or occasionally triadic groupings, rather than in larger units, that the social relationships within the class began to develop. One triad that emerged the very first weekend consisted of the Camp Zion girls — Sylvia, Jeanne, and Claudia — with Sylvia, at the beginning, the most prominent. The three immediately began to relive their camp experience on the Vov weekends.

It should be pointed out that campers, especially those whose overall experience is positive and who succeed in becoming part of a group while at camp, have a perennial and serious problem. That problem, briefly stated, is the formation and the forced dissolution of their social group within a short three, six or eight week period, depending upon the length of the camp session. While summer camping is devoutly desired by many, the inevitable end-of-the-session farewell is often painful. Attempts are made to maintain contact with bunkmates by means of correspondence and participation in annual reunions. But the attempts never quite succeed and the more involved among the young people find themselves leading a twilight existence during the school year. They recreate their camping pleasures in fantasy and literally count the days until the summer returns.

Sylvia, for example, claimed to be involved in regular and active correspondence with no fewer than seventy former Zion campers. By her testimony, Sylvia's correspondence file, attained during the period between the close of camp and March the sum of 236½ points, which she reckoned on the basis of one point for each letter and one half point for each postal card received. She and the other Zion girls could hardly contain themselves in anticipation of the January Camp Zion reunion, which was to include, incidentally, an out-of-town former camper. That the reunion in reality was a recruitment function arranged by the camp authorities bothered the girls not at all. If anything, they were more anxious than the authorities themselves to have their friends sign up. Nor did they spare any effort to induce them to do so. They carried on endless conversations with those they regarded as prospects, including the observer, who they thought should come along as "Camp Rabbi." They distributed camp brochures, underscoring repeatedly that despite rising costs tuition for the next summer had not risen over the previous summer. They brought their out-of-town guest to each session of the Vov Class held during his stay and they reported dutifully the progress of their recruiting efforts to the camp authorities.

Given such a degree of involvement, imagine what it was for these three girls to find themselves in a camp-like environment at Mary Grove in the third week of September. It was to them a boon of exquisite dimensions. They reveled in the outdoors, in the informality of the mess hall, in their favorite camp songs, and in each other.

Drawn to this triad were two other girls, Karen and Bernice. Karen had known Sylvia from public school and both she and Bernice felt at home in the outgoing warmth of a recreated camp atmosphere. Ruth, on the other hand, was not really part of this subgroup. For reasons which will be explained below, she hovered at its periphery but never — not then and not later — did she become a full-fledged member.

Perhaps the most prominent individual to identify with this clique was Roger. It will be recalled that Roger shared the Camping Mystique. He therefore was drawn to the Zion girls, who hung on his every word and delighted in his numerous camping allusions and reminiscences. As the class returned from its second weekend, for example, his and their actions showed the depth of their mutual commitment:

> The bus ride back was rather uneventful and restful. The boys sat in the back of the bus and the girls in the front. Roger was in the first seat. The girls and Roger sang Hebrew songs and a few English songs in a restful relaxed manner. The boys did not participate at all. At one point, they attempted to disrupt the singing, in a kind of halfhearted way, but without success. While the girls sang, they reminisced about Camp Zion and other camps. Roger pointed out to Sylvia that she should guard her camper list, because two or three years after he, Roger, left camp, he would meet former campers at Youth Group conventions and the like and not remem-

ber their names, although he did remember their faces. With the list in hand, he was able to remind himself of the names. (11/1)

Based upon their obvious isolation in the dormitory and at the table, not to speak of outspoken comments on the subject, it was also evident that first weekend, that there was going to be at least one other triad among the girls which, by virtue of its inclinations and loyalties, would constitute an active opposition to the first. This triad consisted of the two cousins, Eve and Susan, and Dorothy. Eve and Susan expressed keen disappointment even before the weekend was over about what was happening. They could not see themselves spending their time all year long in such a fashion, especially since the weekend routine was set within a Jewish framework of Sabbath observance, prayer services and the rest. While it is beyond the ken of the observer to identify the precise causes of their unhappiness, it would seem natural to assume that their opposition was anchored in their previous experiences in the same way as the others' were anchored in theirs. It so happens that both girls stemmed from families in which Judaism was pursued in a manner which can only be described as most energetic. Like their older siblings before them, they had attended the B'nai Israel Religious School somewhat indifferently. According to their teachers, they had learned little and had developed a rather tenuous relationship with things Jewish. Apparently, they had yielded to parental pressure to come to Religious School, but avoided other Jewish contact wherever possible. They attended the same public school and it was known that most of their friends, by design, were non-Jewish. In general, the two girls showed signs, even at this young age, of rebelling against, if not completely rejecting their Jewish identification.

Dorothy, the third member of this opposition triad, was attracted to it for reasons which remain a mystery to the observer and perhaps even to Dorothy herself. Her relationship with Eve and Susan was destined to be a stormy one in which she repeatedly sought but never quite achieved a different identification within the class.

It would be a mistake to think that there was no contact between these two cliques. As it happens, Eve and Susan of the one and Sylvia of the other were students in the same Junior High School. The three thought of themselves as good friends there, and were somewhat at a loss to understand why it was different in the Vov Class. Sylvia in fact regarded both Eve and Susan with some envy, for she saw them as traveling with the highest status girls at school, judged by the criteria of social acceptance and independence from adult control. According to Sylvia and other sources, they were among the "coolest" students at school. It must have been evident to them and to Sylvia that the Vov Class had changed the rules and was going to relate status to quite different criteria.

That Roger identified with the Zion triad might well have been seen as fortuitous from its point of view as from the point of view of its rival — the one because Roger supported their efforts and the other because his action merely confirmed their distrust of teachers and Jewishness, generally. But neither clique, like the observer along with them, had reckoned sufficiently with Roger and his talents. There was a long year ahead and at this early stage, that is during the first several months of the term, it was still far from clear what the class's final social configuration would be.

The boys of the Vov Class classified into subgroups much less neatly than the girls. There was one triad of boys which formed at the start of the year and led, as will be seen, a rather checkered career. It consisted of Bob, by far the tallest and strongest boy in the class; George, who was destined to play a key role both in this clique and in the class as a whole; and Brad, small and mischievous, who never tired of trumpeting the fact that he was being forced to attend the Vov Class against his will. If the basis of the girls' relationship was shared experience or even temperament, such was not the case with the boys. None of the boys had been to camp together and only three of the total of six had attended the same public school. Though Brad and George were among those three, it seems more likely that their relationship was based on boyish concerns, such as making the girls miserable and generally keeping the teachers and everyone else aware of their presence.

The remaining boys — Rich, Bruce and Arnold — were much less developed in these areas than their compatriots. Socially, they were greatly outshone by Bob, George and Brad and were not infrequently used as the butt of pranks and even aggression.

Ruth's repeated shifts back and forth between the two female triads seem to have been related to the interest in boys, particularly the three who made up the boyish triad, which she shared with Dorothy and the two relatives. She, like Dorothy, devoted considerable attention to her appearance and seemed to possess a natural penchant for inviting the awareness of boys. Known among them as The Bod, short for The Body, her manner of dressing made her the object of constant remarks and stares. They also made her a most desirable confederate if not member of the opposition clique.

At the same time as Ruth appeared to enjoy the attention she attracted from the boys as well as the position it afforded her in the opposition clique, she was much fascinated by the descriptions of the pleasures of camping at Zion which wafted about the class from almost the first day. It was not long before the perceptive Zion girls recognized Ruth's interest and identified her as a prime prospect for their recruitment efforts.

> . . . there was a discussion between Sylvia, Claudia and me on the subject of Camp Zion. Sylvia said that she had convinced a number of the girls to go this season. Last season just Claudia, Jeanne and she were there. This year, Karen is going and Bernice, and perhaps Ruth. She later said that Ruth was definite. When I quizzed her as to Ruth's apparent indecision she said that it was a matter of money, that if Ruth could raise the money she would definitely go . . . Ruth seemed very happy during the meal. Her happiness seemed related to the fact that

the Zion girls kept directing their attention to her. (1/15)

In stark contrast to Ruth and to the others in the opposition clique, the Zion girls regarded the boyish boys as undignified and rowdy. They preferred to shower their rather motherly attentions upon Bruce and Rich, both of whom were bright, but rather shy and unaffiliated.

Sylvia looked across the room and said, "Poor Rich looks so sad tonight." I asked her how she meant it and she said, "Well, look at him sitting there. The boys pick on him so much and are so unkind to him." I asked her opinion as to why. She said, "I don't know. He happens to be the only good one in the bunch." Then she added, "With the exception of Bruce." (11/20)

Despite occasional situational shifts, the subgroups seemed to become more rather than less solid as the term wore on. Simultaneously, the isolates seemed to become more isolated which served only to further solidify the cliques. It was obvious that any realignment of the class's social configuration would require a major effort, if indeed it was possible, at all.

The Push Towards Cohesiveness

In many conventional classrooms the establishment of relationships between the teacher and the students proceeds from larger to smaller units. This means to say that the teacher relates first to the class as a whole, and then, as he becomes familiar with individual differences and friendship preferences, to individual students. While in neither case can the process be viewed as linear, Roger and the Vov Class tended to move somewhat differently. As has been pointed out Roger, especially at the start of the year, related primarily to individuals. His whole thrust was the individual — his problems and his needs. Only after one-to-one relationships between him and individual students were firmly in hand did he begin to deal more actively with larger units, first subgroups and finally the totality.

This is not to say that Roger was unmindful of the reality, particularly of the cliques, at every step along the way. In fact, it may be argued that, because he was familiar with the division of the class into cliques rather than despite them, he elected to relate to the individuals qua individuals. To have attempted to deal with his students through their cliques would have perpetuated and deepened cleavages between students which may never have been able to be bridged. By the same token, to have followed his natural inclination — which was to identify with the Zion girls — would have doomed any hope of developing a relationship with the others in the class. Roger's intuitive perception of his task is evident from a section of preliminary planning notes which he wrote in the third month of the term:

> This will be the beginning of a series of value sheets concerning ethics and friendship — ethics because on the fourth weekend our guest will be the President of B'nai Israel, who will do some work with the kids on ethics in Judaism; and friendship because, as I have noted previously, I feel I must attempt to break up the cliques and frictions that are developing especially among the girls . . . hopefully the lesson will help the kids to realize that a lot of their petty differences are not as important as they seem to be. I hope to create a sense of group identity with the kids by splitting them into groups that will divide the cliques. (12/2)

In addition, Roger was not the kind of person who was satisfied to have his leadership refracted through the prism of any intermediary. He yearned to create his own group and to commit it to purposes over which he would have a direct and determinative influence. The main avenue available to him, at least for the moment, was the individual student. Roger wisely saw to it that that avenue was never neglected. Even as the year progressed and he thought in terms of dealing directly through subgroups he carefully maintained individual contact. If all else were to fail, he knew that he would have these personal relationships, at least, upon which to build meaningful Jewish experiences with his students. And he probably knew too that it was these relationships, cultivated as they were in an atmosphere of concern and trust, which would gain him entry ultimately into the clique structure and enable him to attack the problem of welding the students into a single group with himself as leader.

A prerequisite to the formation of a group is the acceptance by its constituent members of one or more superordinate goals.[1] While it is most desirable that the goals be indigenous to the individuals or to the structure of the relationships, it is often possible to provide a goal from the outside which serves to open up lines of communication between the members and causes norms[2] to be established. The desired outcome of the process is that the disparate individuals come to think of themselves as members of a supra-individual body. This is precisely what Roger tried to do the first session of the Vov Class when he suggested and secured the agreement of the class to produce and to present at a later date "Fiddler on the Roof." The vagaries of its fate during the year, including when it was rehearsed and why; which students looked forward to its production and which sought to thwart it and why; constitute like a barometer an accurate guage of the development of the cohesiveness within the Vov Class over the year. Fascinating as it might be to document the process, the fact is however that "Fiddler's" changing fortunes were more a symptom than an agent. "Fiddler's" importance, certainly for the moment, lay in its introduction by Roger so early in the year — indication that he appreciated the need for a superordinate goal of some kind. Alas, he could not have known at that stage that "Fiddler" was not to be that goal. It would do, however, until his relationship with individual students and theirs with each other, nurtured in an atmosphere of trust, would give rise to another.

Simultaneous to the search for a worthy superordinate goal, Roger adopted a number of specific tactics designed to strengthen the lines of communication within the class. For example, the sensitivity exercises, whose original purpose was perhaps self-awareness, soon began to assume a group-building function. Nor should the two purposes be seen as mutually exclusive in any sense. In the same way that "Fiddler" served a number of individual and group needs, at one and the same time, so the sensitivity-type exercises filled certain personal needs even as they operated to increase interaction within the total group.

An excellent example of such an exercise and its double function was the one performed in the middle of October. Roger handed out a sheet of paper to each of the twelve students present and had them complete the following two sentences with a single word or phrase: "I feel best when I am . . ." and "I feel worst when I am . . ." Students were not to sign their names, of course. Roger collected the papers and then listed all of the descriptions side by side. It was the class's job to discuss and decide which student went with which two words or phrases. To give the reader some idea of the type of clues with which they worked, one student responded, "I feel best when I am a cat," and "I feel worst when I am a gerbil." Another wrote, "I feel best when I am hungry or tired," and "I feel worst when I am hungry or tired." Others used terms such as "accepted" and "rejected," "girl" and "stupid," and "Nixon" and "Agnew." The whole exercise, including the decision on which description was written by which student, lasted only a few minutes. As it turned out, each pair of responses was identified correctly with its author, with two exceptions. The exceptions were the two relatives in the class, whose responses were merely interchanged!

The observer's first reaction to what must be seen as an almost unbelievable feat of awareness was not unlike that of Redl and Wineman who were astonished by the accuracy of the personality appraisals of each other made by their youngsters: "Time and time again we were put to shame by the uncanny personality appraisal such children could make of each other, where we ourselves, with all the elaborate tests and case history material at our hands were helpless."[3] Beyond this initial reaction, however, came the understanding that Roger had embarked, in earnest, upon the dual effort of enhancing self-awareness and, at the same time, opening up channels of communication between students which he identified as a necessary condition to the formation of a Vov Class group. That the students were still far ahead of him, at least on the level of cognitive awareness of each other, in no way minimized the importance of his intent. He persisted, although it was clear at the time that the students were not yet ready to form a group under his auspices.

Roger introduced additional exercises with the same purpose in mind. One, mentioned above, consisted of having the students stand in a circle with their arms clasped together. An individual student was chosen to try to crash into the circle. Besides the energy release it afforded, the exercise was designed to illustrate the effects of exclusionary tactics upon certain individuals as well as the power that all individuals have when they work in concert. Again, this exercise and others like it may not have done very much by themselves to fashion the group but they revealed to the class and to Roger himself, in no uncertain terms, what was fast becoming the class's major challenge of the year.

The students' hesitancy to relate to Vov along other than individual or clique lines may be seen in another apparently unsuccessful method used by Roger to increase group cohesiveness. Each Wednesday afternoon, as described above, the class was divided into two units. One unit spent half of the session studying Hebrew with Mrs. Cohen, while the other half remained with Roger. After a short break in the middle of the session the groups exchanged places. Originally, the divisions, which Roger himself made, were based upon knowledge of Hebrew, the more advanced students in one group and the less advanced in the other. Eventually, however, Roger bent the Wednesday division, as he was destined to bend most Vov Class activities, to his goal of fashioning a group. Instead of dividing the class according to Hebrew knowledge, he divided it in such a way as to disturb clique relationships. The relatives in the girls' opposition triad, for example, were separated; the boys of the boyish triad were also divided, unfortunately, from Roger's point of view, the latter into only two units.

Some of the same factors present on weekends which contributed to the creation of an atmosphere of equality and trust in the Vov Class contributed also to enhancing group solidarity. The relative isolation of the weekend settings made interdependence among the participants a fact of life in the Vov Class. From unloading the bus, upon arrival, to the cleanup at the end of the weekend, the entire group worked together. It was only fair, too, that students take turns serving meals, irrespective of clique affiliations. When it became known that Evelyn, the cook, for example, could not be present at a particular weekend, it was natural that all the girls agreed to prepare the food — after all, everyone was going to eat. The same was true of sleeping arrangements. While the students devised ingenious ways of remaining in cliques, the whole thrust was towards union, if not unity. Three or four girls might take their mattresses and situate themselves in a closed square at the far end of the sleeping room away from the others, but the separation thus effected had to fight what amounted to the persistent pressure of the physical setup in the direction of cohesiveness. Similar was the seating at meals. Though one particular clique occupied one corner of the table, usually the one farthest removed from Roger and Sara and went so far as to hoard and ingest only particular items of food, there is only so much separateness available at a single table. The weekends, in short, by their very nature provided significant tools both to Roger and to the class in the general direction of togetherness.[4]

Of equal or perhaps greater significance for the formation of the group was the Jewish framework within which the weekends were lived. Some scholars have attributed what has been described as an intense in-group[5] feeling among Jews and their close family solidarity in part to the influence of Jewish religious and cultural forms.[6] Without taking sides on whether or not the characterization is correct, suffice it to say that many Jewish rituals, especially those associated with the Sabbath, are group and family oriented. A traditional Sabbath, for example, is celebrated primarily within the confines of the home. Each member of the family is apportioned his own special function. Mother cleans the house, prepares traditional foods and ushers in the occasion with the lighting of the candles. Father intones special prayers, instructs the children and leads singing. He also confers blessings upon those present and generally tries to engender what should be, ideally, an intimate, joyous family occasion. Even community worship, so-called, on the Sabbath, occurs within a congregation composed of like-minded family groups rather than individuals. Despite the weakening of traditional forms in modern times there is still a significant residue of knowledge and commitment abroad among Jews. It is not unusual that long after children have grown and have established families of their own they return regularly to their parents' table to taste the old foods, to observe the traditional rituals and to renew family ties.

As has been noted, the students of the Vov Class were conversant with and tied to traditional Jewish forms. Sabbath observance of some kind was present in the home of every single Vov Class student. During weekends, therefore, from the lighting of the candles at sundown Friday through the ritual washing of the hands and the recital of the Sanctification over the wine, from the spirited singing and the Grace After Meals through the various services and study sessions, to the farewell ceremony at sundown Saturday, when the Sabbath queen took her leave, Vov Class students were thrown together in group situations, the legitimacy of which was accepted by even the most reluctant among them. What was true of the Sabbath was true also of a number of other Jewish ritual forms. There was constant stress upon Jewish family-like cohesiveness as both the goal and the method of authentic Jewish expression. Indeed, there were powerful forces at work upon the Vov Class and they all moved in the right direction from Roger's point of view.

A Social Crisis

The Vov Class, however, was still not a group. Worse, it seemed that it would never be, judging by the events of the third weekend, held in November. The third weekend, unlike the first two, was held away from Mary Grove, at the Jewish Community Center facility. The observer noted, almost immediately, a spirit of tension abroad in the class. Students sat at meals but they seemed to want to be elsewhere. They arrived at services, but only after considerable coaxing by Roger. The cliques especially were more clearly demarcated than before. Each sat to itself, resisted contact with the others and generally showed much more concern for its own inviolability than for the program. Even bedtime offered no surcease from the tension.

The observer speculated on the causes. Was it that the hour-long bus ride, which would have allowed a shift in set from the ordinary to the Vov Class experience, was missing? Was it the absence of the woods and its replacement by a game room with its billiard table? Or was it, perhaps, the theme of the weekend — the Cycle of Life — through which everyone, even the youngsters, caught a glimpse of his own aging and eventual demise?

Subsequent careful reflection convinced the observer that none of these was the cause. The cause — to the extent that any complicated social experience can be said to have a cause — in some way was tied to the students' efforts to shake off Roger's and the program's attempt to weld them into a single working unit. There was in progress that weekend a *sub rosa* power struggle involving, besides Roger, the Zion girls, whose ranks had by now been augmented by Bernice and Karen, and the opposition triad, which now also included Ruth as its fourth member. While it is true that the others, the boys and the isolates, were present, they really were in the role of supporting cast. They performed important functions, but the action was carried chiefly by the two girls' cliques.

The struggle reached its zenith Saturday night in an incident which centered about Dorothy, an original member of the opposition clique. The Zion girls, it seems, determined to split her off from her group and bring her into their group. To this end, they took Dorothy aside and confided how difficult these weekends had become because of Eve, Susan, and Ruth. When they are around, they said, the boys pay attention only to them. "And, besides," they added, "they act like babies!" Then shifting the attack they said, "But, you, Dorothy, are different! Why don't you move your bed over to our side?" With this, Dorothy did move her bed and she was quickly surrounded by her new friends. When Eve, Susan, and Ruth, who had been in the bathroom, returned and saw what had happened, they responded by moving their own beds still farther to the other side of the room. If Dorothy was going to separate herself from them, they would help her.

An interesting aside: clued in to what was happening by Sara, the observer went into the girls' dorm ostensibly to bid them good night. He felt immediately the tension in the air. Verbal and visual daggers were darting back and forth between the two warring camps, buffered somewhat by Sara, whose cot stood between them. The observer gravitated towards the Zion girls, with whom he exchanged a few words of greeting. Going to the other side, on his way out, to the opposition clique whose ranks had just been depleted, he was met by stony silence, broken first by his own "Good night," and then by Eve's "That's all right. You can go!" She apparently knew better than he knew himself where his sentiments lay.

The whole of the next day the Zion girls hovered protectively about their conquest, while the decimated opposition clique stalked about planning their next move. Roger who had not been directly involved in the incident, although he was very much aware of it, was thinking of his own next move. It was evident to him that the cliques were more solidly entrenched than ever and that the success of the class, not to speak of his success, was integrally related, if not dependent upon, his ability to restructure them.

A critical feature of the weekends, as has been pointed out, was their ability to serve as focal points of planning and activity during the Sunday and Wednesday sessions which preceded them. Roger was aware of their potential and in part employed the weekends for that purpose. Never did he do so more effectively, however, than he did with the sessions which followed the piracy of Dorothy, leading up to the next weekend in December. It should not be thought that all of the activity during that period was placed in the service of the clique crisis. There were times when other matters, like the demonstration on behalf of Soviet Jewry, commanded Roger's and the class's attention. There were times, too, when Roger seemed to forget about the crisis altogether. He might have been more careful, incidentally, had he noticed how Dorothy was slowly but effectively enticed away from the Zion girls back to her original clique. Evidently the factors which had led to her identification with the opposition clique, in the first instance, still drew her. But there were already enough straws in the wind to convince Roger that he had best prepare carefully for the fourth weekend, if he was to have any hope of mounting a frontal attack upon the clique alignments.

The fourth weekend, held at still another in-town location — the Jewish Student Center across from Jefferson University — had as its theme "people." Roger played records, showed films, conducted services, and delivered speeches which emphasized the need, as he saw it, for the students in the Vov Class to open themselves up to the thoughts and the feelings of their fellow students. Too many people, he said, put up false fronts. They obscure their true selves from themselves and from others and do both a disservice. "People need people," said Roger, and he voiced the hope that all the students would come to appreciate this and allow themselves to know and to be known by the other students in the class.

As might be expected, Roger's words struck a responsive chord in the Zion girls particularly, and among some of the boys. Thus it was that late the first evening of the weekend, these students — about six in number — gathered in the auditorium and together with Roger conducted a frank interchange of their true feelings. Rich criticized Sylvia for what he saw as her insensitivity; Sylvia, for her part, admitted to genuine confusion both about Rich and about herself. All who participated in the discussion felt renewed and took up a firm resolve to communicate more freely with one another, in the future.

Then it happened. The girls' opposition clique, led by George and Bob, appeared at the door of the auditorium. George said out loud for all to hear, "Come on gang, let us have our own discussion. We can have as good a time as they can!" With that, George, Bob, Eve, Susan, Ruth, Dorothy and Brad crossed over the room, went to a far corner and pretended to be immersed in conversation. This was the moment that Roger had been waiting for. He quickly hatched a plan with the students around him: they would rise from their seats, go to the other side of the room, offer their hands in friendship, and actually practice the kind of open communication they had discussed and claimed they wanted for the Vov Class. The following is taken from Roger's own account of what happened as they reached the other group. Roger is speaking.

> I said, "Can we join your group?" George said, "Yes," but all the girls said, "No!" Something like, "You have to pay $25.00 to join our group." As soon as they said "no" and repeated it, all the girls in my (*sic!*) group turned around and left. It was really a frustrating scene . . . we were trying to communicate and they wouldn't even listen. (12/18-20)

The truth, however, is that Roger had sown better than he knew. His foray into the opposition world was destined to yield important results within the next few hours. Later that same evening, George called a secret meeting from which Roger was excluded. Its theme: Roger is trying so hard; maybe we ought to help him. As to the opposition girls, though Roger found a way to gather them together that same evening and tell them a story all by themselves, they were not about to resign the fight. With Dorothy safely back in the nest, Eve, Susan and Ruth decided that the beds in the girls' sleeping room were too hard. When Roger made his rounds, later that night, he found that all four had fallen asleep outside on the corridor floor!

The next morning, Saturday, following services, Roger showed a movie called "Boundary Lines." It dealt with the problems of hate and prejudice which result when people cluster into groups separated from each other by — boundary lines. As he looked up, he suddenly realized that this was precisely the condition of his students the previous evening and also at that moment. On one side of the room sat the Zion girls and a few others; on the other side, sat the opposition girls and George, with Roger and the movie projector astride the dividing line. There was no better time to bring the whole subject out into the open than now. He did, and thereupon ensued a frank confrontation between Roger and the students on the clique problem. Roger held the mirror to each, and the students began to see themselves as they really were. Rationalizations, to be sure, abounded. Some defended their clique affiliation by asserting that the other students were either "too frivolous" or "too serious," as the case was. George defended himself and the boys' clique of which he was a part by asserting that "social mobility," to use his term, enabled a person to identify wherever he wished. Yet, despite these valiant efforts, which rang less than true, when the discussion ended there was general agreement that students in the Vov Class did not know each other and should attempt to bridge the communication gaps between them. Their new-found awareness was symbolized by Bernice who jumped up from her place, planted one foot on either side of an imaginary line running down the center of the room, and declared that she wanted to be part of both groups! Neither she nor the class would ever be quite the same again.

And so it was. During the remainder of that weekend and beyond, the students did interact more freely with each other, irrespective of clique affiliation. Susan, upon occasion, was seen to bracket herself between two Zion girls and Sylvia held on to Eve's feet as the two of them sat in front of the movie screen. In general, there was much more physical contact and conversation among members of opposing cliques. Roger had scored a signal victory in terms of the emerging purpose of the Vov Class, although as of that moment the purpose still had not been articulated.

The effects of the attack upon the cliques which occurred during the fourth weekend were clearly discernible on the fifth. Its atmosphere proved to be much more cordial and relaxed than any of the previous weekends. There was more extensive improvisation on the part of the students. It came as no surprise that the students petitioned Roger for more free time and joined that Saturday night in what was by far the most successful "Fiddler" rehearsal of the year. The rehearsal lasted for a full three and a half hours and everyone enjoyed it and each other immensely. It is interesting too that after the rehearsal was over two girls, none other than Ruth and Dorothy, mounted the stage and continued to rehearse by themselves!

At the same time, however, it must be acknowledged that sleeping arrangements the fifth weekend remained unchanged. Hour-long implorings by the Zion girls, both nights, failed to move the opposition girls into their circle. Whereas the Zion girls by then had had enough of the separation, not so with the opposition. It, like the cat which has nine lives, was in evidence in one form or another, at every one of the nine weekends held by the Vov Class during the year. The restructuring so crucial to the group formation that Roger sought was still a long way off.

The Purpose Emerges

The central importance of the weekend portions of the Vov Class Program in helping to establish an atmosphere of trust, in providing authentic Jewish and group experiences, and in offering a focal point for programming, has already been alluded to. But, these do not exhaust the capability of the total living situation, certainly not from the point of view of Roger's emerging goal. He, like the students, came to look upon the weekends as the object of all their efforts, the end for which the beginning was created. It was almost as though the weekends constituted the real world with everything outside them, including home and the city, being unreal by comparison. Events which occurred on one weekend hung in limbo, as it were, waiting until the next. It is not that the class suspended its activity between weekends; it is just that its activity, whatever its nature, was built upon the shoulders of the anterior weekend and was canonized by inclusion in its successor.

And thus it was with the sixth weekend which was held in February. During its course, a series of events began which as it continued into the seventh, enabled the Vov Class to define to itself and to the world its raison d'être and, at the same time, to march to the brink of its realization. The two principal actors, at the beginning, were George and Claudia, about whom a few words must be said.

George, it will be remembered, was a member of the boyish clique and it was he who led the opposition girls in the "boundary lines" confrontation of the fourth weekend. He was a rather able young man who performed well in school and had a variety of interests, ranging from cameras to newspaper reporting and magic tricks. From the start, George seemed to be tied to a culture which was perceptibly different from that of Roger and his fellow students. For example, he was the only Boy Scout in the class, having risen during the year to the rank of Eagle Scout. While he held generally with the liberal point of view in class discussion, one could see in him a thread of extreme patriotism which caused him uneasiness and sometimes conflict during those discussions. Alone among all the students, for example, George refused to sign a petition sent to Washington by the class urging action on behalf of the Soviet Jews. As pitiful as was their lot, they were, thought George, far less important than the "five million people who might be killed" in the event of an upset in the power balance between the United States and Russia. The students who died at Kent were to blame for what happened, said George at another point, because "you can't get peace through violent protest." More than any other student, George returned again and again to what he saw as the need for Jews to understand Christianity and non-Jews, generally. It was this ecumenism which caused him to urge intermarriage as a weekend theme and to defend his opinion in the face of repeated, almost-universal onslaught, that Hitler, though he did evil things, was one of the great men of all time.

George was also unlike the other students in his relationship with Roger. Whereas everyone else felt that Roger should run the class, George alone felt that a President and Student Council should be elected "to run things." Still he was very cordial towards Roger. He brought him presents, called him at home frequently, and once stopped in with Brad "just to say hello."

At the same session, George could be and was Roger's competitor and his most cooperative ally. It will be recalled that George was the class's most vociferous opponent to the production of "Fiddler." Though Roger guessed the reason to be that "he had such a small part," the truth of the matter is that a whole lot more was involved.

Claudia had been to Zion and found the Vov Class Program very enjoyable. It soon became apparent, however, that she, like George, was not completely comfortable, but for apparently different reasons. One was that Claudia could not or did not establish even the most tenuous inter-personal relationships with her fellow students. After the initial Zion-based ties were augmented by new Vov Class ties, Claudia came to be more and more alone — the proverbial isolate — and remained that way throughout the term. While she would drift into the orbit of one or another clique during the weekends, she would just as easily drift away. She was generally chosen last and forgotten first. She tended to hang on to the adults in the program with whom she was always ready to play cards or ping pong.

Claudia felt and her parents agreed that she was "picked on" by a number of the students, particularly Jeanne, who had been her bunkmate at Zion. Claudia's mother expressed the belief to Roger that it was Claudia's effort to "do the right thing" which excluded her from the friendship of the other girls.

It happened that Claudia and George attended the same public school. Their parents were acquainted before the Vov Class, as were they, as a result of their having been in the same carpool for quite some time. As a matter of fact, Claudia had a party at her house at the beginning of the year and George was the only Vov Class student who attended. By all rights they should have gotten along nicely with each other.

Conflict, however, between them broke out on the sixth weekend. Although the exact details are known neither to Roger nor to the observer, it appears that George was guilty of throwing billiard balls and cue sticks down the corridor. Claudia corrected him or tried to stop him and "the war was on." Events followed in swift succession. Brad, George's clique-mate and the only other Vov Class student to attend public school with Claudia and George, reported that the fight continued there the next day. George made fun of Claudia and called her, among other things, "dog" and various derivations thereof, which offended her greatly and brought matters to a head by the middle of that week.

Before continuing the narrative, it should be pointed out that nicknames of various kinds were used with considerable regularity in the Vov Class. Of course, diminutives of given names were commonplace. Beyond that, however, and quite early in the year, nicknames with in-group connotations replaced more than half of the given names in the class, including that of the observer. In some cases, the names were clearly related to identifiable events or to specific characteristics of their bearers; in others, the origin of the names and their relationship to the bearers were shrouded in obscurity. In all cases the names were known and used by Roger and everyone in the class. It must not be assumed, of course, that all the nicknames conveyed feelings of warmth. Much depended on who used the particular name and the manner in which it was used. Even the same name spoken by the same individual conveyed positive affect under one set of circumstances and negative affect under another.

No such confusion, however, attended George's new nicknames for Claudia. "Dog" and "doggie" spread throughout the Vov Class as well as public school and led to a frantic telephone call from Claudia's mother to George's parents. What had happened between their son and Claudia which had caused her to return from the weekend so disturbed and not to sleep for the two nights following? Not knowing exactly how to answer, George's parents talked first with their son and then put in their own call to Roger. In no way condoning their son's actions, they did express doubt as to the worthwhileness of a program — like the Vov Class Program — which failed to convey the Jewish concept of man's respect for woman and which provided so little supervision over weekends that conflicts could erupt. They urged Roger to call Claudia's mother back and to put the matter straight.

Roger called and learned that Claudia's mother was concerned not just about this conflict but how to put a stop to the name-calling and in general how to integrate her daughter more effectively into Vov Class activities. She feared, she said, that unless a solution were found quickly, Claudia would find it necessary to drop out of the class. Roger then said to Claudia's mother, as he had said to George's parents earlier, that the Vov Class was different from other classes in that the very problem which they were concerned about, namely, Claudia and George's relationship, was in no way incidental to the work of the class but its essence. He promised to deal with the problem in such a way as to help everyone grow by means of it. Meanwhile, he was preparing, he added, an entire presentation on the goals and activities of the Vov Class for the parents' meeting which was to be held about two weeks hence. He urged her attendance.

It is necessary to digress at this point to describe the events leading up to the parents' meeting, for though it came to be scheduled in response to another crisis, one with the administration, it was destined to combine with the Claudia-George crisis to bring to a head, as it were, what indeed was the purpose of the Vov Class and the process by which it was articulated. At mid-semester, Roger, like all the teachers at B'nai Israel, received a notice from the administration that evaluations were due. Since, as has already been stated, written evaluations were contrary to his educational principles as well as to promises he had given to the students, Roger completed only the attendance sheet and then scrawled across its side, "No evaluations will be given!" The reaction was immediate and devastating. The following note from the administration, written on official stationery, was received: "Evaluations will be given! No parents meetings have been called nor have (we) seen any reports. Like all teachers you will not receive next month's check until evaluations are in . . . ."

Roger entered into several conversations with the administration on this subject. Relying on what he saw as his immunity from administration sanctions, he held his ground and eventually compromised on a parents' meeting at which an overall evaluation of the program rather than individual evaluations would be presented.

To return to the main line of the story: after talking with George's and Claudia's parents, Roger had a lengthy conversation with Claudia. He commiserated with her and had her talk out what she considered to be the reasons for her rejection by George and the others. When she laid the blame on her unwillingness to go along with misbehavior, Roger bolstered her by comparing her to the prophets of Israel who stood for principle and, though not popular, eventually were vindicated. More than that, he had an idea and perhaps Claudia could help. He would "contrive" a lesson in which he would "turn the tables" on those who hurt Claudia and others by using disparaging nicknames. He himself would use the names openly and actually show everyone, especially the offenders, how much pain they were causing their friends. Such a demonstration would "teach them" and put a stop to the name-calling in the future. Claudia felt better at the end of the conversation and looked forward to the demonstration lesson, the details of which Roger promised to work out in the next few days.

To state simply that this was a period of great turmoil for Roger is to miss the deep anguish he felt that evening and subsequently. Threatened with Claudia's withdrawal from the class, George's hostility, a mixture of parental curiosity and uneasiness, as well as administration disapprobation, Roger faced the single most traumatic moment of his teaching career. Apart from Claudia, who had only an inkling of what was to be, neither the students nor the observer were prepared for what greeted them at the next session of the Vov Class, the following Sunday. Excerpts from the field notes of that day will convey something of the spirit:

> 9:05 . . . The class is arranged with conventional seating. Kids come in. Roger sticks his head in the door and says, "Boys, put on your Tfillin!" . . .
>
> 9:10 Second bell rings. Roger seems to be in a more

serious (bad?) mood. "Cut the talkin' and let's move." It occurs to me that if Roger has been putting on for my sake (which I do not believe) the ruse will soon break down. Now, he is standing with Talis and Tfillin, against the board, with arms folded, looking (glaring?) at the group. Class gradually calms down as the looseleaf prayer books are distributed. I have forgotten mine.

9:22 Roger tells group to turn to the first prayer.

Ruth: "Roger, this is not going to work out!"

Roger: "There are a lot of tongues wagging this morning. Let's go."

A number of similar comments. Roger says that they are going to go over the prayers with which they are familiar and for which there are tunes so that they will be able to lead the congregation next week. He continues to intersperse his comments with angry phrases like "Keep your big mouth shut!" Group is unusually quiet and attentive . . . . (2/21)

In this fashion, the class began to go through portions of the prayer service. The students, like the observer, were puzzled, to say the least, at Roger's changed behavior. But the change would be still more extreme before they would be let in on what was happening. The notes continue:

9:32 Roger calls on Brad but uses his last name! . . . A moment later he corrects Bob for talking: "All right, Butch, we don't need any cross talk." . . . "Miss Peach (Sylvia's nickname), are you with us?" . . . "Fleece (Jeanne's nickname), are you with us?"

Class giggles.

Roger: "I can't hear anything from Goldstein (George's last name) . . . you guys are singing like you are afraid of your shadows."

Roger quiets Bruce who, as far as I can tell, did not disturb . . .

"O.K. Let's hear it all again, and that includes you, too, Birdseed" (Rich's nickname). . . .

Then, Roger to George, "Come on, you know it! You know everything!" (2/21)

Before he was through, Roger had used every nickname in the class in an authoritarian, if not disparaging, manner. With Bob, he went too far.

9:48 Roger: "No talking, Butch!"

Bob who had made an innocuous comment, rises, removes his prayer shawl and stalks out of the room. As he leaves, he calls over his shoulder to Roger: "See you later, 'Butch?' " (2/21)

The bell signaling the break rang a few minutes later and several of the students gathered about Roger, incredulous at what they had witnessed. "How come you are so aggravated today, Roger?" they asked. As Roger denied being aggravated, Brad, who at that moment was flying out of the room, suggested an answer: "Because he had a fight with his wife!"

It was not until after the break, during which, incidentally, Roger found Bob and induced him to return, that the class and the observer learned what had happened and why. The class sat in subdued mood as Roger wrote on the board each and every nickname in use in the Vov Class. With the aid of the students, he listed five of his own and eleven other nicknames attached to students in the class. He wrote three words upon the board: "continuum," "malicious," and "friendly," making sure that everyone understood their meaning. Then Roger drew a line across the board which he dubbed "the continuum" and placed a big "M" for malicious at one end of it and an "F" for friendly at the other end. Students were called upon to come to the board and enter each nickname by number on the continuum. It should be added that as he called on students he paid special attention to teaming particular nicknames with their creators. After this phase was completed, he had those students to whom the names referred go up to the board and place their own nicknames where they thought they belonged on the continuum. The discrepancies between the apparent intent of the students who created and used the nicknames and the effect upon those to whom the names referred were boldly evident to everyone present. It remained only for Roger to drive home the point. After acknowledging that his whole approach at the beginning of the lesson and his use of the nicknames had been a "put-on with a purpose," he made the point in the following words, "For God's sake, if you want to be a human being you have to respect other people. Individuals may not have the strength to tell how they feel about being called names, but now you see!" Scratching her head in disbelief, Bernice said, "I don't get it. Rich told us he liked being called 'Birdseed.' Now he puts it on the malicious end!"

Roger drove both Claudia and George home that day. When he opened the car door to leave, George said, "Goodbye and thanks" to Roger, and then, turning to Claudia, he added, "So long, Claudia!"

The reticulation of the various strands into a single meaningful pattern occurred at the next session of the Vov Class, which Roger opened with a question written in block letters across the board, "WHAT HAPPENED SUNDAY?" As the students described the atmosphere and reviewed the events of the contrived lesson, which they remembered quite vividly, Roger listed their points on the blackboard. Among the items cited were "Names," "Yelling," "Rows — formal" and "Teacher in front," which Roger then capped with the title "Old Time Hebrew School." The contrived lesson, in other words, from Roger's point of view, was not just a demonstration of what it is like to be called by disparaging nicknames, but also a reenactment of a conventional Hebrew School class. Point by point, the students were then invited to contrast these conditions with those normally in force in their class. They had no trouble whatsoever and soon the board carried two columns of cue words, one describing the "old way" of learning in a Hebrew School, and the other detailing the outcome of the common enterprise to which Roger and the students had committed themselves at the beginning of the year and which they had been putting into practice since.

It was then that Roger confided his problem to the students. Next week there was to be a parents' meeting at which time he would surely be asked what the students in the Vov Class were learning. "In public school there are tests and grades," Roger anticipated the parents saying, "but in Vov you have none of that. The kids may be having a blast, but what do they learn?"

"We have been learning things," acknowledged Jeanne "but it is hard to show what." Bob felt that the class had not been learning anything, certainly not like they were learning at school. Finally, it was Sylvia, directing herself to Roger, who said, "You can say 'we are learning to live with each other this year.'" Then she added wistfully, "But I don't think the parents will accept it."

No sooner were the words out of her mouth than Roger lighted upon them. First, he saw a connection between her statement and the nickname problem. And he also saw a connection between what Sylvia said and his own conception of Jewishness. "Which brings us to last Sunday's discussion," said Roger. "That's one of the main reasons we are here .... Can people live together if they call each other names? Living together, man with man, and not being slanderous and malicious is Jewishness." Roger's statement obviously struck a responsive chord in the students, for each offered his own formulation of the same general theme. Dorothy said, "We're like a family. We know each other better. We communicate better. We feel at ease when we talk to each other." Bruce protested, "But what's Jewish about that? The only Jewish stuff we did was the time we had Havdala, besides Friday night, of course." Other students countered the charge by recalling other Jewish activities. But it was Roger who pulled it together when he said, with all the resolve and uncertain assurance he could muster, "Jewish means much more than dietary laws. Jewish means not hurting other people. Jewish means helping other people. That's what we are doing in this class and that's what I'm going to tell the parents. In the Vov Class, we are learning to live together Jewishly!" As the observer recorded these last words by Roger, it occurred to him, sadly, that two students had missed two out of these last three sessions and one of those students was George!

The parents' meeting came and went. Roger was questioned as he anticipated he would be, and he answered as he said he would. Apart from Claudia's and George's parents, whose comments reflected their own problem, there was in evidence rather widespread approval of the program. According to the parents, the children seemed happy, happier, in fact, than they had ever been in Religious School and though they — the parents — could not claim to understand exactly what had been happening, whatever it was Roger should "keep it up." For his part, Roger was firmly in command of the meeting. His confidence-inspiring demeanor betokened his and his group's new-found resolve regarding the purpose of their enterprise and its future.

What had happened, of course, through this long series of events, culminating in the conviction that the Vov Class was an experience in "learning to live together Jewishly," was that an aggregate of individuals had taken a long stride in the direction of becoming a cohesive interactive group[7] within a Jewish, as Roger defined it, framework. Despite occasional misgivings and doubts, this purpose had been implicit from the start in the people and in the conditions under which they interacted. But now it was explicit and acknowledged more or less universally by all concerned. Though the presumptions which underlay the purpose and its implications needed further definition and delineation, Roger and the bulk of his class acknowledged to themselves, for the first time, that theirs was a commitment to live "Jewishly" with each other in the Vov Class.

A Final Threat

There occurred one last-ditch effort by George and his dwindling corps of co-conspirators to test whether the Vov Class had indeed become a group under Roger's leadership or still was vulnerable either to redirection or internal division. Effort is perhaps too grandiose a word because the truth of the matter is that, following the parents' meeting, no one within or without the class stood a chance of destroying the Vov group-in-formation under Roger's leadership. George must have sensed this too, as is indicated by his willingness to ally himself with Brad whose own peculiar needs were crying for expression.

Brad was by far the most disruptive student in the Vov Class. It will be remembered that he claimed that he was being forced to attend the class. As a result, he made no secret of his right to disturb whatever it was that the class was doing. He seldom paid attention and was constantly involved in mischief of one kind or another. Brad showed not the slightest interest in what was happening in the Vov Class and dedicated himself, with single-minded purpose, to its disruption.

It was really more serious than that. Brad's out of proportion interest in sex caused him to fabricate and use the most wounding nicknames as part of an ongoing campaign of picking on the weaker students. If property destruction occurred, often it was Brad who was involved.

Roger's relationship with Brad followed the same curious pattern as Roger's relationship with George. At the same time as he strongly disapproved of Brad and his antics and at one point even expressed the hope that he would withdraw from the program, Roger accepted Brad for what he was and never sank to outright rejection. With seemingly infinite patience, he tolerated Brad and his machinations and refused to allow Brad to "throw him," as he once termed it. Brad seemed to appreciate Roger's tolerance which he repaid with more or less regular attendance and one or two home visits, if not cooperation.

Joining George and Brad in the final test was Rich, the smallest, one of the most talented, and far and away the most intellectually inclined of the students in the class. Rich's mother had died the year before he entered the Vov Class. The experience of looking after her during her long illness, followed by the events attendant to her death, seemed to have left an indelible impression upon him. He developed a serious preoccupation with death and took a more than casual interest in religious matters. The subject of God, as has been noted, particularly intrigued Rich. For long periods of time, he could be seen sitting quietly on the side, lost in a book or in contemplation. Frequently, Rich would walk around as in a trance. But suddenly, and without warning, he would erupt. Turning to a classmate who sat nearby, he would rain blows upon his head or shoulder with no apparent provocation. It was Rich, it will be remembered, who threw the cue stick at Claudia. On many occasions, Rich would make light of himself or deny his achievements to the point that he permitted others to persecute him as a means of enhancing their own self-esteem. George and Brad could not have wished for a more suitable vehicle through which to satisfy their own needs in their last feeble attempt to challenge the Vov group and its leader.

The seventh weekend, held in March, brought the class back to Mary Grove. Though it had snowed the previous week, when the students boarded the bus Friday afternoon, the skies promised ample sunshine and a welcome spring thaw. The manner in which the students arrived at the camp suggested a real homecoming. They quickly unloaded the bus and embarked upon a weekend that was by far the most intellectually productive of the year. As an accompaniment to their intellectual adventure the group pioneered new lines of social interaction, as well. The girls' opposition clique loosened up considerably. It attempted many more contacts with the Zion girls and with Roger. Leadership of the Zion clique, too, began to move away from Sylvia, although she continued as one of its most respected members. Even Claudia began to be the object of somewhat greater conversational choice, at the same time as she became part of a whole new wave of interest in Zion, the camp's intensified recruiting program having reminded her and the others that the summer was not far off.

It was because of this new social ease within the class that the initials VCL, loudly proclaimed by Brad as the name of a new secret society among the boys, sounded so strange. It seems that he and George had decided earlier in the week on the need for such a society. Bob, their old cohort, who by then was beginning to find real joy in the Vov Class, had been invited to join but declined. They therefore approached none other than Rich who they suggested might want to apply for admission. Rich indicated that he was interested and was informed that the initiation rite, which included "egging" a building and shooting off firecrackers, both of which they knew to be contrary to the rules, would be held that weekend. Whether or not Rich would have carried out the rite remains a question because Roger got wind of the plan and ordered the boys to bed at the precise moment that Rich was supposed to perform. Although the VCL obviously had given George and Brad new vitality and Rich new hope of becoming "one of the boys," its threat to disrupt the weekend remained just that. It was only on the bus ride home Sunday, when the three boys took up the chant "VCL — DESTROY - DESTROY — DESTROY," that one suspected not having seen the last of the society.

The suspicion was well-founded, for the VCL, during the period following the weekend, began to take a more prominent role in the social life of the Vov Class. There were constant allusions to its initials and occasional forays into forbidden activity. Once, for example, Roger entered the room in time to see a pile of desks come crashing to the floor amidst banshee-like screams that the VCL had struck again! It was Bernice who finally revealed to the class what the initials VCL denoted. VCL, she said, meant Vov Class Leftists! It seems that Bernice had been enlisted to establish a girls' chapter of the society and had begun to do so. She even sought the permission of the founding fathers to include some of her friends from public school. The exposure of the sacred letters of their society's name necessitated, of course, a change in designation. In quick succession, VCL became VCR (Vov Class Radicals), and then VCS, VCM, and ELR, the latter three of which were never identified, at least to the observer. During this period, the class was involved in a number of interesting matters and seemed quite unconcerned about the VCL. It was a chance occurrence, however, at public school which provided the boys with an excuse to keep the pot boiling.

Sitting in study hall, one afternoon, Rich observed a bag on Brad's desk. He asked if it contained Brad's lunch. When Brad said, "No," Rich threw it out the window. True, the bag had not contained Brad's lunch; but it had contained his shop project! After quick consultation with George, Brad proudly announced that Rich would be required to stand trial for having injured a fellow VCL'er. Brad was to be the plaintiff and the prosecutor, all rolled into one; George was to be the judge; and poor Rich was to be the defendant. So as to provide a jury of peers worthy of deciding the fate of such a culprit, the trial, they announced, would be held on the next, which was to be the eighth, weekend.

On the bus ride out to Mary Grove the eve of the eighth weekend, spirits ran unusually high. The VCL'ers reminded everyone that Rich's trial would occur late Saturday night and that, in general, their society was going to be much in evidence over the weekend. The boys hurriedly prepared a sign which they displayed in the window of the bus, reminding even passing motorists to be on their guard against the VCL. Despite the fact that half the distance to the camp had to be traversed twice because Roger forgot the meat, nothing could really dampen the enthusiasm of the class, or its enigmatic VCL'ers.

Roger, from the start, had rather gone along with the whole VCL picture. He rightly considered it a negligible threat, if a threat at all. In fact, when he prepared his instruction sheet for the eighth weekend, he added in his own hand, at the bottom, "Printed by VCL Printing Co." Yet, as the bus pulled into Mary Grove, it was clear to everyone that Roger was not his long-suffering self. More unnerving to him than the forgotten meat was the painful boil on the back of his neck which limited not only his head movements but also his patience. He quickly reviewed the rules for the weekend, the last of which was that no destruction of camp property by the VCL or anybody else would be tolerated. Brad shot back, "But, that's the whole point of the VCL!" To which Roger retorted, "Then, you'll have to change the point!"

As long as VCL activity was limited to off-color conversation and disruptive comments during services, Roger displayed forbearance. But, when its activity actually did take the form of property destruction, Roger put his foot down. The boys flooded the bathroom floor, and started a fire on the side of the main building with a broom. Roger delivered himself of a strong lecture on disrespect for the Sabbath and other people's property. He also demonstrated weary disappointment in his students, and mused, "After all we've been through together . . ."

By the time Rich's trial was held Saturday evening, the VCL'ers were much subdued. The whole trial took only a few minutes. Rich was judged guilty and the group, after rejecting George's suggestion that Rich's punishment should consist of kissing "The Dog," ordered him to submit to a whole new initiation ceremony, or to "remain on probation for a million years." The following day, Rich sought out Roger and apologized to him for the destruction the VCL had caused. He had had a talk with his fellow VCL'ers and they had decided that they would clean up the building and not destroy anything anymore. Furthermore, if the others would not be true to their word, he would quit the group. As an afterthought, Rich had heard that Roger and Sara were going to be moving into a new apartment and, with Roger's permission, he would like to help.

By the time the eighth weekend ended, the Vov Class had become a group with Roger its undisputed leader. Apart from one last ineffectual effort by Eve, Susan, Ruth, and Dorothy, in the company of Jeanne and Karen, to create a female counterpart to the VCL, no serious threat to the group emerged again. The girls began to look at each other in an entirely new light. Rich felt a new surge of independence as well as filial-like love for Roger; Brad embraced his marginality with resigned loneliness; and George went home never to return to the Vov Class again, at least not that year. While he made several telephone calls to Roger explaining his decision to quit the class, and sent one message to the class during the last weekend, it was obvious that he was the one student in the Vov Class who lacked either the need or the willingness, or both, to "live together Jewishly" with this group.

The Vov Class as Family

To assert that the Vov Class became a group — even one worthy of being called a "reference group," a "primary group," or a "community"[8] — is to miss, in part, the depth and the flavor of the relationship which had developed between the students and Roger, and among the students themselves. The class, of course, evolved an intricate interpersonal structure in which individuals, as well as cliques, so long as they existed, occupied identifiable, albeit fluid roles.[9] Beliefs, too, both teacher-based and student-based, acquired sentiment and gradually were integrated into a highly stable system of norms.[10] But, beyond that, something more significant happened. The Vov Class became a surrogate family, in which Roger was the father, Sara, in lesser degree, the mother, and the students, the children! It is this fact which places the entire Vov Class experience in the perspective it deserves. It is this fact more than any other which locates the nexus between the "living together" and the "Jewishly" parts of its purpose. After all, it is only a family or family-like group — even if it be an orientative rather than a procreative one[11] — because it has no need to justify its existence to itself or to the world, which is capable of combining social purpose with a religious and cultural tradition like Judaism and have it yield a meaningful life experience. Yet, this is precisely what happened in the Vov Class. Nor was there anything else that happened which approached, much less rivaled its importance. The Vov Class became a family!

It is no accident for example that Roger and Sara invited the students to their family table on the second weekend or that Roger came to refer to the students as his kids. It is no accident either that often in apparent jest students would address Roger as father, or that Roger would express the kind of pride or disappointment in them that one would more readily associate with a parent than a teacher. When the class went to a movie, for example, the students were admonished in typical family fashion not to do anything that would embarrass them. Even more telling is the exchange between Eve and Roger in which she mentioned that she had recently acquired a "gorgeous boy friend." Roger's reflex response, which will be recognized by every Jewish parent as his own, was "Is he Jewish?"

One of the most revealing, however, of all of Roger's behaviors and student response to it which showed the family-like nature of the Vov Class had to do with food. Food for obvious reasons is closely associated with families. This is especially true among Jews. Not only are certain foods peculiar to Jewish families but certain attitudes towards food are, too. For example, among Jews, food in great abundance is regarded as essential to health and vitality. Also, one of a Jewish parent's main functions in life is to supply his offspring with food in such quantity, even as one of the child's main functions in life is to consume all of the food that is put on his plate by his Jewish parent.

Roger had acquired from his grocer grandfather and from his restaurateur mother, both of whom he loved dearly, a deep commitment to these culinary principles which were associated in his mind with the proper interactive relationship between an adult and a young person in a Jewish setting. Thus, at breakfasts, held after services on Sunday mornings, and at weekends, Roger could be seen flitting about among the tables, making sure that all of his kids had enough to eat and were enjoying their food. He would provide "seconds" and "thirds" for those who gave the slightest indication of their willingness to consume more and then hover over them until they did.

There was really only one offense which when committed by his kids consistently caused Roger to lose his temper. That offense was throwing food or otherwise wasting it when they should have known that people "in Asia and Africa are starving." Many was the speech Roger delivered regarding the appropriateness or the inappropriateness of certain behavior at the table. Many was the time, too, that he and Sara expressed the hope that one day they would have their own biological progeny gathered around them on the Sabbath, just as the Vov Class was gathered on weekends.

Paradoxically, it was during the course of the year that Roger decided to go on a diet. It seems that he had tried to lose weight many times in the past but had never succeeded. Whether because the Vov Class experience had bolstered his self-confidence or for some other reason, one day he announced to the class that he was going to lose sixty pounds by the end of the year and that failing to do so, he would treat everyone to, of all things, a dinner! Soon, Sara decided to join Roger on the diet. They affiliated with an organization, the purpose of which was to provide instruction on how to lose weight as well as incentives for doing so effectively, and made arrangements with Evelyn to be served special food on weekends.

Overnight, Roger's and, to a lesser extent, Sara's diet became a major concern of the Vov Class. The fit of Roger's clothes, the weekly, if not daily, progress of his weight-trimming efforts, the problems and the temptations he faced — all became standard fare at each and every session of the class. Students would refer to Roger alternately as "Fats" or "Skinny" in a good-natured manner and remind him when he needed reminding that this or that item of food was fattening. On the whole, students felt themselves very much a part of their teacher's effort to lose weight.

Just as Roger's behavior was like that of a Jewish parent, the students' behavior was like that of Jewish children. Not that the students felt obliged to eat everything on their plates — for a new food culture had developed between Roger's youth and theirs — but they came to exhibit a pride in the Vov Class which can only be described in family terms. Midway through the year, for example, students began to bring their friends from public school to witness what they were doing and to see for themselves "what it is like to be Jewish." Though weekends were reserved exclusively for Vov students, Sunday and Wednesday sessions saw a number of friends, some Jews and many non-Jews, welcomed into the family orbit. When guests were present, the group pursued its normal activities. Guests were free to participate or not, as they wished. It is apparent that the Vov Class was sufficiently secure within itself to receive outsiders and yet not be disrupted by their presence.

Perhaps the most convincing testimony to the family-like solidarity which had developed was the near panic the students and Roger began to feel when they realized that the term was drawing to a close and that the Vov Class was almost over. The field notes record that it was on the seventh weekend that the question of "what to do next year?" was raised by the students:

> Roger mentioned that this past week he talked to the three classes which would enter the Vov Class Program next year. He told the students that if they really wanted to find out about the Vov Class they should talk to kids in the present class . . . . This provided the springboard for a whole discussion about continuation. Sylvia turned to me (the observer) and said, "You'll be in charge of the Shul next year, right?" I smiled assent. "Well, we demand" and she mouthed the words with all the determination at her command, "We demand a continuation of the Vov Class next year!" . . .

> Jokingly, Bob said that he volunteers to teach the boys in next year's class how to get along. Brad said, "Yes, like throwing rocks, like spreading shaving cream, and the like." Somebody mentioned that when they are very old they should have a reunion of the Vov Class. Roger went around the room and said, "Yes, it will be interesting to have Mr. and Mrs. Bernstein come and Mr. and Mrs. Serkes and Mr. and Mrs. Corn." This was the occasion for Eve to say, "Boy, those teachers are going to be surprised next year when I walk in and say, 'Bullshit, teacher.'"

> Roger answered, "Well, isn't the Vov Class really the same as Hebrew School, since we meet on Sunday and Wednesdays?" "No," came the reply from someone, "you're the teacher on Sunday and Wednesday, which makes it different." (3/26-28)

Though he was highly complimented by this ground swell of desire to continue, Roger gave the students mild encouragement, at best. He was unsure of his own program for the following year and even more unsure of what the administration's reaction would be.

At the two sessions following the seventh weekend, however, the desire to perpetuate the experience in some fashion jelled into a specific plan. The students loudly proclaimed that the Vov or Sixth Grade Class would simply become the Zayin or Seventh Grade Class and Roger would continue as its teacher. Unable to remain neutral any longer, Roger stated that he was "for it" but that a decision of this magnitude was up to Rabbi Katz and the School Board. Should the students decide to bring the matter to their attention, they should be sure to point out that he, Roger, had not "put them up to it."

The students did bring the matter to Rabbi Katz as forcefully as they knew how. They tramped into his office one day and stated, in no uncertain terms, that they wanted a Zayin Class next year with Roger as its teacher. Rabbi Katz responded more or less favorably, reminding the students that there were a number of problems that would have to be worked out. One of these was the plan to establish a new Vov Class which Roger was going to be invited to teach. How could he do both? The administration promised to consider the matter and to get back to the students, as soon as possible.

By the time the eighth weekend came around, the class had begun to flex its muscles in earnest. Apart from George, Eve, Susan, Brad, and Dorothy, who were still uncertain about continuing, there was universal agreement that they would not accept "no" for an answer. Parents were approached and Rabbi Levy was reminded that he would be well-advised to look to their demand.

Meanwhile, Roger was searching himself in order to determine whether or not he could hope to shoulder the double responsibility of a Zayin Class and a new Vov Class. At the same time, the parents and the administration were experiencing a mixture of elation and consternation in the face of the unusual, to say the least, spectacle of a religious school class, especially one on the post Bar and Bat Mitzva level, literally demanding the right to continue.[12] In an unprecedented move, Roger was invited to a School Board meeting to help it reach a decision. His presentation was confident and convincing. The School Board reacted with guarded enthusiasm, and a tentative commitment that if Roger could arrange his schedule it would agree to a continuation of the program.

Most of the students greeted the news with jubilation. Brad flatly declared that he would not continue. In fact, since George by then had dropped out, he was not even going to attend the final weekend. Susan and Eve might come to the weekend, they said, but they had "better things to do with their time next year."

The Year Ends

The final weekend was the most poorly attended of all. Through no fault of their own, Ruth and Dorothy had to miss. Brad had grass-cutting commitments, which he claimed not to be able to get out of, and George was off on a vacation. Before leaving, however, George did pause to jot a note to the class, which Claudia delivered for him. It read:

> To Roger and Vov Class, Sorry I couldn't make this last overnight and graduation, but I'm sure that there is no great loss . . . By the time you read this . . . and are at the Synagogue, I'll be either water-skiing, fishing, and swimming with Connie (an old friend of mine) or I'll be giving her a ride in my boat. Eat your hearts out. (Signed) George.

George's "sour grapes" advice to the group was not followed. His fellow students merely absorbed the implied insult and then settled down to being together for three full, largely uninterrupted days. They played games, piled on top of one another, took long walks, waded in a park pool, and wallowed in the warmth of their association. Whatever intellectual or religious content there was to the weekend, it was incidental. The students and Roger were together as a family group and that is all that seemed to matter.

This is not to say that there was not some residual separatism which showed up from time to time. But it was the exception rather than the rule, and short-lived. For example, on the first night, the girls' sleeping quarters still saw Eve and Susan to one side, by themselves. However, the second night they were joined by Karen, and the third night by the rest of the girls, all of whom slept within touching-distance of each other.

There was no division among the boys whatsoever. George's and Brad's absence allowed Rich and Bruce to blossom in a way they had not before. Both became much more outgoing and vocal as they exhibited a degree of relief and release which was a marvel to behold. Even Bob seemed to be free of the millstone of his former clique-mates.

It was at the final banquet, however, the last official gathering of the Vov Class for the year, that the group's new-found solidarity asserted itself most strongly. Following seemingly endless reminiscences and frank confessions of how, as the term progressed their fear had turned into trust,[13] Sylvia and none other than Eve and Susan produced a surprise which they had prepared together. It was a yearbook, a copy of which they distributed to everyone present. It consisted of twenty-eight pages of exuberant well-being. The opening page, which follows in full, gives something of its spirit. The style is patterned after the prologue to "Fiddler."

> "A Vov Class like ours, sounds crazy, no? But in our little (?) synagogue of B'nai Israel you might say, each one of us is a real nut, trying to live through nine weekends without killing himself. You may ask, why do we go if they're so hard to survive? We go because B'nai Israel is our synagogue. And do we enjoy it — that — I can tell you in one word — Roger! Because of Roger, *a few* of us have managed to retain our sanity. Here in our Vov Class, Roger has taught us many things. How to eat (a weight watcher's dinner). How to sleep (?) (at 4:00 a.m.) even how to wear clothes (football grubbies). You

may ask, how did we learn these miraculous things? I'll tell you. We don't know . . . Because of Roger each one of us knows who he is . . . and what he *isn't* expected to do ("If you don't want to be here, you can leave"). Well . . . we would like to lovingly (believe it or not) thank the greatest, most wonderful, super-duper, spectacular, marvelous, peechy-keen, and yes — even *skinny* teacher — Mr. Roger — (What'd you say your last name was?)"

After this introduction, Roger was portrayed pictorially before his weight loss and after. A page was devoted to each of the adult participants and to each student, although, as might have been anticipated, Claudia was inadvertently omitted. Among the questions with which the year book closed was one which bespoke a normal family concern: Will Sara get pregnant next year?

It was while thumbing through the year book that one of the students said, "Wouldn't it be wonderful if we could all pick up and go to Israel this summer together!" The subject had been mentioned once or twice previously but never quite so boldly. Rabbi Levy, who was sitting at the banquet table, digesting the high spirits as well as the food, decided to end his year-long silence. He secured quiet and asked if the suggestion was a serious one. If it were, he wanted to help. Thereupon ensued an exchange during which each student offered his personal reaction to the idea of a class trip to Israel and what he might hope to derive from it. It occurred to Rich that the class had not learned much Hebrew during the year and that they would make up for it in this way. Bob saw the trip as an opportunity to fulfill a long-standing dream of his to work on the land. Injected into the conversation were also some of the realities such as cost and parental permission. But the encouragement given by Rabbi Levy was sufficient to convince the students that the idea was within the realm of possibility. Agreeing that it was too late to consider for that summer, however, every single student present — with the exception of Eve, who suggested that she wanted to go to Israel, but not with the class — declared his intention of spending the following year in the Zayin Class, earning money, and doing whatever else was necessary to bring about a class trip to Israel. The students had finally hit upon a superordinate goal worthy of their allegiance, and they knew it. Roger and Sara agreed that they would accompany the group and Rabbi Levy promised to help in any way that he could.

It was at that moment that Karen and Jeanne dimmed the lights and flashed a transparency that they had prepared upon the screen. Superimposed above the crossed out initials VCL was another set of initials — VCU — which the girls proposed as the new name for the class. VCU stood for Vov Class United! There was general assent, but someone in the group observed that a more fitting name would be ZCU. And thus it was settled. The Vov Class, after having meandered through a difficult yet exciting year, in which they had learned much about Judaism and each other, would be known, henceforth, as the Zayin Class United!

As the students gathered their gear together to depart, animated conversation could be heard on all sides. No one was saying goodbye to anyone else, because plans were already afoot for several summer get-togethers. Some students talked about going over to Roger and Sara's apartment the following week to help celebrate their move and their wedding anniversary. Also, Bob was looking forward to having everyone over to his house for a swimming party. By then, too, the girls knew — all of them except Eve and Susan, whose parents were taking them on a long motor trip — that they would be together at Camp Zion most of the summer.

As the parents arrived and they took leave of each other that evening, Claudia was heard to call to the group, in the traditional Hebrew phrase recited by Jews twice each year as part of the Holy Day services, "Next Year in Jerusalem!" Arnold, with just a tinge of embarrassment, declared that he had made an important decision. No more did he want to be called Arnold. From that moment on he wanted to be called by his middle name, Abraham. Subsequent questioning revealed that Arnold, or rather Abraham, did not know what had come over him to inspire such a change. But the observer suspected that the change represented a change in this boy's self-identification, creditable, in greater or lesser degree, to the experience he and fourteen of his fellow students had just completed in "Learning to live together Jewishly."

Chapter Five

Implications

The Vov Class as Community

Whatever other consequences have derived from the conditions of life in modern America, one of the most serious is the weakening of dialogic relationships among people.[1] Concepts such as anomie, alienation, and estrangement, though seldom defined clearly, point to the decline in the interpersonal relationships which are so crucial to the fulfillment of human potential.[2] If this condition characterizes the community at large, it characterizes also the Jewish community, as the experience of B'nai Israel in Graceville shows.

Less than twenty-five years before the present study was undertaken, Congregation B'nai Israel still thought in terms of a Jewish neighborhood. It located its combination synagogue--

school structure in what was then a substantial residential area inhabited largely by Jews. Members' homes were within walking distance of a number of significant institutions, from kosher butcher shops to public schools, in which the enrollment of Jews in some cases was 90% of the total. The synagogue and its Hebrew School were accepted elements of life even among those who did not consider themselves "religious." Members, many of them, walked to Sabbath services and their children reached after-school Hebrew School by foot, with time to spare, in the half-hour which intervened between the 3:30 P.M. closing of public school and the 4:00 o'clock bell.

With propinquity went a sense of community,[3] that is, a feeling of mutual dependence and shared destiny expressed by means of participation in a common culture. It is not surprising that the children growing up in and around B'nai Israel should have experienced a similar sense of community. They were Jews, irrevocably, and they saw their future and that of the Jewish community as bound together inextricably. It is not surprising either that the Hebrew School they attended performed rather successfully its major function of acculturating young people to the Jewish community by providing knowledge of its past and the opportunity to participate in its present.

In the space of one or perhaps two generations, many changes occurred. B'nai Israel families moved to the suburbs of Graceville, some ten miles from the synagogue-school building. Although they tended to congregate in the same general suburban area, the conditions of their association were quite different from what they had been. Not only was the synagogue not within walking distance, nothing was, except perhaps the neighbors on either side. Several public schools did have a large percentage of Jewish students but seldom did it approach what it had been in the old neighborhood. The new spatial diffusion of B'nai Israel families seemed to be accompanied by a social diffusion as well. Friends, both among adults and children, tended to be drawn from a wider circle than formerly. In general, whatever the needs of B'nai Israel families, they came to be satisfied increasingly outside B'nai Israel and even outside the Jewish community.

One of the most significant outcomes of these changes was that Jewish education, on both an adult and child level, was not nearly as successful as it had been. After all, if there was no Jewish community, what sense did the intensive study of its forms and values make? If there was no Jewish community, to what end the study of its modes of communication and expression? The effort to teach Hebrew and other subjects of traditional content, not to speak of the effort to engender commitment to ritual observance and prayer, faltered. In evidence was a growing malaise which expressed itself in low teacher morale and an eagerness on the part, particularly of the young, to rid themselves of the burden of Jewish education as quickly as possible. While exceptions, here and there, creditable to an especially engaging teacher or to an especially interesting program were to be found, by and large there was a gradual and unmistakable diminution of interest on the part of the young Jews and their teachers in Jewish schooling. It was in partial response to this condition that the heads of B'nai Israel decreased the number of sessions of Hebrew School per week from four to three and moved classes to a more convenient rented facility in North County. It was in partial response to this very same condition that the Jewish leadership of Graceville, like the leadership of numerous other places throughout the United States, conducted the survey referred to above and feverishly searched for new and it was hoped more effective instruments of Jewish education.

It is against this background that the importance of the Vov Class experiment must be assessed. For the single most important fact about the Vov Class is that Roger and the students, in satisfaction of their felt need for community,[4] created one of their own. That which Jewish life in Graceville no longer supplied, they supplied for themselves. Nor was the community they created merely a community of people who happened to be Jewish. It was a Jewish community. It was Jewish in that its religio-cultural frame of reference was Jewish. It was Jewish in that its forebears, its sponsorship, and its hopes for the future were expressed in Jewish terms. It was Jewish in that it chose to relate to the total Jewish community, including the vestige of it which still existed in Graceville, with some intimacy.

It cannot be claimed that the creation of a Jewish community was in the minds of the program's originators when they conceived it. Their purpose was merely to "teach Judaism" more effectively. They had some rather imprecise intuitions, derived from their experience in Jewish camping, about how this might be done. But community, as a concept and surely as a purpose, was far from their minds. It was not until long after the year ended, in the analytic phase of the research, when the data were coded and analyzed, that the push towards community came to be identified as the central achievement of the class.

Nor can it be claimed that Roger ever consciously sought the creation of a community within the class. He, like the program's originators, had many dissatisfactions regarding conventional education, Jewish and general. Yet, he had only the vaguest of notions regarding alternatives. Community was not one of them.

If not the program's originators and if not Roger, certainly not the students. They were involved with their own problems — problems relating to school, to parents, and to peer relationships. Participation in a new Vov Class community, in their view, held no solutions for these. At best, the reputation of Roger and the new Vov Class promised a respite from the usually disagreeable contact with religious school they had come to expect. ·

Still, as one studies the total Vov Class experience, it turns out that each of these in his own way — the originators, by means of the conditions and the tools they made available for the experiment; Roger, by means of the personal and Jewish qualities he brought along with him; and the students, by means of their need to come into possession of their own identities through interaction with the world around them — contributed to the creation of a Jewish community within the Vov Class.

So demanding did the community formation purpose of the class become that most of what happened in it, in whatever area, became its handmaiden eventually. This was true of both the experiential portion of the curriculum and the instructional. Though students learned a great deal about a great many subjects, especially Jewish subjects, the acquisition of knowledge was not their first concern. More than that, after a certain point in the term, as the participants began to sense the true goal of their association as well as the directions of its possible fulfillment, the inclusion of particular subject matter in the curriculum found its justification in terms either of its intrinsic value as perceived by the group,[5] or its effect upon the community formation process. Roger's contrived lesson on nicknames and at least four of the weekend themes are cases in point.

Let it not be thought, however, that because of its secondary role, the cognitive content was unimportant to the experience. On the contrary, it is difficult to conceive of the Vov Class becoming a community, much less a Jewish community, without its emphasis upon such content. One reason relates to the nature of Judaism.

If Judaism includes within its purview all that is relevant to human welfare, it regards the study of Holy Writ or Torah as the key to an understanding of the nature of that welfare and the means for its attainment. The cognitive mastery of Torah and those works inspired by it, followed by the translation of their dictates into action, constitute the highest calling of the Jew, child and adult. Despite the primacy of the community formation goal, therefore, Judaism's insistence upon study was forever looking over Roger's and the students' shoulders, as it were. Every time the group was engaged in a service or exchanged information about Judaism, this emphasis kept thrusting itself forward. It is true that Roger and the students did not always heed the implications of this emphasis. But they were aware of its ubiquitous presence and of its promise to assert itself when the time would be ripe.

A second reason that cognitive content was important was that Roger was the teacher of the class. He was a thoroughly Jewish, cultured person. He had high regard for the role of knowledge in the education of the young and naturally insisted upon its inclusion in the program. The only questions in his mind related to the kind of subject matter which should be presented, the method of its presentation, and the timing.

A third reason that cognitive content was important relates to the nature of the students who comprised the class. It would be a mistake to think that students who had come as far as these in their Jewish and general education, were not themselves eager to acquire a knowledge of Judaism. Within the confines of their primary purpose and evolving interests, the students were desirous of learning about the world, particularly the segment of it defined as Jewish, and their relationship to it.

When people associate with one another over as long a period and as closely as Roger and the students did, obviously they undergo an infinite number as well as an infinite variety of experiences. As these experiences become integrated into the life space of the people involved, they yield meaning on various levels. They yield meaning to each individual in terms of his own needs and capacities. In addition, to the extent that the experiences are shared by several of the participants, they yield supra-individual, relational meaning in terms of the totality's needs and capacities. The two combine to form the developing history of the group which feeds back constantly into the emergent individual histories. It is small wonder that the researcher hesitates to place such a mass of experience upon the block of speculative summation and pronounce over it a single categorical, perhaps even dogmatic judgment. Yet, the data and their analysis permit no less. Roger and the Vov Class succeeded in constituting themselves not just a community in the generic sense but a Jewish community with Jewish family-like characteristics. On behalf of their community its members were willing to make sacrifices and even to fight. More than that, from the security of their community, they reached out to what was surely the most palpable Jewish community in the world at the time, that of Israel. They resolved to fashion a future for their small community in league with that large one and to cap the relationship, which they hoped would result, with their physical presence the following year.

If, as is claimed, then, the single most significant fact about the Vov Class experience is that it resulted in the emergence of a Jewish community, an analysis of the process by means of which it did so is crucial both to an understanding of the experience and to the applicability of some of its elements to other educational situations, particularly Jewish ones. That is accomplished perhaps most expeditiously by reference to the four original working hypotheses or guiding hunches which underlay the founding of the program.

A Fresh Start

In various educational establishments, goals or objectives are laid down by curriculum fabricators of one kind or another on the basis of what in their view is important to the present or future welfare of students under their charge. Fleshed out with suggested techniques and materials, the resultant list of objectives and their concretization in the form of a curriculum, are handed to teachers, usually in bound form, in advance of the school term. It is made clear to the teachers that it is their task to say the words and to do the things which will lead to the achievement of the objectives, as evidenced most often by individual students' ability to play back particularly the cognitive portion of their lessons on demand. If students are able to perform the playback with a faithfulness somewhere in the neighborhood of 60% of the total, it is presumed that the curriculum has been covered and that the objectives have been achieved. The students are then ready to ascend to the next higher curriculum level, which by virtue of their successful completion of the previous one, they can be expected to undertake and eventually to master.

While at various times and in various schools, this admittedly extreme approach to the formulation of educational objectives and curriculum has been modified, it is hard to conceive of a situation, certainly one which is within an established school system, in which it has been modified more than it was in the Vov Class. It has been noted already that no one — neither school board nor principal — had set out a curriculum for the class to follow. Even broad objectives for the year had not been formulated, neither for the class as a whole nor for the individuals within it. It was up to Roger and the students to set their own objectives as well as the means for their attainment.

And this they did. In near countless hours of discussion and simple conversation, as well as in numerous more formal evaluation sessions, what precisely were the Vov Class's goals and how they could be realized formed the group's major occupation or perhaps preoccupation. At best, the outcomes of the effort were rough approximations of formal objectives and largely tentative in the sense that they remained in force for a certain period and then were replaced or augmented by other objectives. Even the same objectives changed over time to the point of becoming unrecognizable. Some were embraced by certain people and others by other people. Roger's objectives frequently differed from those of the students and theirs differed from each other. Nor could it be ascertained with any real certainty much of the time either by the participants or by the observer what objectives were in operation at a given moment and for whom. In short, the educational objectives in the Vov Class were every bit as complicated and as fluid as the people who struggled with their formulation.

Yet, whatever the status of particular objectives in their multifarious operations over the course of the year, the objectives of the Vov Class and their ultimate translation into curriculum emanated primarily from Roger and the students. They were the product of their desires, their needs and their ingenuity rather than someone else's. It is true that those desires in part were compounded of and influenced by Roger's and the students' previous educational experiences and by what was regarded as the parents' and the school's expectations for them. It is true also that the Vov Class experiment of the previous year provided Roger with some curriculum guides. However, to the extent that young people and a teacher operating within the orbit of a parental and religious structure can be said to pursue goals which are theirs and which represent their concerns and their orientation, Roger's and the students' goals did so indeed.

How the freedom to set their own objectives and then to pursue them in a manner largely of their own choosing functioned can be documented by tracing the operation of the well-nigh universal resolve within the Vov Class to create a Jewish educational experience different from and in their terms better than the ones which had been so repugnant to them in the past. Of all the possible bases of joint endeavor between them, it was this above all which unified Roger and the students, especially at the beginning of the term. Roger and the students knew from the very moment they came together that they wanted something different although neither of them foresaw how that something different would relate to their need for community. It is difficult to overestimate the importance, in the life of the Vov Class, of the desire for more satisfying education. Unlike those educational objectives which because they are set by outsiders or for whatever reason fail to tap the real concerns of the people involved, the effort to create a new and better educational experience commanded the allegiance in some degree of each and every student in the class as well as that of the teacher. It joined them all in a common enterprise and very early took on the character of a superordinate goal.[6] Most significantly, it joined the teacher and students in radical experimentation.

Young people entering upon adolescence often hone their identities on an abrasive interaction between them and extant societal institutions. Such interaction frequently takes the form of rebellion against or rejection of those institutions. Nor can one conceive of any institution better suited to be the object of this adolescent need than the schools, not just by virtue of the immediate and intimate knowledge that adolescents possess of the schools, but also by virtue of the schools' conservative, often reactionary, character. While common sense tells us that communities fashion themselves around goals which may not be radically new, the anti status-quo nature of the Vov Class goal seems to have endowed it with special potency. It is this last property which underscores the function of several structural features of the Vov Class Program. One was the class's exemption, not from Sunday attendance, but from Sunday School attendance.

B'nai Israel, unlike many Conservative congregations, required those of its students who attended Hebrew School to attend its Sunday School too. Each Sunday morning, Hebrew School students found themselves grouped with non-Hebrew School students in one-day-a-week classes, the composition of which was dictated largely by public school grade levels rather than by the level of Hebrew knowledge as was the case with the Hebrew School classes. Because of this fact and because Sunday classes frequently were taught by teachers whose own backgrounds were wanting, the course of study tended to be limited to Bible stories, holiday observances, history, and superficial social activity. Particularly the more apt among the Hebrew School students came to view Sunday School as vapid and irrelevant to their concerns. It is for that reason that the unprecedented exemption from Sunday School attendance granted the Vov Class was of such importance to the development of the program. Roger and the students were able to maintain the integrity of their association on Sundays as well as on Wednesdays and on the nine weekends. They were able to establish their own community with a minimum of outside interference.

The second structural feature of the Vov Class Program which permitted the pursuit of a radically new approach relates to the nine weekends held at Mary Grove and at the in-town facilities. Permitted to remove themselves physically from the B'nai Israel building one weekend each month, the students could give expression to their radicalism. They could reject the "institutional sanctity"[7] of B'nai Israel and at the same time explore alternatives in a temporary and relatively risk-free environment.[8]

A third factor was Rabbi Levy's presence as observer and its importance in providing the class immunity from criticism.[9] Rabbi Katz who naturally considered it his right, even his obligation, to be involved in every facet of B'nai Israel's school during Rabbi Levy's sabbatical, repeatedly expressed concern regarding certain practices in the Vov Class program. Yet, he was consistently denied access to authentic information by Roger who as a matter of principle considered himself and the program outside the purview of the school and its accepted procedures. Many an innovative program in education has died for want of adequate protection during its formative stages and such might well have been the case with the Vov Class Program, 1970-1971, had it not been for its identification with Rabbi Levy and his work at the university. For, despite serious misgivings on the part of Rabbi Katz and others within the administration, Roger, the program, and its non participant observer enjoyed a year of virtual immunity from criticism and even supervision.

These structural features of the Vov Class Program combined with radical changes in educational practice gave the experience a certain underground quality. Though eminently fair to Rabbi Katz and the administration, there was no dissension from the conviction that they were "the enemy." Rabbi Levy, by virtue of his Sabbatical detachment, was spared this designation. Yet, the class was constantly on the lookout for other candidates who could be identified similarly. It was not accidental that at the first session of the Vov Class, which was the orientation session, Roger took the students into the synagogue and allowed them to run all over the pulpit. He also activated the microphone on the lectern and permitted them to speak into it. In short, Roger and his students were involved in revolt against long-standing tradition. The structure of the Vov Class and the protected environment created by exemption from Sunday School, weekends away, and Rabbi Levy's presence, gave them rich opportunity for its expression.

Martin Buber wrote, "The real beginning of a community is when its members have a common relation to the center overriding all other relations."[10] And thus it was with the Vov Class. Once the goal of creating a better educational experience was identified, accepted and then acted upon by Roger and the students, it became a powerful force towards cohesiveness. The participants began to interact intensely and meaningfully with each other. As the body of shared experience grew, there developed a common culture, with a new set of group norms.[11] Gradually additional goals took root with the result that a mere conglomerate of disjointed parts began to be a community in which each individual, at the same time as he fulfilled his own needs, contributed to the need fulfillment of his fellows.

While it would be presumptuous to assume that it is the only objective capable of moving a class towards community, there can be no question that the pursuit of a more satisfying educational path can act as a powerful force in this direction. The reason is that beyond providing the group with a superordinate goal of significant proportion, a spirit of revolt against the status quo draws its motive strength from deep inside young people. A break with an educational establishment, legitimated but not co-opted by that establishment, possesses a special potency for the formation of a community of young people at this age.[1][2]

In the light of the foregoing it is possible to state the following proposition which seems to derive from the Vov Class experience:

> In order to create a community, at this age level, within a Jewish framework, teacher and students must be free to choose and pursue their own objectives and the means for their attainment.

An Origin-like Climate

A class does not become a community merely because it possesses and exercises the freedom to choose its own objectives and the means for their pursuit. Nor does it become a community merely because one of those objectives happens to be the search for a new and more satisfying educational experience. Required in addition, according to the originators of the Vov Class Program, is a certain type of climate or atmosphere, the character of which was set out in the second of the four working hypotheses which underlay the program's founding. It will be recalled that this working hypothesis related to the importance of engendering an atmosphere in which the human beings involved would perceive themselves to be in essential control of their destinies. Known variously as an Origin-like climate, a democratic atmosphere, or an atmosphere of mutual respect and trust, what was sought was a situation in which students and teacher alike would be regarded as ends in themselves, in possession of the right of ultimate decision in matters affecting them. It was anticipated that such a climate would enhance learning and at the same time convey, as none other, Judaism's approach to people in general and to students in particular.[13] It was not anticipated, however, that such a climate would contribute, as it seems to have contributed, to the formation of a community in the Vov Class.

That Roger fostered in his students the feeling that they controlled their own behavior hardly requires reiteration. Suffice it to say that the right to say no, the right to leave the room at will and to differ with the teacher, as well as the other rights which have been enumerated in detail above, inspired the conviction in the students that in the final analysis they were the arbiters of their fate. Each student felt himself to be the authority of his own acceptance or rejection of the class, its activities, and of Roger himself. Nor was that authority suspended even when, in its exercise, the purposes of the totality were thwarted. The example of George and Brad's adamant opposition to the production of "Fiddler," which doomed a passionate and year-long hope of Roger and many of the students, is a dramatic, in more senses than one, case in point.

While it may not be possible to identify the precise dynamics of the process, one suspects the existence of a functional connection between the character of Roger's relationships with individual students and the character of what came to be the group's climate. It is obvious that different individuals require different lengths of time, not to speak of different kinds of reassurance before they are ready to commit themselves to a group, especially one with a purpose such as that which emerged in the Vov Class. Students frequently experience misgivings and even travail as they flirt with and test the conditions of group membership. Needed is the freedom to move in and out of the group's orbit at will until such time as a commitment can be made. While this happened — and it happened to virtually every student in the Vov Class at one time or another — the individual student's personal relationship with Roger was that which prevented him from wandering too far or giving up entirely. If the distance between the individual student and the group can be thought of as a tight rope which individuals had to traverse before group membership could be achieved, it is a fact that many students, unable to maintain the necessary balance, fell or jumped from the rope. Yet, they never fell very far. Their relationship with Roger acted as a safety net which invariably caught them before they hit the ground. And Roger himself was there too, waiting to pick the students up and help them climb onto the rope again for another try. Nor did there seem to be a limit to the number of times either that the students were willing to test Roger's availability or that Roger was willing to extend himself on their behalf. It was up to them to join the group when they were ready and they knew it.

Whatever the dynamics, suddenly a point was reached in the Vov Class after which the individual relationships — particularly those involving Roger and the students — ceased to be individual only. The participants, including the observer, came to the realization that they were immersed in a total situation which was trustful, accepting and cordial. It was not just each student's relationship with Roger or even each student's relationship with fellow students which bespoke this awareness. It was the relationship of each person to a new corpus which was somehow comprised of individuals and yet was known to be supra-individual. Suddenly each person — the students, Roger, the observer — began to think of himself as an integral part of this new corpus. His personal needs and desires were legitimate and somehow deserving of satisfaction by the totality. It was then that each and every person responded with a measure of warm acceptance towards the others in the group and particularly towards its leader who in some vague way was known to be largely responsible for what had occurred. It was then, too, that the individual sought the continuation of his participation in what could be termed now a climate. It was then, in a word, that a new community sprang into existence and that each individual sensed his membership in it. This process, the effects of which the observer saw both in the students and in Roger, suggests the following second proposition:

In order to create a community, at this age level, within a Jewish framework, it is necessary first that Origin-like, supportive, interpersonal relationships between the teacher and individual students be established.

A Total Living Situation

Once the Vov Class identified objectives worthy of its allegiance and once Origin-like interpersonal relationships were established, particularly between Roger and individual students, the class was well on its way to becoming a community with Roger as its leader. What was needed were conditions within which the process and the experimentation attendant to it could occur. Provision for these conditions was anticipated in the third of the four working hypotheses which underlay the founding of the Vov Class: the need for a total living situation.

It will be remembered that the program's originators, basing themselves upon the example of Jewish camping, deemed it crucial to involve students in monthly residential experiences. They felt, first, that heightened exposure would result in greater influence than is found in a conventional classroom situation; second, that a total living situation would convey an understanding of authentic Judaism also not available in a classroom; and, finally, that a total living situation would shield the group from the sometimes inimical influence of current culture.

The actual experience of the Vov Class seems to support the basic validity of these hopes. In fact, based upon its operation in the Vov Class, it is difficult to conceive of a structural tool more valuable to serious educational endeavor, especially if a major purpose of that endeavor is to create a community. For it was primarily the monthly total living situations which provided Roger and the students with the laboratory in which group processes were fostered and in which ultimately the conversion of the class from an aggregate of individuals to a community took place. A perusal of the story reveals that the critical moments in the community's formation occurred in connection with weekends, either during or immediately after weekends. The biweekly sessions in between weekends, while important from the point of view of consolidating group gains and for that matter digesting defeats, were inert by comparison. It was in the total living situation that the community yearned to come into existence, fought off its adversaries, licked its wounds, submitted to the teaching efforts of Roger, slowly took shape, and ultimately breathed life. Thus it was the fourth weekend which saw the "Boundary Lines" confrontation, in which Roger and certain members of the class achieved their first glimpse of their community-to-be. The sixth weekend saw the Claudia-George fight, which was to prove such a powerful group learning experience, culminating in the articulation of the class's purpose. On the seventh, the group progressed to the point that the subject of continuation into Zayin was broached for the first time. It was on the eighth weekend that the last feeble attempt by George and Brad as well as the girls' opposition clique to wrest control of the class from Roger was mounted. Not so coincidentally, it was the day after the eighth weekend, too, that word was received of George's decision to quit. And it was on the last and longest of the total living situations of the year, the ninth weekend, that the Vov Class faced in earnest the prospect of going to Israel.[14]

Not only did the total living situations contribute to the Vov Class's becoming a community; they assured its becoming a community within a Jewish framework. Judaism is described best in what is perhaps an overworked phrase as a "way of life." This description of Judaism removes it, as it is meant to, from all delimiting conceptions of its character. Judaism is not a matter just of belief or of faith, even belief or faith buttressed by a body of ritual. It is civilizational, in the sense that it includes within itself whatever is germane to human life. From the Day of Rest, therefore, which began almost immediately as the weekend began and remained in force throughout its largest portion, to the traditional Jewish foods eaten at each of the six meals on a weekend, students made contact — some for the first time — with the life-embracing, hence authentic character of Judaism.

Actual experience offers support as well for the third contention of the program's originators, namely, that the weekend total living situations would shield the class from the influence of current culture and provide in its stead contact with another and it was thought superior culture. And thus it seems to have been. Separated one weekend a month from the din of the popular media and from the necessity to travel by automobile; separated, in general, from the routines imposed upon them by urban society, the students found themselves in a new, relatively pressure-free environment whose values, to a greater extent than any other they knew, were those of an honored religious culture. It is not that this monthly experience divorced them in a categorical sense from the American milieu which produced them and which they shared with their non Vov Class contemporaries. It is simply that periodically they had rather intensive contact with another cultural milieu, governed by different and in the opinion of their elders superior values. That the students themselves gave growing acceptance to this same bias is indicated by the fact that as the term progressed they came to regard Vov Class weekends as oases in their calendars and looked forward to their arrival with keen anticipation. As the year ended, the observer was gripped by a sense that the total living experiences on weekends had exerted a positive influence upon the students, with respect to both their general development and their acquaintance with and acceptance of Jewish values.

In view of the foregoing it seems reasonable to extract from the experience of the Vov Class the following third proposition:

> In order to establish a community within a Jewish framework, a monthly total living situation is a valuable, if not a crucial structural tool.

The Influence of Nature

The fourth of the original working hypotheses which underlay the founding of the Vov Class was the importance of nature. Again, based upon the example of Jewish camping, it was felt that usually neglected aspects of Judaism relating to its rural-agricultural origins could be conveyed more accurately in a rural, as distinguished from an urban, setting. In addition, it was felt that, in general, there was something about contact with nature which would contribute to more successful Jewish education.[15]

The experience of the Vov Class seems not to have supported these expectations, at least not in the form in which they were posited.

It will be recalled that three different weekend sites were used during the course of the year: Mary Grove, a camp some fifty miles from Graceville; and the Jewish Community Center and the Jewish Student Center, both in the city. The group used Mary Grove for four of its nine weekends (September, October, March and April), the Jewish Community Center for two (November and February) and the Jewish Student Center for three (December, January and May). The use of the in-town locations rather than Mary Grove was dictated by the early onset of the Sabbath during the winter months as well as by administrative considerations totally irrelevant to the nature issue. A comparison of the content of those weekends held in the rural setting with those held in the city fails to indicate any significant difference in the emphasis upon Judaism's rural character. Even the recreational activities in which the group engaged, which might well have been different depending upon site, showed no divergence. If nature was important to the experience, Roger and the students found as much of it as they desired at the in-town locations as at the camp. The chief importance of the sites, as indeed the chief importance of most of what occurred during the year, related not to nature but to the Vov Class's effort to become a community.

On the final weekend, student reactions to the several sites were solicited. Mary Grove was overwhelmingly preferred by the students, followed by the Jewish Student Center and the Jewish Community Center, in that order. Discussion indicated that Mary Grove was the students' choice simply because it afforded the group the isolation they felt they required in order to pursue their community formation purpose. The Jewish Community Center, though its facilities were far more inviting than those of the Jewish Student Center, was open to the public for five hours on Saturday afternoon and for that reason was considered least desirable. Thus the following fourth proposition, largely serendipitous to the original study plan, seems to derive from the experience:

In order to create a group within a Jewish framework spatial isolation is a valuable, if not a crucial factor.[16]

Conclusion

By the time the 1970-71 Vov Class Program came to an end, Eve, Susan and Dorothy, all of whom at one time had expressed uncertainty about continuing in the Zayin Class, decided to continue. In fact, all the girls, with the exception of Eve and Susan, made arrangements to attend Camp Zion the following summer. It was only Brad and George, the latter having officially withdrawn a month before the end of the term, who remained adamant in their resolve to quit. Soon, however, Brad declared his desire to go on with the group and George contacted the B'nai Israel school office requesting permission to return. Thus it turns out that each and every one of the fifteen students of the Vov Class and their teacher reached a decision, apparently without outside compulsion, to continue their experiment in "learning to live together Jewishly."

While there are any number of criteria which may be used to evaluate the success of a Jewish educational endeavor, the evocation among students of a desire to continue their education, in the estimation of the researcher, is a significant one, particularly when applied to post Bar and Bat Mitzva students. Apart from the welcome contrast to the customary dropout rate at this age level,[17] the Vov Class students' universal decision to continue indicated movement in the direction of substantive Jewish identification and learning. The group's first order of business, as has been stated repeatedly, was the creation of a Jewish community. But, once having accomplished this, the group was ready to embark upon a program involving contact with Israel and the acquisition of the Hebrew and general Jewish knowledge needed for that contact.

This is not to say that community was a one-time achievement, which once attained would cause the group to turn its gaze outward. No doubt, the effort would require good teaching and at best occur only gradually. "The realization of community," Martin Buber pointed out, "like the realization of any idea, cannot occur once and for all time: always it must be the moment's answer to the moment's question and nothing more."[18] With the onset of a new term, however, especially one with the goal of a trip to Israel at its end, it could be hoped that the class would devote itself in increasing measure to the satisfaction of needs beyond those related to its community formation purpose. Among those needs, Jewish study and further involvement in Jewish community affairs could well occupy an important place. It could be hoped, too, that concomitantly the Jewish commitment of the individual participants would broaden and deepen. "Group interaction," wrote Muzafer Sherif, "is seen as the major determinant in attitude formation and attitude change, and other phenomena of vital consequence to the individual."[19]

In summary, the Vov Class experience was more than a transitory educational experience. It was more even than an educational experience which gave promise of exerting lasting influence upon those who participated in it. The Vov Class experience was midwife to the birth of a living community which gave indication, as the year ended, of persisting in life and performing many of the functions natural to a viable organism. If the students, in the one year, did not plumb Judaism to its fullest depth — and who would argue that they did — they both identified the existence of that depth and created an instrument by means of which they could continue to plumb it in the future.

Beyond its effect upon the young people who were involved in it, the Vov Class Program may prove one day to have been a significant experiment in effective Jewish education. It seems to be an example of the kind of innovative program which, if multiplied and improved, could help to turn the tide of Jewish indifference and ignorance among the youth of this country. To be sure, many questions remain to be considered. One set of questions relates to the replicability of the Vov Class experience. What indeed were the subtle influences exerted by the presence of Rabbi Levy and how drastically would the results have been altered had he not been present? The entire Hawthorne Effect,[20] so-called, will never be known in its entirety. To what extent was Roger, his personality and his personal magnetism, rather than the passage to community, responsible for the outcome of the experience? While it is true that no educational experiment can be or should be considered independently of the teacher who conducts it, one suspects a special measure of influence on the part of this teacher.

Indeed, before the Vov Class approach can be viewed as a viable alternative in Jewish education, these and many questions like them need to be subjected to further systematic and disciplined research. It is the fervent hope and humble prayer of this researcher that such continuous inquiry will be forthcoming. For the Vov Class insight — the importance of community in the educational process — may contain implications far beyond the confines of the Jewish community. Martin Buber said, and this researcher agrees, that a new and better world "will never build itself up out of individuals but only out of small and ever smaller communities...,"[21] communities, in the researcher's estimation, not unlike the Vov Class, 1970-1971.

Chapter Six

Methodological Approach

The Genesis of the Study

Although Rabbi Levy had deep interest in the program, his actual contact with the Vov Class during its first year, because of his extensive Rabbinical duties, had been minimal. However, having come to B'nai Israel some twenty years earlier as a Rabbi-educator rather than as a pulpit Rabbi he had never lost his fascination for Jewish educational problems nor his hope that a better path could be found. Rabbi Levy, like Roger, had studied at Jefferson University — albeit many years earlier — and had completed all of his work towards a doctorate in education, with the exception of the dissertation. After being granted a year's partial sabbatical for the year 1970-1971 by the congregation, he approached the Graduate Department of Education at the university and requested permission to return as a full-time student. Together, the university authorities and he explored a topic for the dissertation. In the course of the exploration, he expressed his confidence, if not in the actual Vov Class Program, in the principles upon which it was founded. It was not long before the possibility occurred of his studying the new Vov Class Program by means of the non participant observation method.

The Method of Non Participant Observation

While non participant observation can be described as a naturalistic method, there are certain guiding constructs which are crucial to its employment. The first derives from the inability of even the most astute observer to perceive everything in a social situation with uniform interest and accuracy. Choices are necessarily made, whether consciously or unconsciously. What guides the choices are the observer's natural proclivities and the situation's inherent demands.

It was Bronislaw Malinowski in a classic social anthropological study[1] who delineated the steps involved in the process. He called attention to "fore-shadowed problems" by which he meant the initial foci of the observation which result from an interplay between the observer and his perception of the situation. The observer's background, interests and native ability, as well as his hunches, lead him to particular emphases within the situation being observed. This is quite different from "preconceived ideas," another of Malinowski's terms, in which the investigator seeks to find in the situation support for his preconceptions, a dangerous tactic to say the least. Research guided, however, by "foreshadowed problems," eventually leads to theory which is molded according to the facts, not the other way around. This should not be construed to imply that only those data which seem to have relevance to the "foreshadowed problems" are noted. Quite the contrary. The narrative, that is, a faithful portrayal of what actually happened, is emphasized above all. Much of what is thought at the time to be unimportant often turns out, in the analytic phase, to have considerable importance.

Although this approach to research was developed first in anthropology, it was later taken over by sociology. The emphasis here, like with its sister science, became the interaction of people rather than individual behavior and the flow of events rather than isolated occurrences. Howard S. Becker, *et al.*, for example, spoke of a "sociological mode of analysis" which is concerned with "social unit or units" rather than "individuals."[2] J. Von Velsen, however, averred that the subject is somewhat more complicated than this. Whereas the earliest researchers whom he calls the "pre-structuralists" failed in that they concerned themselves primarily with isolated "customs," the "structuralists" in their search for a social morphology also missed the mark. The latter, since they based themselves primarily upon norms[3] as revealed verbally, tended to obliterate individual differences such as may result from norm conflict, in which people select particular norms to fit their purposes. What is required, therefore, is a "post structural" approach resting upon observed behavior which it is thought yields a much more accurate portrayal of the social process.[4]

Be that as it may, the typical stance taken by the researcher-observer is perhaps best conveyed by what Abraham H. Maslow referred to as the "idiographic" as opposed to the "nomothetic" approach to human situations. This means that if one desires real understanding of a human situation he does not achieve it by applying lawful, general categories, usually arrived at a priori, but by adopting a "noninterfering global, waiting" approach.[5] The ideal is a combination of spectator-type "scientific" knowledge combined with "experiential naiveté" which is identified as the "ability to see freshly as a child sees, without a priori expectations or demands, without knowing in advance what they will see."[6]

More recently the method of non participant observation began to be employed by educators who investigate what Louis M. Smith has called "classroom microethnography." While acknowledging his debt to Fred Strodtbeck for the term, it was Smith who developed the implications of the method in the study alluded to above, which he coauthored with William Geoffrey.[7]

Just as the collection of data involves an ongoing interactive process, data analysis and theory building from the data do likewise. Barney G. Glaser and Anselm L. Strauss[8] present the concept of "theoretical sampling" by which they mean the joint collection, coding and analysis of data, which guides further collection as the theory begins to emerge. The researcher finds clusters of data, that is incidents, which resemble other incidents in some respect, as well as concepts which derive from those clusters. The concepts, in turn, guide the search for other incidents in the notes or, for that matter, in other relevant investigations, which both clarify and modify the concept.

Glaser and Strauss argue that this whole general process which they call "the comparative analysis of groups" is done as effectively, or perhaps even more effectively, in the study of one group as opposed to several. One, they say, may *"make comparisons of an array (of acts and social structures) characteristic of a single case — one array at a time — to generate grounded theory."*[9] The important thing is that the researcher continually moves from data to concepts and back again from concepts to data. The reporting of the concepts should of course contain samplings of illustrative incidents.

The researcher in the course of his investigation should seek "slices of data" which means various kinds of data taken from different vantage points. Such a collection process has the effect of providing a more complete, hence a more accurate understanding of the situation. Muzafer Sherif, *et al.*, emphasize the very same point when they write that ". . . only through . . . a combination of methods, applied to the flow of interaction process without chopping it into disjointed pieces, can we hope to attain generalizations with some bearing on the persistent group problems of actual life situations."[10]

If "slices of data" can be viewed then as the breadth of the situation, so depth must also be taken into account. It is up to the researcher to identify the various levels of meaning and then to plumb those levels to whatever depth is necessary to grasp the real character of the situation.

It is understood that the foregoing process of data collection and analysis is guided by flexibility and theoretical sensitivity. Obviously, the researcher must be prepared to follow where the data lead, it is hoped not too far afield, but still in directions that he may not have anticipated.

At some point along the line, the concepts begin to turn into propositions, that is, theoretical statements of relations between elements which extend beyond the particular situation being investigated. These propositions eventually link together to form substantive middle range theories, as described by Glaser and Strauss as well as Hans L. Zetterberg,[11] that is, plausible explanations of what has happened and what is likely to happen in similar situations in the future. In more technical language, the investigator begins to link the antecedents and consequences of the events which he has observed into a theoretical framework.

While it is difficult for a researcher to be sure that he is doing his work correctly there are certain criteria that he can use to judge his success. One is clarity, which implies that both the concepts and the relationship between concepts are carefully and clearly specified and speak to others as well as to him. Important, too, is good fit which implies a sense of the rightness of the interpretation — this theory offers a better conceptualization of the data than would others.

But such criteria notwithstanding, it all comes together, as it were, at some point. What emerges is "grounded theory" to use the Glaser and Strauss term, or "empirical generalizations" as opposed to "a priori generalizations" to use Maslow's term. The data, in other words, in appreciation for the many long hours during which they have been cleaned and curried, confer upon the researcher an insight that saturation has been achieved and that the categories are properly understood. When this happens, the researcher relies upon his own sensitivity to convince him that he has indeed identified as many of the properties of the data as they are inclined to yield and as he is capable of teasing to the surface.

Rabbi Levy as Non Participant Observer

While it was agreed that the method of non participant observation would be the most suitable for understanding the Vov Class, Rabbi Levy's role as the observer in this particular situation presented two serious methodological questions: first, to what extent would Rabbi Levy's presence affect the program? and second, to what extent would findings which derive from an observation of this kind be valid and generalizable?

The first question stems from the fact that, due to his position in the congregation and previous, in many cases, intimate association with the participants, students and teachers alike would be very much aware of Rabbi Levy's presence and would remain so from the moment he would enter the class until he would leave. Despite studied effort on Rabbi Levy's part to be as unobtrusive as possible, everyone would know that he was observing and recording his actions. Under such conditions there could be no doubt that Rabbi Levy would affect the situation materially.

It is a fact, however, that every study based upon non participant observation must face similar contamination problems. George J. McCall called attention to the "reactive effect" in which "the observer does not have the opportunity to observe the very thing that he had hoped to observe and that he may in fact believe he is observing."[1][2] Thus it is that no study, with the possible exception of one based upon a technique in which subjects are not aware that they are being observed, is immune to the charge. The real issue, therefore, is not the presence or the absence of a contaminating effect but the suggestion implied by some that it can be factored out and described. This study, therefore, makes no such pretense. It presents neither data nor speculation on the effect of Rabbi Levy's presence or, to phrase it another way, how the experience might have been different were he not present. The reality of Rabbi Levy's presence is accepted as one fact among many which characterize the experience.[13]

It was the second question, however, relating to the validity and generalizability of the findings, which, in a sense, constituted the more serious methodological concern if the study would lay claim to being anything more than an interesting anecdotal account of one isolated situation. Long before he contemplated the study, Rabbi Levy was personally committed to the importance of religious education for the young people of his congregation. Moreover, he was committed, as has been stated, if not to the Vov Class program itself, then to the principles which underlay it. The program was in a sense "his idea." How could he be relied upon to conduct valid research on the properties of the Vov Class experiment?

Long reflection convinced the researcher as well as the Faculty Committee responsible for approving the research method that, far from detracting from the validity of the findings and their generalizability, Rabbi Levy's commitments would serve to enhance the findings. They rested their conviction on a particular view of what constitutes valid scientific research in such an area. That view is the one which contends that, in the final analysis, all knowledge is derived from individuals who are deeply involved in and committed to particular situations which they explore and then describe. Michael Polanyi in his book *Personal Knowledge,*[14] presented perhaps the most sophisticated theoretical underpinning for this point of view.

Polanyi began his by-now classic monograph by critiquing present-day science, which he accused of pursuing a will-o'-the-wisp in the form of detached, so-called objective knowledge. While such an effort may have been useful at one particular period of history, it has come not to be so. In the present age, knowledge rests upon unformalized rather than formalized meaning. Truth, which is really the claim to universal validity, is similarly based upon commitment and asseveration, that is, belief, on behalf of which the scientist is willing to stake his professional life. In Polanyi's words:

Desisting henceforth from the vain pursuit of a formalized scientific method, commitment accepts in its place the person of the scientist as the agent responsible for conducting and accrediting scientific discoveries.[15]

Two things follow from this point of view: first that the scientist operating as a whole person, with his opinions and his biases, his intuitions and his fears, suddenly assumes pivotal importance in the discovery of scientific knowledge. Nor is it just a matter of the scientist being the person who selects and then filters through himself those aspects of a particular situation regarded as significant. More profoundly, it is by being a person that the scientist is able to perceive altogether that which is significant in a situation involving other persons. While it may be true that the scientist as non-person might be able to identify and describe certain behaviors in other people, when he attempts to assign motives to those behaviors, he finds that he must do so by attaching them to concepts. The concepts in turn are known to him only through their identification with concepts which he himself has experienced or learned about from the reported experience of other human beings who, like himself, were subject to the same process. Thus it is that the personal characteristics and qualities of the scientist, together with his personal perception of the motives and concepts which underlie human behavior, far from hampering discovery, are the soil out of which it grows. "The process of examining any topic is both an exploration of the topic and an exegesis of our fundamental beliefs in the light of which we approach it."[16]

The second outcome of such a view is that a specific situation in the hands of a specific investigator is quite capable of yielding conclusions universally significant. Polanyi asked the question of himself: "How can we claim to arrive at a responsible judgment with universal intent if the conceptual framework in which we operate is borrowed from a local culture . . .?"[17] The answer is, " . . . compulsion by universal intent establishes responsibility. The strain of this responsibility is the greater — other things being equal — the wider the range of alternatives left open to choice and the more conscientious the person responsible for the decision. While the choices in question are open to arbitrary egocentric decisions, a craving for the universal sustains a constructive effort and narrows down the discretion to the point where the agent making the decision finds that he cannot do otherwise. *The freedom of the subjective person to do as he pleases is overruled by the freedom of the responsible person to act as he must.*"[18]

While it hardly seemed necessary to pursue the subject beyond Polanyi, he is not the only scholar who adopts such a point of view. From a somewhat different perspective, P. W. Bridgman[19] arrived at the conclusion that all collection of data and their analysis are "operational," by which he meant that scientific investigation is and should be characterized by immediacy, first person concerns, rather than illusory, objective and therefore static abstraction. To the extent that we are all individuals, the accusation of solipsism can always be made and perhaps never adequately answered, unless the accuser is disposed to accept the answer.

It is not accidental that this point of view, when applied by committed human beings to the study of other human beings, especially those involved in intricate social interaction, results in highly significant, theoretically very provocative material. Fritz Redl, for example, who was both the originator and director of Pioneer House in Detroit, was committed to a particular approach to the treatment of "children who hate." He operationalized his commitment to a residential setting with five young people over a period of two years. The study which emanated from that experience[20] remains a singular contribution to the understanding of all human behavior. The same is true of the seminal work of A. S. Neill at Summerhill,[21] the example of which remains a source of inspiration to educators the world over.[22] For these reasons, Rabbi Levy's deep involvement in every facet of the Vov Class came to be regarded as a strength rather than a weakness. Because of his involvement and the passion engendered by it, not in spite of it, could he hope to fathom the depth of meaning in what would be a very complex social-educational situation. While humility and ultimate uncertainty would necessarily accompany the effort, refuge was found in Polanyi's assertion that ". . . the higher the level of success we are contemplating the more far-reaching must be our participation in our subject matter."[23]

In time, provisional approval for the study was granted by the Faculty Committee including the head of the Institute. At a later date, representatives of the various wings of the Institute met and expressed confidence in the approach, and the study was launched.[24]

The Data Base

Data for the study were culled by means of a multi-method, multi-situation, multi-variable, multi-person approach. Of first importance were the longhand field notes written during sessions of the Vov Class, beginning October 4, 1970. "These. . . records grew," like those of Louis M. Smith, "to a horrifying quantity." The reason is that the observer was present for 78% of the total of 71 official meetings of the class. His longhand field notes reflect 302 hours and 50 minutes of direct observation.[25]

These notes, including interpretive asides which occurred to the observer during the sessions, were immediately typed and reread to guard against errors and significant omissions. Frequently, summary observations on particular aspects of the experience were recorded between sessions. In one or two cases the proceedings were taped and transcribed primarily as a means of checking the accuracy of the observer's notes. It was found that this procedure was not rewarding and was therefore discontinued.

In addition, there were numerous documents, formal and informal, official and unofficial, emanating from teachers, the administration, and in some cases the students, which were in the observer's possession and formed part of the data base.

The study also made use of what has been called by Louis M. Smith the "inside-outside" technique.[26] The teacher faithfully recorded his plans as well as his post-situational summaries and evaluations of all sessions and made them available to the researcher. These proved to be very valuable. In addition to providing data on those sessions for which the observer was not present, they provided information on the teacher's perception of situations for which the observer was present. Apart from their inherent value, such information served as a corrective to what the observer sometimes overlooked or misinterpreted.

Another major portion of the data base consisted of materials written by the students in class. As was pointed out, the teacher frequently had the students write their opinions on a variety of subjects. Copies of all such materials were in the possession of the researcher. It should be added that the researcher had complete files on the students' entire religious school background, including written records of previous communications between him and them, as well as between them and the congregation. Available to him also was considerable background material on the parents and families of Vov Class students and the record of numerous conversations held with them and with others who had either direct or indirect contact with the program. Information on parents was augmented by the self-administered questionnaire on Jewish identity referred to above.

Finally, student IQ scores, the results of one Hebrew comprehension test and the Origin Climate questionnaire, probing the students' estimate of classroom atmosphere, also described above, were used by the researcher.

The Scope of the Study

Because of the many unique aspects of the present study it may be helpful to set out in some detail what the study is, or at least what it attempted to be and what it is not or did not attempt to be. First, the study is not a study of the methodology of a non participant observation which employs a highly involved investigator as the observer. Although the issues which emanate from such an observation are both fascinating and important they were not in any sense the major concern of the study. To be sure the temptation to turn the research spotlight upon the relationship between the investigator and the class was present at every step along the way. Nor was there any lack of data which if described and analyzed might not have yielded significant insights regarding the opportunities as well as the pitfalls offered by such an investigation. Yet these were not pursued beyond the point that the researcher considered necessary for a valid description and analysis of what became the major focus.

In like fashion the study did not attempt an historical-philosophical critique of conventional Jewish educational forms. Long personal experience in the field augmented by the experience of other Jewish educators with whom he had contact were sufficient to convince the researcher both of the inadequacy of present forms and of the need for bold experimentation in the pursuit of better ones. Yet this does not imply that a systematic appraisal of extant forms was undertaken. That such an appraisal is lacking and long overdue cannot be denied. But again this study of the Vov Class makes no pretense to filling the need.

By the same token, the study does not attempt to provide a new general theory of Jewish religious education which is presumed to be superior to those theories presently in force. While values, explicit or implicit, are present in all conceptual activity of this kind, their organization into an hierarchal scheme involves a leap which the study avoids meticulously. More than that, the study does not even lay claim to the discovery of new knowledge. Very little of what has been written purports to be a "contribution to science," unless the reorganization of widely known principles culled from a number of branches of the humanities and their application to Jewish education in a particular place at a particular time can be so termed.[27] It is quite possible that the study combined with others of a similar stripe might one day yield a grand treatment of what religious education in America "ought to be," but this is not that treatment.

If the study is not a systematic critique of conventional Jewish educational forms and if it is not the presentation of a new theory it is certainly not a laboratory comparison between the two. Such an enterprise necessarily involves subjecting experimental and control groups to experiences which are equated in all but those elements which have been isolated for comparison, the techniques for which have been established and carefully described in the canons of classical experimental research. No such groups were in existence and no such comparison was undertaken.

If not these, then what? The present study of the Vov Class, 1970-1971, is an idiographic, microethnographic study of a class involved in an innovative program of Jewish religious education. Based upon a non participant observation by the investigator, it is an attempt to describe and understand the intricacies primarily of the interactions of fifteen young people and their teachers who were engaged in a Jewish educational endeavor. These interactions led to highly complicated restructuring by individuals of their personal lives as well as to plethoric and constantly changing social relationships among those individuals. The interactions, particularly those involving the teacher in relation to the students, led within the class again to highly complicated and constantly changing perceptions about life in general, about the nature of Jewishness, and about the place of the individual in confrontation with both. And the interactions, all of which occurred within an evolving context, physical and otherwise, led to the formation of a *sui generis* entity whose perimeters were delimited by that context. It is the attempt to describe and understand the properties of that entity, with emphasis upon the factors which gave it its character, which forms the primary focus of the study.

Additionally, the study attempts to draw out of the experience tentative general theoretical propositions of the middle range variety which may or may not be applicable to other Jewish educational situations. If in time they prove to be applicable to other Jewish schools it is likely that they will not be so in any literal and direct sense. As John Dewey once said, "We do not expect to have other schools literally imitate what we do. A working model is not something to be copied; it is to afford a demonstration of the feasibility of the principle and the methods which made it feasible."[28]

For organizational purposes, the theoretical propositions were considered within the framework of the original working hypotheses by means of which the program was conceptualized. But in so doing, the study implies neither that these propositions are the only ones obtainable from the experience nor that this formulation of the propositions is the most beneficial. The researcher is the first to acknowledge that people, especially as they interact with other people, are bigger than this attempt to describe them much less analyze them, and that education in general and Jewish education in particular are far too broad to be confined either to a single experimental program or to a study which seeks to conceptualize its properties. It is sufficient for the researcher that the Vov Class Program demonstrates that alternatives for educating American Jewish youth to an understanding of their heritage are possible and that disciplined techniques employed in the sciences of human behavior may be brought to bear upon the description and analysis, including the broader implications for Jewish education, of one such alternative.

Chapter Seven

Epilogue

It was in the middle of May, 1975, that Rabbi Levy relived and savored again the kind of weekend which had figured so prominently in the life of the Vov Class, 1970-1971. The occasion was the Senior Farewell Shabbat sponsored by the B'nai Israel Synagogue Youth Group. By then — four years later — the original Vov Class no longer existed. It had fallen prey, two years earlier, to a mindless decision by the Synagogue administration as well as to the changing interests and fortunes of the individual students.

It will be recalled that when the Vov year ended, in 1971, the class had reached two decisions: one, to remain together the next year in what was to be called the Zayin Class; and the other, to try to spend the summer following as a group in Israel.

After three months of uncertainty, the B'nai Israel School Board did agree to form a Zayin Class, with Roger as its teacher. Its purpose — clearly discerned both by Roger and the students but hardly by the School Board and the parents — was to prepare for and to spend the summer of 1972 in Israel.

The story of what happened in the Zayin Class and why, while fascinating and extremely important, is outside the purview of this work. The story has been incisively documented with meticulous concern for detail by Ronald Wolfson in his *A Description and Analysis of an Innovative Living Experience in Israel — the Dream and the Reality.*[1] Suffice it to say that the Zayin Class, comprising thirteen of the original fifteen Vov Class students, did indeed spend the entire next year preparing for Israel. Contact was established early with a group of Israel youngsters of the same age, residents of a small agricultural collective which, in many ways, was a near perfect example of the integrated organic Jewish community which their own group had come to approximate. Exchanges of letters, pictures, and tapes, as well as programmatic anticipations of what they would encounter during their stay, formed the substance of the curriculum content. When the summer arrived, the students were eminently well-prepared for what they were to experience, as much as students can be said to be prepared to live and work in an environment so different from their own. The stay itself from the point of view of the quality of the experience, Jewish and general, as Wolfson describes it, was extraordinary.

However, upon the group's return from Israel at the end of the summer of 1972, the B'nai Israel administration decided that the youngsters had separated themselves from the rest of the school long enough and that it was time for them to be integrated into the existing structure. Their request therefore that they be allowed to designate themselves by the next letter of the Hebrew alphabet, Chet, and to perpetuate their class was denied. The reasons given were, in retrospect, as questionable as the decision itself. It was claimed that while the youngsters had benefited greatly from their two-year association in the Vov and Zayin Classes, they had to learn now to relate to fellow B'nai

Israel students who were not part of their group. It was hoped, too, that some of the deep commitment to the synagogue and to Jewish modes of behavior which they had achieved during the previous two years, would somehow rub off on those who had not been part of the program. Also, the administration and a few parents felt that it was important that all the youngsters participate together in the Religious School graduation ceremony which traditionally was held at the end of the 10th grade. Protests from the students and from those of the parents who identified with their request were of no avail, especially since the administration now had two more Vov classes and one Zayin class with which to concern itself.

Indeed the Vov Class idea had caught on at B'nai Israel. By dint of reputation and the experience of older brothers and sisters, the overwhelming majority of post Bar and Bat Mitzva youngsters had come to expect participation in the Vov Class and later in the Zayin Class. In fact, so widespread was this expectation that it was not long before the traditional one-day-a-week Sunday School at this age level, which had been standard at B'nai Israel and was still standard throughout Graceville, fell into virtual disuse. It was the exceptional B'nai Israel child for whom a one-day-a-week Jewish educational experience, post Bar and Bat Mitzva, was sufficient. The experiment had ceased to be experimental and was now the mode at B'nai Israel.

As to the original group, what had grown up among them was not about to be dissipated by a school board decision. While precise data are lacking regarding number and frequency, there can be no doubt that during the following two years, that is, until their graduation from high school, most of the group maintained close contact with each other, with Roger, and with Judaism. Some were among the most active youth in the synagogue. They assumed positions of leadership and accepted responsibility of various kinds. Many attended services with regularity and a number adopted life styles much more traditionally Jewish than any in their immediate families. Some also became active in B'nai Israel's Synagogue Youth Group and were now among the seniors in whose honor the Farewell Weekend alluded to above, with Rabbi Levy and his wife in attendance, had been arranged.

The weather was especially inviting that weekend. It had been a mild, wet spring in Graceville and the May countryside was luxuriantly verdant. Even though the present site was not one of those used four years earlier when the Vov Class study was done, the gentle intensity of the sun and the mingling of youthful voices with the sounds of the outdoors, so warmly reminiscent of those earlier weekends, invited Rabbi Levy to another look at the Vov Class experiment and its meaning for Jewish education in our time.

It is a truism that, once the child reaches adolescence, the environment educates, in the broadest sense of the term, more than the school or even more than the home. It is a fact too that the American environment in which Jewish youth experience their adolescence is not Jewish — neither in form nor in content. Not only is the environment not supportive of Jewish values, modes of behavior and ritual observances, but it is often inimical to them. Identification with Judaism, on the part of the adolescent, therefore, requires a degree of assertiveness and commitment which few, with even the best of intentions, are able to call forth. Yet, this is precisely what most current Jewish educational programs expect of young people. On the strength of sporadic classroom exposure and some superficial "youth group" activity, young Jews are urged to become conversant with and dedicated to a profound and highly sophisticated cultural tradition and religious regimen which under the most favorable of circumstances is not easy to achieve. It is not difficult to guess why most educational programs for this age group prove to be abysmal failures.

The Vov Class program, on the other hand, as described and analyzed in these pages and as demonstrated subsequently with at least six more groups, has shown that *the creation of a small, cohesive social enclave, in which the student locates himself psychologically and emotionally, as well as physically, constitutes a powerful instrument for the transmission of Jewish culture and religion.*

The community, once it is formed, becomes the focus of the educational effort. It is the group rather than the individual student which is acted upon by the instructor and the school. Only after the group adopts, as its own, modes of operation and values which are Jewish are individual students inspired to identify personally with and commit themselves to those same modes and values. And experience has shown that an unusually high percentage of young Jews, when approached in this manner, do so identify and do so commit themselves. May their example spur those charged with the education of our youth to refine and adapt these insights to their own institutions.

APPENDIX A

The Schedule of Weekends

Weekend Number	Month	Place	Theme
1	September	Mary Grove	Awareness
2	October	Mary Grove	Sabbath
3	November	Jewish Community Center	Cycle of Life
4	December	Jewish Student Center	Friendship
5	January	Jewish Student Center	Peace
6	February	Jewish Community Center	Love
7	March	Mary Grove	God, The Messiah, Life-After-Death, Freedom
8	April	Mary Grove	The Holocaust
9	May	Jewish Student Center	– – – – –

APPENDIX B

Sessions and Elapsed Waking Time of Vov Class Meetings

	Number of Sessions		Hours		Total	
Wednesday	29	X	1:30	=	43:30	
	1	X	1:00	=	1:00	
	2	X	2:00	=	4:00	
	32					48:30
Sunday	22	X	1:40	=	36:40	
	1	X	5:00	=	5:00	
	23					41:40
Weekends	7	X	28:00	=	196:00	
	1	X	32:00	=	32:00	
	1	X	51:00	=	51:00	
	9					279:00
Special Events	5	X	2:00	=	10:00	
	1	X	5:00	=	5:00	
	1	X	6:00	=	6:00	
	7					21:00
	71					390:10

GRAND TOTALS: 71 Meetings = 390 Hours, 10 Minutes

Sessions During Which the Observer was Present

	Number of Sessions		Hours		Total	
Wednesday	25	X	1:30	=	37:30	
	1	X	1:00	=	1:00	
	1	X	2:00	=	2:00	
	27					40:30
Sunday	20	X	1:40	=	33:20	
	20					33:20
Weekends	5	X	28:00	=	140:00	
	1	X	32:00	=	32:00	
	1	X	51:00	=	51:00	
	7					223:00
Special Events	3	X	2:00	=	6:00	
	3					6:00
	57					302:50

GRAND TOTALS: 57 Meetings = 302 Hours, 50 Minutes

APPENDIX C

VOV CLASS ATTENDANCE

According to Hours

Name	Wed. T.	Wed. %	Sun. T.	Sun. %	Weekends T.	Weekends %	Special Events T.	Special Events %	Total T.	Total %
Arnold	22:30	48%	30	72%	219	79%	7	33%	278:30	71%
Bob	42	87%	38:20	92%	247	89%	9	43%	336:20	86%
Brad	40	83%	40	97%	204	73%	5	24%	289	72%
Eve	43	89%	35:40	85%	251	90%	11	52%	340:40	87%
Susan	45	93%	38:30	93%	251	90%	11	52%	345:30	89%
Claudia	34:30	71%	25:50	62%	279	100%	5	24%	344:20	88%
Ruth	42:30	88%	30:30	73%	172	62%	6	30%	251	64%
Dorothy	46	95%	37:10	90%	228	82%	7	33%	318:10	82%
Bernice	41	85%	36:40	88%	251	90%	17	81%	345:40	89%
George	23:30	48%	26:40	64%	228	82%	5	24%	283:10	73%
Bruce	42:30	88%	37:10	90%	209	75%	11	52%	299:40	77%
Karen	41:50	86%	33:10	80%	279	100%	19	95%	373	96%
Sylvia	45:30	94%	39:50	95%	279	100%	21	100%	385:20	99%
Jeanne	46:30	96%	36:40	88%	279	100%	9	43%	371:10	95%
Rich	44:50	92%	38:10	92%	279	100%	11	52%	373	96%
Totals	601:10		524:20		3655		154		4934:30	
Average & %:	40	83%	35:30	84%	244	87%	10	49%	329:30	84%
Girls:	43:20	89%	35:10	84%	252	90%	12	57%	342	88%
Boys:	36:30	76%	35	85%	231	83%	8	38%	310:30	79%
Rabbi Levy	40:30	83%	33:20	80%	223	80%	6	29%	302:50	78%

According to Sessions

Name	Wed. T.	Wed. %	Sun. T.	Sun. %	Weekends T.	Weekends %	Special Events T.	Special Events %	Total T.	Total %
Arnold	15	46%	16	69%	7	78%	2	29%	40	56%
Bob	28	88%	21	91%	8	89%	3	43%	60	85%
Brad	27	84%	22	96%	7	86%	1	14%	57	81%
Eve	29	91%	19	83%	8	89%	4	51%	60	85%
Susan	30	94%	21	91%	8	89%	4	51%	63	89%
Claudia	23	72%	19	83%	9	100%	1	14%	52	73%
Ruth	28	88%	16	69%	6	67%	3	43%	53	75%
Dorothy	31	97%	20	87%	8	89%	2	29%	61	86%
Bernice	27	84%	20	87%	8	89%	7	100%	62	87%
George	16	50%	14	61%	8	89%	1	14%	39	55%
Bruce	28	88%	20	87%	7	74%	4	57%	59	83%
Karen	28	88%	19	83%	9	100%	7	100%	63	89%
Sylvia	30	94%	22	96%	9	100%	7	100%	68	96%
Jeanne	31	97%	20	87%	9	100%	3	43%	63	89%
Rich	30	94%	21	91%	9	100%	4	57%	64	90%
Totals	401		290		119		53		864	
Average & %:										
Girls:	27	84%	19	84%	8	89%	4	50%	58	81%
Boys:	29	89%	20	85%	8	91%	6	59%	61	89%
Rabbi	24	75%	19	83%	8	86%	2½	36%	53	75%
Levy	27	84%	20	87%	7	78%	3	43%	54	76%

Notes

Preface

1 Alexander M. Dushkin and Uriah Z. Engelman, *Jewish Education in the United States*, The American Association for Jewish Education, New York, 1959, p. 4.

2 See, for example, Oscar I. Janowsky, *The American Jew a Reappraisal*, The Jewish Publication Society of America, Philadelphia, 5725-1964, pp. 153-172. Also, Walter I. Ackerman, "An Analysis of Selected Courses of Study of Conservative Congregational Schools, Part I," *Jewish Education*, March 1970, Vol. 40, No. 1, pp. 7-23, and "Part II," *Jewish Education*, Summer 1970, Vol. 40, No. 2, pp. 37-48.

3 The names of all persons and places have been coded to preserve anonymity.

4 Samuel Dinin, *Report on the Status of Jewish Education in . . .*, American Association for Jewish Education, New York, July 1966 (mimeographed).

5 *Ibid.*, p. 27

6 Michael Polanyi, *Personal Knowledge*, Harper Torchbooks/The Academy Library, Harper & Row, Publishers, New York, 1964, p. 300.

Chapter I *Introduction*

1 For a complete description of this concept see Richard deCharms, *Personal Causation*, Academic Press, New York, 1968, particularly Part IV.

2 The approach of deCharms seems to this researcher to be very much in the spirit of the pragmatic-experimental philosophy which flowered in the work of John Dewey. For an overview of Dewey's philosophy, particularly as applied to education, see Arthur G. Wirth, *John Dewey as Educator*, John Wiley & Sons, Inc., New York, 1966. In similar fashion deCharms seems to draw inspiration from the work

of Kurt Lewin and his concept of democratic group atmosphere. See Kurt Lewin and Ronald Lippitt, "An Experimental Approach to the Study of Autocracy and Democracy: A Preliminary Note," *Small Groups Studies in Social Interaction*, A. Paul Hare, Edgar F. Borgatta, Robert F. Bales (eds.), Alfred A. Knopf, New York, 1955, Chapter 10, pp. 516-523.

3 The term "total living situation" was borrowed from Donald R. Hammerman and William M. Hammerman, *Outdoor Education*, Burgess Publishing Co., Minneapolis, Minnesota, v. 55415, p. 338. Other terminology referring to the same approximate approach might have been used. John Dewey, for example, spoke of "an environment educationally controlled." (Quoted by Arthur G. Wirth, *The Vocational-Liberal Studies Controversy Between John Dewey and Others (1900-1917,)* U.S. Department of Health, Education & Welfare, Office of Education Bureau of Research, 1970, p. 274.) Fritz Redl & David Wineman make reference to "total residential design." (*The Aggressive Child*, The Free Press of Glencoe, Inc., 1957, p. 34.) Also, Bruno Bettelheim & Emmy Sylvester spoke of "total environmental design." ("The Therapeutic Milieu," *American Journal of Orthopsychiatry*, XVIII (1948), pp. 191-206.)

4 See Jacob Neusner, *Judaism in the Secular Age,* Ktav Publishing House, Inc., New York, 1970.

5 Samuel Dinin, *op. cit.*, p. 17.

6 Jack Rothman said that adolescence "is the period during which the process of identification is at the center of attention, consciously and unconsciously, and during which the eventual pattern becomes crystalized." (*Minority Group Identification & Intergroup Relations*, Research Institute for Group Work in Jewish Agencies in cooperation with The American Jewish Committee, Ann Arbor, Michigan, 1965.)

7 Erik H. Erikson, *Identity Youth and Crisis*, W.W. Norton & Company, Inc., New York, 1968, p. 156.

8 Lawrence Kohlberg and Rochelle S. Mayer, *Preschool Research and Preschool Educational Objectives; a Critique and a Proposal*, Harvard University, n.d. (mimeographed), p. 33.

9 Charles E. Silberman, *Crisis in the Classroom*, Random House, New York, 1970, p. 325.

10 Much of the information on the families was derived from a 297-item questionnaire on Jewish Identity, self-administered by the parents at the request of the researcher. The questionnaire bears the title *Study of the Changing Jewish Community*, Account No. 70173 (p. 129). It was developed by Leonard J. Fein of Brandeis University.

11 An excellent review and critique of the attempts to measure Jewish identity, or Jewish identification, as it is sometimes called, is contained in "Jewish Identity Scales – A Report," by Ralph Segalman, *Jewish Social Studies*, Vol. 29, 1967, pp. 92-111. Special note should be taken of *Minority Group Identification and Intergroup Relations*, by Jack Rothman, (*op. cit.*) Although the major purpose of the latter work is to examine Kurt Lewin's theory of Jewish group identity in relation to out-group attitudes, it presents *en passant* a thorough overview of the field capped by the conclusion that "there exists presently no scale for measuring Jewish identification which is generally accepted . . . in the field." (p. 126) By far, the most complete listing of available materials on the subject is contained in

Bibliographies on Jewish Identity prepared by Norman Feinstein and Stanley Feder under the direction of Leonard J. Fein, Massachusetts Institute of Technology, 1966 (mimeographed). The companion work, *Studying Jewish Identity: Observations*, by Leonard J. Fein, Cambridge, Mass., 1966 (mimeographed) offers a broadside criticism of the literature, from both the conceptual and methodological standpoints. It says, quite correctly, "...the work that has been done is grossly inadequate. In almost every case, one finds total weaknesses in sample selection, or in questionnaire design, or in data analysis, or in interpretation, or more fundamentally, in problem definition or, finally, in all too many cases, in more than one of these areas . . ." (p. 19).

12 Another girl started the year with the class but withdrew almost immediately. She attended no weekends and in the observer's judgment had negligible influence upon the experience. She will not be included beyond this point.

13 I.Q. scores based upon Henmon-Nelson or Lorge-Thorndike tests administered by the public schools in the sixth or seventh grade yielded a range of 103-150, a median of 120, and a mean of 120.87.

14 This conclusion seems justified by the fact that only one student in the class stated unequivocally that he had been forced to come, while another upon occasion claimed that she had been forced but at other times denied it.

15 In 1970, Roger received a BA in Religious Studies from Jefferson University. The following year — the year in which the study was conducted — he earned an MA in Education, also at Jefferson, and passed the bulk of his entrance exams to Rabbinical School.

Chapter II *Setting the Climate*

1 For a detailed analysis of the implication of different seating arrangements, particularly sociopetal seating, see Robert Sommer, *Personal Space* (Prentice-Hall, Inc., Englewood Cliffs, N.J., 1969), p. 51, note 3 p. 121, p. 137, etc.

2 Fritz Redl & David Wineman (*The Aggressive Child, op. cit.*, p. 447 ff.) call this technique "self bouncing." In general a number of the techniques employed by Roger in the Vov Class were presaged in their excellent volume. Several others are "regrouping" (p. 423 ff.), and "post situational rub-in" (p. 455).

3 To the best of the observer's knowledge, information gleaned in this fashion was divulged neither to the administration nor to other members of the faculty.

4 Roger of course preferred volunteers. For an analysis of the effects when teachers solicit volunteers rather than "direct pupils" see Louis M. Smith, *The Microethnography of the Classroom* (Ocassional Paper Series Number 1, 1966, Central Midwest Regional Educational Laboratory, p. 4.)

5 See Richard deCharms, *Personal Causation* (*op. cit.*), p. 312 ff., for an experiment which he and Bridgman conducted to explore "the feelings of the student toward a teacher (or a follower toward a leader) when a student feels that he can have some control in determining the course of events in the classroom situation." The results of the experiment were "interpreted as showing that when group members feel that they have some freedom to control the situation . . . their feelings toward the leader and willingness to work for him will be much more positive than if they feel they have no say in the procedure . . ."

6 Appendix A presents the schedule of weekends, including the location and theme of each.
7 For a precise definition of awareness and its operation in a classroom, see Louis M. Smith and William Geoffrey, *Complexities of an Urban Classroom,* Holt, Rinehart & Winston Inc., N.Y. 1968, pp. 102 ff., 235. As with Redl and Wineman, so with the work of Smith, the writer is deeply indebted for many of the concepts of teacher behavior found in this section.
8 See note 2.
9 See note 7.
10 One is reminded of the comment by Herbert R. Kohl, in *The Open Classroom*, (A New York Review Book, Vintage Books, 1969). "...the things that work best in class, ... are the unplanned ones, the ones that arise spontaneously because of a student's suggestion or a sudden perception." The teacher, he added, "trusts his intuitions and isn't too upset to abandon plans that had consumed time and energy." (pp. 40-41).
11 The concept of "conditional acceptance" is identified as "Rogerian" by Chris Argyris in "Interpersonal Competence and Organizational Effectiveness" (*Interpersonal Dynamics,* Warren G. Bennis, *et al.* (eds.), The Dorsey Press, Homewood, Illinois, 1968, pp. 583-597), p. 588.
12 For a discussion on "the extent to which teachers differentiate on the basis of intellectual, motivational, or physical dimensions" as opposed to differentiation "on the basis of personal social constructs" see Louis M. Smith and Paul F. Kleine, *Minor Studies in Teacher-Pupil Relationships* (Technical Report Series, Number 5, 1969, Central Midwestern Regional Educational Laboratory), p. 25.
13 Jack R. Gibb & Lorraine M. Gibb, "Role Freedom in a TORI Group," *Encounter*, Arthur Burton (ed.), Jossey-Bass, Inc., Publishers, San Francisco, 1970, p. 55.
14 "One fact seems to generate from the literature: any individual who wishes to be influential among his fellows in a free society needs to exhibit a behavior which reflects this quality of warmth, supportiveness, or acceptance." Louis M. Smith & Paul F. Kleine, *Minor Studies in Teacher-Pupil Relationships, op. cit.*, p. 7.

Chapter III *The Curriculum Content*

1 While the concept of curriculum or curriculum content is sometimes considered in the narrow sense as referring to cognitive aspects of classroom activity exclusively or in the broad sense as referring to virtually everything that happens in an educational situation, the approach of this chapter is somewhere in between. It resembles Gordon N. Mackenzie's conception of curriculum as "the learner's engagements with various aspects of the environment which have been planned under the direction of the school." (p. 402, "Curricular change: participants, power, and processes," *Innovation in Education*, edited by Matthew B. Miles, Bureau of Publications, Teacher's College, Columbia University, New York, 1964, pp. 399-424.)
2 The term was suggested by Louis M. Smith.
3 For a complete listing of weekend themes see Appendix A.
4 Shabbat is the English transliteration of the Hebrew original of the word Sabbath.
5 The small-town Jewish community of eastern Europe which persisted until World War I and in some places until World War II. An excellent description of the

culture of the Shtetl is found in *Life is With People, the Culture of the Shtetl*, by Mark Zborowski and Elizabeth Herzog, Schocken Books, New York, 1967.

6 Havdala, which means separation, is the name of the traditional ceremony which officially closes the Sabbath at sundown on Saturday.

7 The Feast of Weeks, commemorating the Giving of the Pentateuch to Moses on Mt. Sinai.

8 The class's nickname for the observer.

9 See *Tradition & Change, The Development of Conservative Judaism*, Rabbi Mordecai Waxman, (ed.), The Burning Bush Press, New York, 1958.

10 Upon occasion, Roger involved his students in community events which he considered important. Typically, he would inform the class of a forthcoming event, often by means of specially prepared materials, and then urge attendance in his and Sara's company. If the event in question was to occur during other than school time, he would advise students to secure their parents' permission. In some cases, he suggested that students invite their parents. During the year, students joined Roger in a march and rally on behalf of Soviet Jewry and two film showings, one an Israel-produced film and the other a full-length film depicting a Blood Libel incident in Russia at the turn of the century. In addition, five students found their way to one or more sessions of B'nai Israel's annual weekend study seminar and all but five came to the annual Purim Service.

11 As the Hebrew consonant Vov represents six, so Tet represents nine. Bob was suggesting a performance of "Fiddler" at the end of the ninth grade, three years hence.

12 Technically, there is no such distinction in traditional Judaism as clergy and laymen. Any male Jew may lead the service and usually does on weekdays. By the same token, the Rabbi who is merely the teacher of the community and the Cantor who is distinguished because of his musical talent, have no religious duties or privileges other than those which devolve upon every Jew.

13 A Talis is a prayer shawl, and Tfillin, sometimes known as phylacteries, are small leather boxes containing Biblical quotations. Male Jews wrap themselves in the Talis and strap the Tfillin to their forehead and arm during daily morning prayer.

14 Whereas women are invited to the daily service, few attend. The reason has to do with Jewish law which exempts women from the obligation, as well as with the fact that traditional Jewish practice bars women from equal participation in the service. Women, for example, are not counted in the Minyan, the Hebrew term for the quorum necessary to conduct the service as an official community service rather than as an aggregate of individual services.

15 The development of cohesiveness in the Vov Class and its effect upon various aspects of the program is the subject of Chapter IV.

16 Late in the year, an attempt was made to measure the Hebrew knowledge of the Vov Class. Entitled "Test on the Fundamentals of Hebrew — I, Lower Level" by the Committee on Tests of the American Association for Jewish Education, the instrument relies on grammar and the translation of Hebrew words. It was administered to the twelve students present by the School Administrator. For comparative purposes, the same test was administered to the three classes in the grade just below the Vov Class, called Hay. A significant difference was found between the four groups ($p < .01$). The difference, however, between the Vov Class and two of the groups was not significant; whereas the difference between the Vov Class and one

was significant at $p < .05$. (H. Scheffé, *The Analysis of Variance*, New York, Wiley, 1959.)

17 While universally reliable norms have not been established for the Origin-climate concept, a test for measuring comparative Origin climates in a relatively restricted area was developed by Sharon Koenigs of Washington University. Called the Origin Climate Questionnaire, the test purports to measure student perception of classroom climate by means of six variables: Internal Control, Goal Setting, Instrumental Activity, Reality Perception, Personal Responsibility, and Self-Confidence. In March, the Vov Class was randomly divided into two groups of eight and six students, one student having been absent that day. Administered by the test's author, one group reacted to the climate in Mrs. Cohen's room while the other reacted to the climate in Roger's room. The results in Mrs. Cohen's case were: n=8, range=39-97, mean=65.5; in Roger's case: n=6, range=108-120, mean=115.1. The contrast between the Origin climates in the two rooms is readily apparent.

18 Carl Ransom Rogers, *Freedom to Learn*, C.E. Merrill Publishing Co., Columbus, Ohio, 1969.

19 Colloquial Yiddish for Grandmother and Grandfather.

20 Richard L. Rubenstein, *After Auschwitz*, The Bobbs-Merrill Company, Inc., 1969.

Chapter IV *From Aggregate To Group*

1 The term is borrowed from Muzafer Sherif, *et al.*, whose experiment in group interaction is a classic in the field. See *Intergroup Conflict and Cooperation, The Robbers Cave Experiment* The Institute of Group Relations, The University of Oklahoma, Norman, Okla., 1961, especially Chap. 7. See also, Muzafer Sherif (ed.), *Intergroup Relations and Leadership*, Wiley, New York, 1962 and Muzafer Sherif and Carolyn W. Sherif, *Reference Groups*, Harper & Row, Publishers, New York, 1964.

2 A norm is regarded, according to the definition supplied by Louis M. Smith and William Geoffrey, as a "group variable indicating common sentiment for activities or behavior to be carried out by individuals, roles, or groups." *Complexities of an Urban Classroom, op. cit.*, p. 266.

3 *The Aggressive Child, op. cit.*, p. 175.

4 The comparative influences of a residential camp environment with a home environment on a nine-year-old were studied by Paul V. Gump, Phil Schoggen and Fritz Redl, ("The Behavior of the Same Child in Different Milieus," *The Stream of Behavior*, Roger G. Barker, ed., Appleton-Century-Crofts, New York, 1963, pp. 169-202). They found "obvious supports and invitations to particular play forms which were inherent in the home and camp milieus." Noting the differences in behavior in the same child, they observed that "the presence of these supports lends credence to the judgment that the differences obtained . . . were a result of environmental differences opposed to differences resulting as from mood or special circumstances." (p. 179)

5 According to Herbert H. Hyman and Eleanor Singer (eds.), (*Readings in Reference Group Theory and Research*, The Free Press, New York, 1968), Sumner first used the felicitious terms "in-group" and "out-group" in 1906.

6 See Stanley R. Brav, *Jewish Family Solidarity; Myth or Fact*, Nogales Press, Vicks-

burg, 1940; Benjamin Kaplan, *The Jew and His Family*, Louisiana State University Press, Baton Rouge, 1967; and Benjamin Schlesinger, *The Jewish Family*, University of Toronto Press, Toronto, 1971.

7   Robert Sommer's definition of a group "as a face-to-face aggregate of individuals who have some shared purpose for being together" is accepted. (*Personal Space, op. cit.*, p. 58).

8   The literature fails to yield a clear distinction between a "reference group" and a "primary group." For example, Muzafer Sherif claims that the former "can be characterized simply as *those groups to which the individual relates himself as a part or to which he aspires to relate himself psychologically*." (Italics in the original.) ("The Concept of Reference Groups in Human Relations," Hyman; Singer, eds.; *op. cit.*, p. 86.) Close indeed is Charles Horton Cooley's assertion that "a primary group is characterized by intimate face-to-face association and cooperation," the result of which "psychologically, is a certain fusion of individualities in a common life and purpose of the group . . . . It involves the sort of sympathy and mutual identification for which 'we' is the natural expression." (*Social Organization*, New York, Charles Scribner's Sons, 1911, pp. 24-25), quoted by Murray B. Seidler and Mel Jerome Ravitz in "A Jewish Peer Group," *The American Journal of Sociology*, Vol. LXI, No. 1, July, 1955, p. 12.

A similar ambiguity attends the use of the term "community." One study, "Definitions of Community: Areas of Agreement," by George A. Hillery, Jr., (*Rural Sociology*, XX, 2, June, 1955, pp. 111-123) classified no fewer than ninety-four definitions of the term community. All three terms obviously connote an intimate interpersonal association among individuals who are joined in some common purpose or task.

9   The term is used here in its technical sense as "a repertoire of behavior patterns which must be rattled off in appropriate contexts." (Sidney M. Jourard, "Healthy Personality and Self Disclosure," *Interpersonal Dynamics, op. cit.*, p. 723.)

10   For an incisive description of the process involved in the passage from beliefs to norms, see Smith and Geoffrey, *op. cit.*, p. 48, 70ff.

11   The terms are drawn from James H. S. Bossard and Eleanor Stoker Boll, *The Large Family System*, University of Pennsylvania, Philadelphia, 1956, p. 46. "The family of orientation" designates "the family group in which and through which the child receives his orientation in the larger society" as distinguished from " 'the family of procreation' which is confined to the procreative unit of parents and children."

12   See above, p. xii, for national and local figures on post Bar and Bat Mitzva continuation in Religious School.

13   The process is reminiscent of the statement by Jack R. Gibb and Lorraine M. Gibb, *op. cit.*, pp. 42-57. "As groups grow, they reduce fears and build a climate of increased trust . . ." (p. 43)

Chapter V *Implications*

1   See Roland L. Warren, *The Community in America*, Rand McNally & Company, Chicago, 1963, p. 53, particularly the Introduction and Chapter 3, in which the

author documents his feeling that "something is wrong with the system." (p. 14) Compare, too, Martin Buber's statement that "just as his degenerate technology is causing man to lose the feel of good work and proportion, so the degrading social life he leads is causing him to lose the feel of community," *Paths in Utopia*, Translated by R. F. C. Hull, The MacMillan Company, 1950, p. 132. Another worthwhile source is Maurice R. Stein, *The Eclipse of Community*, Princeton, N.J., 1960. See the author's discussion of religion in suburbia, which he considers "one more status symbol counting well below most others in the all important secular realm." (p. 226) "Man's alienation from his neighbors" and its relationship to spatial matters is treated by Robert Sommer, *op. cit.*, especially p. 60ff. Finally, man's loneliness and its relationship to the cult of individualism is dealt with by Philip Slater, *The Pursuit of Loneliness*, Beacon Press, Boston, 1970.

2 Compare the assertion of George Herbert Mead that "the individual experiences himself as such, not directly, but only indirectly from the particular standpoints of other individual members of the same social group, or from the generalized standpoint of the social group as a whole to which he belongs." *Mind, Self & Society*, The University of Chicago Press, Chicago, Illinois, 1934, p. 138.

3 Although a number of terms might have been employed to describe the same general phenomenon, the term community seems most felicitous. For its relationship to other terms which have the same or similar meaning, see above, p. 219, note 8.

4 The need seems to be particularly acute at this age. As Muzafer Sherif observed: in his "state of instability and conflict, the adolescent tries to belong *some place*." "The Concept of Reference Groups & Human Relations," *Readings in Reference Group Theory & Research, op. cit.*, p. 92. (Italics in the original.)

5 The contrast between the extrinsic motivation of behavior, which he calls "instrumentalism," and behavior which is "intrinsically determined within the conditions of its own context," has been pointed up by Sigmund Koch in "Behavior as 'Intrinsically' Regulated: Work notes towards a pre-Theory of Phenomena called 'Motivational,'" *Nebraska Symposium on Motivation*, 1956, Marshall R. Jones, editor, University of Nebraska Press, Lincoln, 1956, pp. 42-86.

6 See above, p. 218, note 1.

7 The term is Robert Sommer's, *op. cit.* See p. 80 where he has pointed to the inhibiting influence of institutions in which "the customary becomes fixed and natural."

8 Matthew Miles has found that "temporary systems," such as conferences and juries, and presumably weekends such as those conducted by the Vov Class, are particularly well-suited to educational innovation. Freed from the protective machinery usually surrounding "permanent systems," they are moved to use time judiciously, to redefine goals in terms of individual influence, to create predictable, controllable and compelling procedures, to restructure roles leading to greater socialization, to set up new and more honest feedback loops, to channel sentiments more constructively, and to establish norms relating to equalitarianism, authenticity, inquiry, hypotheticality, and newism. See his "On Temporary Systems," *op. cit.*, Chapter 19, pp. 437-490.

9 See below, Chapter 6 for a full treatment of Rabbi Levy's status in the class.

10 *Op. cit.*, p. 135.

11 Basing himself upon the work of Kurt Lewin, Matthew B. Miles agrees that "isolation from the ordinary environment tends to shear away the person's (or group's) preoccupation with, and allegiance to, 'things as they are.' Thus there is a reduction of resistance to change based on the group norms of permanent systems, and a gradual substitution of new norms aiding change . . ." *Op. cit.*, pp. 454-5.

12 The relationship between individuals and groups in revolutionary settings has been studied by Eric Hoffer in *The True Believer*, Perennial Library, Harper & Row, Publishers, New York, 1951.

13 Compare Martin Buber's identification of "Judaism's profound sense that man has been appointed 'as an originator of events,' as a real legitimate partner in a real dialogue with God, 'empowered to speak his own independent word from out of his own being.' " (Quoted in Paul E. Pfuetze, *The Social Self*, Bookman Associates, New York, 1954, p. 127, n. 211.)

14 The importance of a total living situation to group formation of course is well known. An example is the work of David C. McClelland whose effort to teach Achievement motivation relies, among other factors, upon a "retreat"-like milieu. He observes that "the effect of this retreat from everyday life into a special and specially labeled experience appears to be twofold: it dramatizes or increases the salience of the new associative network and it tends to create a new reference group." See his "Towards a Theory of Motive Acquisition," *American Psychologist*, 20, 5, 1965, p. 329.

15 The salutary effect of nature upon young people seems to be accepted as a matter of faith, usually in a rather dogmatic manner, by devotees of camping both recreational and educational. See, for example, William H. Freeberg and Loren E. Taylor, *Philosophy of Outdoor Education*, Burgess Publishing Co., Minneapolis, Minn., 1961, and *Programs in Outdoor Education*, by the same authors, 1963. Also, M. Alexander Gabrielson and Charles Holtzer, *The Role of Outdoor Education*, The Center for Applied Research in Education, Inc., New York, 1965; Donald R. Hammerman and William M. Hammerman (compiled by), *Outdoor Education, op. cit.*, and Julian W. Smith, *et al.*, *Outdoor Education*, Prentice Hall, Inc., Englewood Cliffs, N.J., 1963. For additional works within what has come to be a vast literature on camping, see *Bibliography of Studies and Research in Camping and Outdoor Education*, American Camping Association, Bradford Woods, Martinsville, Indiana, 1962; *Cumulative Index to Camping Magazine*, (mimeographed) by the same organization; also its *Research Related to Camping*, 1963; *Outdoor Education A Selected Bibliography*, compiled by Eulyne Fulton and Charlotte Loomis, Educational Resources Information Center, New Mexico State University, Las Cruces, New Mexico, 1970.

16 This proposition is supported by the statement of Robert Sommer that "Spatial segregation is a pervasive principle of social organization" since it "protects the in-group against undue external influence." *Op. cit.*, p. 41.

17 See above, p. xii.

18 *Op. cit.*, p. 134.

19 *Op. cit.* "The Concept of Reference Groups & Human Relations," p. 85. Sherif and his associates have explored the influence of the group upon attitude formation and change most extensively. In addition to the works cited above, see *Groups in Harmony & Tension*, Harper, New York, 1953, Muzafer Sherif & Carolyn W. Sherif; *Problems of Youth: Transition to Adulthood in a Changing*

World, edited by Muzafer Sherif & Carolyn W. Sherif, Aldine Publishing Co., Chicago, 1965; *Attitudes and Attitude Change*, Carolyn W. Sherif, Muzafer Sherif & Roger E. Negergoll, Saunders, Philadelphia, 1965.

20 See Henry A. Landsberger, *Hawthorne Revisited*, Cornell University, Ithaca, New York, 1958, for an analysis of the intricacies and subleties of the Hawthorne effect and the misconceptions surrounding it. See also "Educational innovation: the nature of the problem," Matthew B. Miles, *Innovation in Education, op. cit.*, p. 11, note 6.

21 *Op. cit.,* p. 136.

Chapter VI *Methodological Approach*

1 *Argonauts of the Western Pacific*, E. P. Dutton & Company, Inc., N.Y., 1922.

2 *Boys in White*, The University of Chicago Press, 1961, p. 18.

3 See above, Chapter IV, note 2.

4 "The Extended Case Method and Situational Analysis," *The Craft of Social Anthropology*, A. L. Epstein, ed., Tavistock Publications, London, 1967, pp. 129-149.

5 *The Psychology of Science*, Harper & Row, Publishers, New York & London, 1966, p. 11.

6 *Ibid.*, p. 64.

7 Numerous other works describing the intricacies and subtleties of the method have flowed from his pen. Several of the most prominent are *Go, Bug, Go! Methodological Issues in Classroom Observational Research*, (Central Midwestern Regional Educational Laboratory, Inc., Jan., 1970) coauthored with J. A. M. Brock and *Grounded Theory and Educational Ethnography* (CA1 Fieldwork Methodology, Appendix I) coauthored with Paul A. Pohland, and most recently, *Anatomy of Educational Innovation*, John Wiley & Sons, Inc., New York, 1971, which he coauthored with Pat M. Keith.

8 *The Discovery of Grounded Theory*, Aldine Publishing Company, Chicago, 1967.

9 *Ibid.*, p. 153. (Italics in the original).

10 *Intergroup Conflict and Cooperation, The Robbers Cave Experiment, op. cit.*, p. 148.

11 *On Theory and Verification in Sociology*, The Bedminster Press, 1965.

12 "Data Control in Participant Observation," *Issues in Participant Observation*, edited by George J. McCall and J. L. Simmons, Addison-Wesley Publishing Co., Reading, Mass., 1969, p. 128.

13 Actually, the program was well underway when Rabbi Levy began to observe. It had already held an initial orientation session, five Wednesday and Sunday sessions, and one weekend. Roger later noted his opinion that this was a most desirable circumstance for whatever influence Rabbi Levy's presence came to exert upon the experience, it was surely not present during the period when the major thrust of the program as well as its general tone were in the process of being established. Subsequent observation tended to substantiate this judgment especially after Rabbi Levy, in the best tradition of non participant observation, assumed a neutral and noncommittal stance. As any newcomer to a classroom situation, he

was subjected to certain trials, that is, students did certain things and uttered certain profanities in his presence and then waited to see his reaction, particularly whether or not he would report them to the teacher. They waited in vain because Rabbi Levy was present in no capacity other than observer and did not participate in the group any more than was absolutely necessary. A similar conclusion based on a similar reaction was noted by Howard S. Becker, *et al.*, *Boys in White, op. cit.,* "The best evidence that our presence did not noticeably alter their behavior lies in the fact that they were willing to engage in behavior the faculty disapproved of while in our presence." (p. 26)

14 *Op. cit.*
15 *Ibid.*, p. 311.
16 *Ibid.*, p. 267.
17 *Ibid.*, p. 322.
18 *Ibid.*, p. 309, (Italics in the original).
19 *The Way Things Are*, Harvard University Press, Cambridge, Mass., 1966.
20 *Op. cit.*
21 *Summerhill*, Hart Publishing Co., N.Y., 1960.
22 Though different in a number of respects, William Foote Whyte's *Street Corner Society* (The University of Chicago Press, 1943) and, somewhat later, Leon Festinger's *When Prophecy Fails* (University of Minnesota Press, Minneapolis, 1956) seem to draw sustenance from the same general thrust.
23 *Op. cit.*, p. 381.
24 See Chapter I for details.
25 See Appendix B for the number and type of sessions held by the Vov Class and the distribution of the sessions during which the observer was present. Appendix C presents the breakdown of individual student attendance according to the type and duration of sessions.
26 See his and William Geoffrey's *The Complexities of an Urban Classroom, op. cit.,* p. 3, 14.
27 Polanyi seems to feel that they should be so termed. He wrote: "The power to expound hitherto accepted beliefs far beyond the scope of hitherto explored implications is itself a preeminent force of change in science." (p. 277) *Personal Knowledge, op. cit.*
28 *The School and Society*, The University of Chicago Press, Chicago, Ill., 1900, p. 84.

Chapter VII *Epilogue*

1 Unpublished doctoral dissertation, Washington University, 1974.

Bibliography

Ackerman, Walter I., "An Analysis of Selected Courses of Study of Conservative Congregational Schools, Part I," *Jewish Education*, March 1970, Vol. 40, No. 1, pp. 7-23; "Part II," Summer 1970, Vol. 40, No. 2, pp. 37-48.

_____. "Jewish Education — For What?" *American Jewish Yearbook 1969*, Vol. 70, American Jewish Committee and the Jewish Publication Society, 1969, pp. 3-36.

American Camping Association, *Bibliography of Studies and Research in Camping and Outdoor Education*, Bradford Woods, Martinsville, Indiana, 1962.

_____. *Cumulative Index to Camping Magazine*, (n.d.) (mimeographed).

_____. *Research Related to Camping*, 1964.

Argyris, Chris, "Interpersonal Competence and Organizational Effectiveness," *Interpersonal Dynamics*, Warren G. Bennis, *et al.*, (eds.) The Dorsey Press, Homewood, Illinois, 1968, pp. 583-597.

Barker, Roger G. & Herbert F. Wright, *Midwest and Its Children*, Row, Peterson and Company, Evanston, Illinois, White Plains, N.Y., 1954.

Becker, Howard S., Blanche Geer, Everett C. Hughes, Anselm L. Strauss, *Boys in White,* The University of Chicago Press, 1961.

Becker, Jerome, "The Influence of School Camping on the Self Concepts and Social Relationships of Sixth Grade Children," Teachers College, Columbia University, *Journal of Educational Psychology,* 1960, Vol. 51, No. 6, pp. 352-356.

Bettelheim, Bruno and Emmy Sylvester, "The Therapeutic Milieu," *American Journal of Orthopsychiatry,* XVIII (1948), pp. 191-206.

Blumenfield, Samuel M., "John Dewey and His Contribution to Jewish Education," *Chicago Jewish Forum,* Spring 1950, VIII, iii, pp. 169-176.

Bossard, James H. S., and Eleanor Stoker Boll, *The Large Family System,* University of Pennsylvania Press, Philadelphia, 1956.

Brav, Stanley R., *Jewish Family Solidarity; Myth or Fact,* Nogales Press, Vicksburg, 1940.

Bridgman, P. W., *The Way Things Are,* Harvard University Press, Cambridge, Mass., 1966.

Buber, Martin, *Paths in Utopia,* Translated by R. F. C. Hull, The Macmillan Company, New York, 1950.

deCharms, Richard, *Origin Pawns and Educational Practice,* first draft to appear in G. S. Lesser, (ed.) *Psychology and the Educational Process,* Scott, Foresman & Co., 1969.

_____: *Personal Causation,* Academic Press, New York & London, 1968.

_____, Janet R. Collins, K. R. Jackson, D. J. Shea, *Can Motives of Low Income Black Children Be Changed?,* Symposium prepared for the American Educational Research Association Meeting, Feb. 7, 1969, Los Angeles, California.

Dewey, John, *Democracy and Education,* New York, The Macmillan Co., 1916.

_____. *Experience & Education,* The Macmillan Co., New York, 1954.

_____. *The School and Society,* The University of Chicago Press, Chicago, Ill., 1900.

_____, and James H. Tufts, *Ethics,* Henry Holt and Co., N.Y., 1908.

Dinin, Samuel, *Report on the Status of Jewish Education in "Graceville,"* American Association for Jewish Education, 1966, (mimeographed).

Dushkin, Alexander M., Uriah Z. Engelman, *Jewish Education in the United States, Report of the Commission for the Study of Jewish Education in the United States,* Vol. I, sponsored and published by the American Association for Jewish Education, 1959.

Erikson, Erik H., *Identity Youth and Crisis,* W. W. Norton & Co., Inc., N.Y., 1968.

Fein, Leonard J., *Study of the Changing Jewish Community,* Jewish Identity Questionnaire, Account No. 70173, Brandeis University, (n.d.).

_____. *Studying Jewish Identity: Observations,* Cambridge, Mass., 1966, (mimeographed).

Feinstein, Norman and Stanley Feder, *Bibliographies on Jewish Identity,* under the direction of Leonard J. Fein, Massachusetts Institute of Technology, 1966, (mimeographed).

Festinger, Leon, Henry W. Riecken, Stanley Schachter, *When Prophecy Fails,* University of Minnesota Press, Minneapolis, 1956.

Franzblau, Abraham N., *Religious Belief And Character Among Jewish Adolescents,* Teachers College, Columbia University, Contributions to Education, No. 634, N.Y., 1934.

Freeberg, William H. and Loren E. Taylor, *Philosophy of Outdoor Education,* Burgess Publishing Co., Minneapolis, Minn., 1961.

_____. *Programs in Outdoor Education,* Burgess Publishing Co., Minneapolis, Minn., 1963.

Fulton, Eulyne and Charlotte Ann Loomis, (compiled by), *Outdoor Education A Selected Bibliography,* Educational Resources Information Center, New Mexico State University, Las Cruces, New Mexico, 1970.

Gabrielson, M. Alexander and Charles Holtzer, *The Role of Outdoor Education,* The Center for Applied Research in Education, Inc., N.Y., 1965.

Gibb, Jack R. and Lorraine M. Gibb, "Role Freedom in a TORI Group," *Encounter,* Arthur Burton, ed., Jossey-Bass, Inc., Publishers, San Francisco, 1970, pp. 42-57.

Glaser, Barney G. and Anselm L. Strauss, *The Discovery of Grounded Theory,* Aldine Publishing Co., Chicago, 1967.

Gordon, Milton M., *Assimilation in American Life,* The Role of Race, Religion and Natural Origins, N.Y., Oxford University Press, 1964.

Gross, Neal, Ward S. Mason, Alexander W. McEachern, *Explorations in Role Analysis,* John Wiley & Sons, Inc., N.Y., 1958.

Gump, Paul V., Phil Schoggen & Fritz Redl, "The Behavior of the Same Children in Different Milieus," *The Stream of Behavior,* Roger G. Barker, ed., Appelton-Century-Crofts, New York, 1963, pp. 169-202.

Hammerman, Donald R. and William M. Hammerman (compiled by), *Outdoor Education: A Book of Readings,* Burgess Publishing Co., Minneapolis, Minn., v. 55415.

Hare, A. Paul, Edward F. Borgatta, Robert F. Bales, (eds.) *Small Groups Studies in Social Interaction,* Alfred A. Knopf, New York, 1955.

Heschel, Abraham J., *The Insecurity of Freedom,* The Jewish Publication Society of America, 1966.

Hillery, George A., Jr., "Definitions of Community: Areas of Agreement," *Rural Sociology,* XX, 2, June 1955, pp. 111-123.

Hoffer, Eric, *The True Believer,* Perennial Library, Harper & Row, Publishers, New York, 1951.

Hyman, Herbert H. and Eleanor Singer (edited by), *Readings in Reference Group Theory and Research,* The Free Press, N.Y., 1968.

Janowsky, Oscar I., (ed.) "Jewish Education," Chapter VI, *The American Jew, A Reappraisal,* The Jewish Publication Society of America, Philadelphia, 1964.

Jourard, Sidney M., "Healthy Personality and Self-Disclosure," *Interpersonal Dynamics,* Warren G. Bennis, *et al.* (eds.), The Dorsey Press, Homewood, Illinois, Revised Edition, 1968, pp. 720-730.

Kaplan, Benjamin, *The Jew and His Family,* Louisiana State University Press, Baton Rouge, 1967.

Kilpatrick, William Heard, *Philosophy of Education,* The Macmillan Co., N.Y., 1951.

Koch, Sigmund, "Behavior as 'Intrinsically' Regulated: Work Notes Towards a Pre-theory of Phenomena called 'Motivational,'" *Nebraska Symposium on Motivation,* 1956, Marshall R. Jones, editor, University of Nebraska Press, Lincoln, 1956, pp. 42-86.

Kohl, Herbert R., *The Open Classroom,* a New York Review Book, Vintage Books, 1969.

Kohlberg, Lawrence, *The Development of Modes of Moral Thinking and Choice in the Years 10 to 16,* Unpublished Doctoral dissertation, the University of Chicago, Dept. of Psychology, December, 1958.

_____, and Rochelle S. Mayer, *Preschool Research and Preschool Educational Objectives; A Critique and a Proposal,* Harvard University, (mimeographed).

Landsberger, Henry A., *Hawthorne Revisited,* Cornell University, Ithaca, N.Y., 1958.

Lewin, Kurt and Ronald Lippitt, "An Experimental Approach to the Study of Autocracy and Democracy: A Preliminary Note," *Small Groups Studies in Social Interaction,* A. Paul Hare, Edgar F. Borgatta, Robert F. Bales (eds.), Alfred A. Knopf, N.Y., 1955, Chapter 10, pp. 506-523.

Malinowski, Bronislaw, *Argonauts of the Western Pacific,* E. P. Dutton & Company, Inc., N.Y., 1922.

Maslow, Abraham H., *The Psychology of Science,* Harper & Row, Publishers, New York & London, 1966.

McCall, George J. and J. L. Simmons, (eds.) *Issues in Participant Observation,* Addison-Wesley Publishing Co., Reading, Mass., 1969.

McClelland, David C., "Toward A Theory of Motive Acquisition," *American Psychologist,* 20, 5, 1965, pp. 321-333.

McGrath, Joseph E., Irwin Altman, *Small Group Research,* Holt, Rinehart & Winston, Inc., New York, 1966.

Mead, George Herbert, *Mind, Self & Society,* The University of Chicago Press, Chicago, Illinois, 1934.

Merton, Robert K., and Alice Kitt Rossi, "Contributions to the Theory of Reference Group Behavior," *Readings in Reference Group Theory and Research,* edited by Herbert H. Hyman & Eleanor Singer, The Free Press, N.Y., 1968, pp. 28-68.

Miles, Matthew B. (ed.) *Innovation in Education,* Bureau of Publications, Teachers College, Columbia University, N.Y., 1964.

_____. "On Temporary Systems," *Innovation in Education,* Teachers College, Columbia University, N.Y., 1964, Chapter 19, pp. 437-490.

Neill, A. S., *Summerhill,* A Radical Approach to Child Rearing, Hart Publishing Co., N.Y., 1960.

Neusner, Jacob, *Judaism in the Secular Age,* Ktav Publishing House, Inc., New York, 1970.

Pfuetze, Paul E., *The Social Self,* Bookman Associates, N.Y., 1954.

Pilch, Judah (ed.) *A History of Jewish Education in the United States,* The National Curriculum Research Institute of the American Association for Jewish Education, N.Y., 1969.

Polanyi, Michael, *Personal Knowledge,* Harper Torchbooks/ The Academy Library, Harper & Row, Publishers, N.Y. & Evanston, 1964.

Redl, Fritz and David Wineman, *The Aggressive Child,* The Free Press of Glencoe, Inc., 1957.

Rogers, Carl Ransom, *Freedom to Learn,* C. E. Merrill Publishing Co., Columbus, Ohio, 1969.

_____. "This Is Me," *Interpersonal Dynamics,* Warren G. Bennis, *et al.* (eds.), The Dorsey Press, Homewood, Illinois, Revised Edition, 1968, pp. 703-714.

Rothman, Jack, *Minority Group Identification and Intergroup Relations,* Research Institute for Group Work in Jewish Agencies in cooperation with the American Jewish Committee, Ann Arbor, Michigan, 1965.

Rubenstein, Richard L., *After Auschwitz,* The Bobbs-Merrill Company, Inc., 1969.

Scheffé, H., *The Analysis of Variance,* Wiley, N.Y., 1959.

Schlesinger, Benjamin, *The Jewish Family,* University of Toronto Press, Toronto, 1971.

Segalman, Ralph, "Jewish Identity Scales — A Report," *Jewish Social Studies,* Vol. 29, 1967, pp. 92-111.

Seidler, Murray B., and Mel Jerome Ravitz, "A Jewish Peer Group," *The American Journal of Sociology,* Vol. LXI, No. 1, July, 1955, pp. 11-15.

Sherif, Carolyn W., Muzafer Sherif & Roger E. Negergoll, *Attitudes and Attitude Change,* Saunders, Philadelphia, 1965.

Sherif, Muzafer, "The Concept of Reference Groups & Human Relations," *Readings in Reference Group Theory and Research,* Herbert H. Hyman & Eleanor Singer (eds.), The Free Press, New York, 1968.

_____, et al., *Intergroup Conflict and Cooperation, the Robbers Cave Experiment,* The Institute of Group Relations, The University of Oklahoma, Norman, Oklahoma, 1961.

_____. (ed.) *Intergroup Relations and Leadership,* Wiley, New York, 1962.

_____, & Carolyn W. Sherif, *Groups in Harmony and Tension,* Harper, New York, 1953.

_____ ____ _____, (eds.). *Problems of Youth: Transition to Adulthood in a Changing World,* Aldine Publishing Co., Chicago, 1965.

_____ ____ _____. *Reference Groups,* Harper & Row, Publishers, N.Y., 1964.

Silberman, Charles H., *Crisis in the Classroom,* Random House, New York, 1970.

Slater, Philip, *The Pursuit of Loneliness,* Beacon Press, Boston, 1970.

Smith, F. Tredwell, *An Experiment in Modifying Attitudes Toward the Negro,* Teachers College, Columbia University, Contributions to Education, No. 887, Bureau of Publications, Teachers College, Columbia University, N.Y., 1943.

Smith, Julian W., *et al., Outdoor Education,* Prentice Hall, Inc., Englewood Cliffs, N.J., 1963.

Smith, Louis M., *Classroom Ethnography and Ecology,* Central Midwestern Regional Educational Laboratory, Inc., April, 1969, (mimeographed).

_____, *The Micro-ethnography of the Classroom,* Occasional Paper Series, Number 1, 1966, Central Midwestern Regional Educational Laboratory.

_____, and J. A. M. Brock, *"Go, Bug, Go!" Methodological Issues in Classroom Observational Research*, Central Midwestern Regional Educational Laboratory, Inc., Jan., 1970.

_____, and William Geoffrey, *The Complexities of an Urban Classroom*, Holt, Rinehart and Winston, Inc., 1968.

_____, and Bryce B. Hudgins, *Educational Psychology*, Alfred Knopf, N.Y., 1964.

_____, and Pat M. Keith, *Anatomy of Educational Innovation: An Organizational Analysis of an Elementary School*, John Wiley & Sons, Inc., New York, etc., 1971.

_____, and Paul F. Kleine, "The Adolescent and His Society," *Review of Educational Research*, Vol. XXXVI, No. 4, pp. 424-436.

_____ _____ _____. *Minor Studies in Teacher-Pupil Relationships*, Technical Report Series, Number 5, 1969, Central Midwestern Regional Educational Laboratory.

_____, and Paul A. Pohland, *Grounded Theory & Educational Ethnography*, (CAI Fieldwork Methodology, Appendix I).

_____ _____ _____. *Participant Observation of the CAI Program*, Central Midwestern Regional Educational Laboratory, Inc.

Sommer, Robert, *Personal Space*, Prentice-Hall, Inc., Englewood Cliffs, N.J., 1969.

Stein, Maurice R., *The Eclipse of Community*, Princeton University Press, Princeton, N.J., 1960.

Velsen, J. Van, "The Extended Case Method and Situational Analysis," *The Craft of Social Anthropology*, A. L. Epstein, (ed.), Tavistock Publications, London, etc., 1967, pp. 129-149.

Warren, Roland L., *The Community in America*, Rand McNally & Company, Chicago, 1963.

Waxman, Rabbi Mordecai, (ed.), *Tradition & Change, The Development of Conservative Judaism,* The Burning Bush Press, New York, 1958.

White, Robert W., "Motivation Reconsidered: The Concept of Competence," *Psychological Review,* Vol. 66, No. 5, 1959, pp. 297-333.

Whyte, William Foote, *Street Corner Society,* The University of Chicago Press, 1943.

Wilson, John, Norman Williams, Barry Sugarman, *Introduction to Moral Education,* Penguin Books, Balto., Md., 1967.

Wirth, Arthur G., *John Dewey as Educator,* John Wiley & Sons, Inc., N.Y., 1966.

_____. *The Vocational-Liberal Studies Controversy Between John Dewey and Others (1900-1917),* U.S. Department of Health, Education and Welfare, Office of Education Bureau of Research, 1970.

Wolfson, Ronald, *A Description and Analysis of an Innovative Living Experience in Israel — the Dream and the Reality,* Unpublished doctoral dissertation, Washington University, 1974.

Zborowski, Mark and Elizabeth Herzog, *Life Is With People, the Culture of the Shtetl,* Schocken Books, New York, 1967.

Zetterberg, Hans L., *On Theory and Verification in Sociology,* The Bedminster Press, 1965.